Orysia Hrudka, Bo

# Dark Days, De

Stories from Ukraine

MW01257471

With a foreword by Myroslav Marynovych

# UKRAINIAN VOICES

Collected by Andreas Umland

The book series "Ukrainian Voices" publishes English- and German-language monographs, edited volumes, document collections, and anthologies of articles authored and composed by Ukrainian politicians, intellectuals, activists, officials, researchers, and diplomats. The series' aim is to introduce Western and other audiences to Ukrainian explorations, deliberations and interpretations of historic and current, domestic, and international affairs. The purpose of these books is to make non-Ukrainian readers familiar with how some prominent Ukrainians approach, view and assess their country's development and position in the world. The series was founded, and the volumes are collected by Andreas Umland, Dr. phil. (FU Berlin), Ph. D. (Cambridge), Associate Professor of Politics at the Kyiv-Mohyla Academy and an Analyst in the Stockholm Centre for Eastern European Studies at the Swedish Institute of International Affairs.

Orysia Hrudka, Bohdan Ben

# DARK DAYS, DETERMINED PEOPLE

## Stories from Ukraine under Siege

With a foreword by Myroslav Marynovych

**Bibliographic information published by the Deutsche Nationalbibliothek**
Die Deutsche Nationalbibliothek lists this publication in the Deutsche
Nationalbibliografie; detailed bibliographic data are available on the Internet at
http://dnb.d-nb.de.

Bibliografische Information der Deutschen Nationalbibliothek
Die Deutsche Nationalbibliothek verzeichnet diese Publikation in der Deutschen Nationalbibliografie;
detaillierte bibliografische Daten sind im Internet über http://dnb.d-nb.de abrufbar.

Cover picture: © copyright by Sofiia Afanasieva, Kyiv, 2024.

Sonia Maryn kindly provided editorial assistance for this book project.

ISBN (Print): 978-3-8382-1958-5
ISBN (E-Book [PDF]): 978-3-8382-7958-9
© *ibidem*-Verlag, Hannover • Stuttgart 2024
All rights reserved.

# Contents

"*Watching the pain of Ukrainians almost continuously for the past few years has been excruciatingly difficult. This book unfolds the daily sacrifices Ukrainian soldiers and volunteers make, in their own words.*"
—Michael Bociurkiw, Sr. Fellow—Atlantic Council (Washington DC), global affairs analyst (CNN, BBC, Al Jazeera), and former OSCE spokesperson.

"*Dark Days, Determined People vividly chronicles the Russia-Ukraine war by providing a clear and intimate account of the motivations, hopes, anxieties, and worries of Ukrainian defenders and civilians. In the process, it reveals the profound depth and extent to which Ukraine and its survival matter.*"
—Bohdan Kordan, PhD, Professor Emeritus, Political Studies, University of Saskatchewan.

"*This book tells the stories of ordinary Ukrainians who became heroes by fighting on the frontline and supporting their country's defense against Russia's aggression. Anyone who wants to understand the reality of war should read this book.*"
—Winfried Schneider-Deters, Director of the Friedrich Ebert Foundation's Kyiv Office, 1996-2000, author of books and essays about contemporary Ukraine.

# Foreword
## The Power of the Unnoticed

The Ukrainian defense against Russian military aggression has been unfortunate in that it does not have a single unified narrative in the world. It is described differently depending on political and ideological preferences. However, there is one radar on which the chronicle of this war is being reflected most accurately: the radar of the human spirit. It is on this screen that courage to stand against obliteration shines brightest, and only on this screen does the suffering of the innocent gain a higher meaning.

The collection of stories presented here is literally transcribed from these radars of the spirit. For only the human spirit can convince ordinary young men to rush to evacuate the wounded and desperate civilians, ignoring the constant bombardment. It is the spirit that encourages a warrior to remain on the battlefield and cover his brothers-in-arms, realizing that he may be seeing daylight for the last time. It is the human spirit that prompts farmers to sow bread amidst hidden mines, not knowing if they will be able to harvest it. When you stand on the side of Light, the possibilities of your inner strength become virtually limitless.

In each of these stories, we see the blatant and triumphant evil of the occupier who has been given the command: "Attack!" I want to believe that all these documents will one day be laid on the table of the International Tribunal, which Ukrainians now confidently call "Nuremberg 2," although this name is probably unfair to the current residents of this peaceful German city. For Ukrainians, however, this name is important because it reminds the whole world that the actions of the communist regime in the USSR were not qualified as crimes, the perpetrators were not held accountable, and those who supported this regime did not repent. And the seeds of these unatoned crimes have today borne terrible fruit in the regime of Putin's "Rashism." Thus, it is not surprising that Putin acts according to Stalinist textbooks. And until the world finds the strength to condemn the latest crimes, punish the criminals, and incline Russian society to repentance, the 21st century will not advance beyond the streak of "dark times."

This was and is quite obvious to me, a human rights activist and political prisoner of the Brezhnev era, as well as to all my companions in the infamous Gulag, who shared with me the title of "especially dangerous criminals against the state." And those of us who are still alive today warn the world in one voice against the temptation to quickly reconcile the Ukrainian and Russian peoples in the style of Realpolitik, allegedly for the sake of saving people, by exempting aggressors and war criminals from responsibility. It is not for nothing that the saying goes, "The road to hell is paved with good intentions."

I write these words in the days when the master of the Kremlin has come out with new and cunning "peacemaking" initiatives, which are an undisguised ultimatum to Ukraine. And once again, there are so many politicians and just good people who have forgotten Clausewitz's warning that "the aggressor is always peace-loving;" he seeks to conquer only "peacefully." May God guide the minds and hearts of those who will make crucial decisions in the world today.

The world has sufficiently researched how Nazism originated and has placed clear warning red flags along this path. Today, humanity must decode how Rashism originated and what it does. After all, it again combines the satanic triad of drivers: deception, hatred, and violence. And behind the "Russian world" doctrine, the ambitions to reincarnate the Russian Empire, which is impossible to imagine without Ukraine, are already openly manifesting. That is why the national identity of Ukrainians, which Russians have been distorting or simply uprooting for centuries, is a recurring theme in many of the stories in this book. However, the world saw only the effects of this trauma: at best, the identity of Ukrainians was undefined for it.

That is why even in 2020, one of the documents of the Munich Security Forum proposed something unprecedented: to "launch a new national dialogue about identity." "This dialogue should include opinion-makers, top scholars, and internationally recognized experts. Efforts should be made to engage with perspectives from

Ukraine's neighbors, especially Poland, Hungary, and Russia."[1] And the sad irony is that Russia took it upon itself to fulfill this wish of Western experts in its own way, by sending troops to reinforce its claim that "Russians and Ukrainians are one people."

Thus, Ukrainians had to make a sacrifice to prove that they indeed have a national agency. And the manifestation of it amazed even themselves. After 24 February 2022, in an instant and without any command from above, society turned into one huge hive of people who managed to protect the state itself.

This book invites readers to rethink many long-standing stereotypes, as it will give them the opportunity to see how significant Havel's "power of the powerless" (in contemporary Ukraine, power of individuals' contribution to the cause) is—and how shameful a people becomes when it seeks its "greatness" in "forcing love". Russia's war against Ukraine will make world democracies wonder whether they retain, in an age of post-truth and new weapons of mass destruction—fakes—their ability to distinguish truth from deception, and therefore good from evil.

However, the eye of a former Gulag prisoner sees not only the crimes of the occupiers, who are responsible for numerous graves of the murdered, cars with the inscription "Children" shot at, entire cities leveled to the ground, people expelled from their homes, widespread torture, the numbness of orphaned children and helplessness of mothers locked with their infants in the basement. And this list is far from exhaustive. In the introduction to my camp memoirs, I wrote: "Far more important to me than any condemnatory testimony, however, is the love of those dear to me, the camaraderie of my friends, the nobility of sacrifice, and the spark of humanity in criminals. For surely the chronicle of Satan's deeds is not as majestic as the shining traces of God's light, which warmed my soul in bondage. His light can brighten the darkness of any prison."[2]

1    The statement was published in February 2020 (https://securityconference.or g/assets/02_Dokumente/03_Materialien/EASLG_Statement_Ukraine_FINA L.pdf).
2    Myroslav Marynovych. The Universe behind Barbed Wire. Memoirs of a Ukrainian Soviet Dissident / Translated by Zoya Hayuk. Edited by Katherine Younger. With a foreword by Timothy Snyder - University of Rochester Press, 2021, p. 2.

So I invite all readers to feel the truth of this conclusion, which is also reflected in these stories. I can only admiringly note that both of its authors — Orysia Hrudka and Bohdan Ben — managed to capture and highlight new "shining traces of God's light" in the grim days of war. It is thanks to these manifestations of love and mutual support, resilience and self-sacrifice that the book — despite its undoubted tragedy — is not pessimistic. This book accurately conveys the truth of the famous quote by Erich Maria Remarque: "In dark times, bright people are clearly visible." Through their self-sacrifice, these bright people are defining the history of Ukraine today. And the light they radiate is capable of overcoming the greatest darkness of dark times.

Myroslav Marynovych

# Preface

For more than two years since 2022, every day an average of over 50 Ukrainian soldiers have given their lives defending the country from Russian military aggression. More than 10,500 civilians have been killed according to most moderate estimates.[3] Each of these people had their dreams and plans for the future, families and friends for whom they were beloved and dear. Overshadowed by top politicians and major events, "little individuals" frequently go unnoticed, while the country becomes an abstract territory where front lines are drawn and bombings occur.

The heroes of these stories were caught in extraordinary conditions and had to put their lives on hold to protect what is valuable to them. If it were not for the hundreds of thousands of Ukrainians ready to defend their country and the millions willing to help them, President Volodymyr Zelenskyy's rumored response to the foreign leaders' evacuation offer, "I need ammunition, not a ride," would never have been possible. And if it were not for hundreds of thousands of Russians ready to die in a war of aggression, there would be no war at all.

This book describes Ukraine at war, where fighting and the killing of civilians happen every day. But it also depicts life in the country under siege. In 2022, Russian forces surrounded Ukraine from the south, east, and north, but the siege is not just about this physical dimension. In a siege, people cannot afford to focus on their personal goals; instead, they postpone them to protect the very possibility of living in their home, in their community, with the

---

3    On 25 February 2024, Ukrainian President Volodymyr Zelenskyy revealed for the first time that since February 2022, 31,000 Ukrainian serving military personnel had been killed in action. The figure included only identified and confirmed cases, without numerous missing soldiers. According to the UN Human Rights Monitoring Mission in Ukraine, more than 10,500 civilians were killed in Ukraine from the start of the full-scale war, from February 2022 to February 2024. However, this number of civilian casualties is significantly undercounted in cities that were occupied after the intensive fighting in 2022—such as Mariupol, Lysychansk, Popasna, and Sievierodonetsk, where it was impossible to determine and verify the exact number.

people dear to them. Ukrainians saw that freedom is not personal, it is ultimately political – the freedom of self-expression, movement, and choice is impossible without a free state and nation. Since 1708, the year Moscow conquered the then capital of the Ukrainian Cossack State, Baturyn, and massacred all its residents, Russia's perception of international relations has not significantly changed. To this day, Russia does not treat Ukraine and other neighbors as equal parties, choosing to wage wars rather than focusing on developing its vast territories.

Each of these stories reveals an important theme of life during wartime: how the "Ukrainian hive" functions during war, using the example of one town; how it is to live under Russian occupation; how the defense of Ukrainian cities was bolstered by units formed by civilians without military experience; how quiet villages in the forests suddenly became places of torture and murder; what life is like after having a limb amputated; what strategic technological goals Ukraine has set to gain an advantage in the war; how Ukrainian children grow up during the war; how it feels to fight for ten years; and more.

During 2022–2024, while working for Euromaidan Press, the independent Ukraine-based English-language publication, we conducted over 300 interviews across various regions of Ukraine, writing hundreds of articles about the critical events in the Russia-Ukraine war. At the same time, we gathered stories that would become the foundation of this book. The vast majority of what is written here, including the smallest details, is either what we saw ourselves or what our interviewees told us, and we kept all the recordings of these conversations and photos in our archive. In the rare cases when we used secondary sources, except for well-known facts, we indicated them in footnotes or within the main text. We made every effort to verify all stories and provide their broader historical and political context. Overall, these stories can be read in any order; however we did not provide the same context repeatedly throughout the book if it had been described previously. The idea to write this book arose in April 2022 but we continued collecting stories until May 2024, when the last story included here was recorded.

These stories are primarily, of course, about the years 2022–2024. But telling them would be impossible without delving into the past and exploring the vision of the future that drives the individuals featured in this book. After the collapse of the Soviet Union in 1991, Ukrainians were finally able to breathe freedom during the subsequent years of independence. A new generation was born and grew up in an atmosphere inspired by the possibilities of creating a new political system, rediscovering their own national culture — which had been banned for centuries — and establishing institutions and businesses where totalitarianism once reigned. That is why it is a great pity for Ukrainians to interrupt everything they had just begun to implement and go to a war which they did not choose. They were only left to choose their role in it. This book also reflects how a war of this scale affects society and changes the lives of artists, entrepreneurs, farmers, scientists, politicians, educators, the military, and many more — all of whom are the heroes of these stories.

We tried to depict the life during the war as it is — with all its difficulties, hesitations, and inner conflicts — and how two realities, peaceful and military, coexist in constant tension. We hope this book will give its readers the opportunity to immerse themselves in Ukrainian reality and will help to explore how Ukrainians perceive this war and what gives them faith and strength.

# Navigating Hell

In 2014, Russia started the war against Ukraine, occupying Crimea and sending its troops into Ukraine's easternmost Luhansk and Donetsk regions, ostensibly to support local separatists. The 2014 and 2015 Minsk ceasefire agreements only partially limited hostilities but failed to completely halt them. In 2022, Russia attacked Ukraine in a full-scale invasion from north, east, and south, aiming to capture Ukraine's capital Kyiv in a matter of days.

Irpin, a town bordering Kyiv to the northwest, suddenly found itself on the very front line in February 2022. The town was split into three zones: Ukrainian-controlled, Russian-controlled, and the so-called gray zone. Thousands of civilians had not fled Irpin early enough and found themselves trapped in their flats and yards. At the same time, the Ukrainian army was holding the defense line around Kyiv, preventing Russian troops from entering the capital.

***

At 5:30 am, Anton awoke to a phone call from his mother.

"The war has begun," she said.

At first, outside, there was only silence. Anton and his wife Inna spent the time walking in circles around and around their Kyiv apartment. They heard explosions in the distance and decided to wake up their 18-month-old son Mark and leave. Anton watched from the window as neighbors in the opposite apartment building started to stir. Lights were being turned on, and very soon people were loading their vehicles, getting ready to depart. It was 24 February 2022. Russia had escalated the 2014–2021 war into a full-scale invasion.

Anton and Inna had packed nothing in advance. However, Anton had purchased a paper map three days earlier to work out escape routes. At the time, he chuckled to himself, "Why am I doing this?" — thinking it was completely pointless.

"When we decided to leave, I found myself mentally bidding a final farewell to closets, rooms, beds, and cactus plants," Anton tells us three months later.

Anton is a scientist and was due for work that February morning at the Institute of Physics, part of the National Academy of Sciences. "I had a funny feeling that I should call the boss and ask for some time off," he laughs. "Why?" asked his boss. Thus news about the war spread quickly from one phone call to another.

At 7:30 am, Anton, Inna, and little Mark were on their way, leaving Kyiv. Russian troops were advancing towards the capital from the north, and the family had to get to a safe place as soon as possible. Like many Kyiv residents that day, they were using less crowded back routes heading west. In the cities the family passed through, smoke was rising from explosions caused by missile strikes. Ukrainian soldiers in military vehicles were speeding past them towards Kyiv, their faces tense.

The volume of traffic kept increasing while the gas stations on these rural roads kept decreasing. Anton had containers with 70 liters of fuel stored in the boot of his car—it proved to be a godsend.

\*\*\*

Meanwhile, in another part of Kyiv, the war was already reaching Anton's good friend Andriy, a fitness trainer.

They had met several years back during another decisive event in Ukraine's history—the 2014 Revolution of Dignity. They, along with hundreds of thousands of Ukrainians, assembled on Maidan Square in the center of Kyiv to protest then-President Viktor Yanukovych's decision to abandon Ukraine's EU integration plan. The demonstration, initially entirely peaceful in nature, lasted three months. It turned violent when shots rang out and snipers on rooftops fired into the crowd, killing dozens. This only served to exacerbate the growing number of protesters to the point of revolution. "Maidan," as it has come to be known, is one of the few modern-day revolutions that resulted in the disgraced president fleeing the country; in February 2014, Yanukovych fled to Russia.

Andriy learned of the war when he woke up to a loud explosion. Initially he thought he must be mistaken. Only when he heard his upstairs neighbors clamoring about did he accept the reality.

Oksana, Andriy's wife, and their three-year-old daughter, Daryna, were still sleeping. He knelt quietly beside his wife and whispered:

"Oksanochka, the war has begun."

"What?" she exclaimed.

"Let's get up, have some coffee, and make a plan. Daryna is still asleep, so we have time to figure out what to do next."

Despite the shock, the couple was ready long before this day arrived. In early winter, while the Russians were assembling their military around the borders of Ukraine, Andriy signed up with the Kyiv Territorial Defense Forces — the reserve military that civilians could join in their local community. "I realized the Russians were not going to back away from our borders. It was only a matter of time before things spiraled out of control." Andriy had only attended a couple of early training sessions. From an internet article, they learned about the first steps in escaping invaders and the risk that evacuees would need to abandon their vehicles because of destroyed roads or lack of fuel. The day before the invasion, they called a friend in Hlevakha, a village quite a distance from Kyiv, and asked if their friend's home could serve as a temporary shelter for his family in case of an emergency. The answer was, "Yes, of course. But I can't imagine what would have to happen for a war to break out."

Andriy and Oksana did not need much time to pack — they had prepared their clothes in advance. When their daughter woke up, Andriy told her, "The adventures we talked about have begun. We were attacked by Orcs."

They left at 4 pm, when the Russian troops started moving closer to Kyiv, drove for two nights without stopping, and slept for the first time in Zakarpattia, Ukraine's westernmost region, which borders four countries: Poland, Slovakia, Hungary, and Romania. Oksana and Daryna's destination was the Slovakian border.

Andriy remained with them in the border queue for 36 hours until their final parting. With one last wave goodbye, he turned back, his heart heavy, not knowing when he would see them again. But there was no time to waste—he sped as fast as he could, knowing that Anton, whose family had already gone abroad, was waiting for him.

*** 

The two friends met up in Lviv, a city in the west of Ukraine. "We got in the car, and our war began," Andriy says. They were driving in an empty lane to Kyiv, while a long stream of cars from Kyiv was passing by them heading west. He adds, "We kept asking ourselves why we were going, where we were going, and which military unit we should join."

Suddenly, their car broke down. A repair shop next to the road was closed, but the mechanics were still inside. The two friends banged on the doors and appealed to them, saying they were going to Kyiv.

"To Kyiv? Then come in," and one of the mechanics opened the garage door. Even though they did not have the necessary spare part, the mechanics repaired the car so that it could drive a few hundred kilometers more.

While driving, Andriy and Anton soon learned that the weapons for the Kyiv Territorial Defense had already been handed out. "You'll have to stand in line for too long," Anton's friend from the territorial defense told him over the phone. He advised them to volunteer at the Kryyivka Vilnykh Foundation,[4] which was assisting defense units. "Don't try to learn something new. Do what you know well," he said, referring to their experience of volunteering from 2014 to 2016 during the initial years of Russia's war against

---

4    One of numerous Ukrainian foundations collecting donations and providing material aid to the army, such as radios, drones, and body armor, in the early stage of the war. "Kryyivka" was a hiding place of the UPA (Ukrainian Insurgent Army) during World War II, typically located in underground bunkers. The Ukrainian word "vilnyi" literally means "free" and originates from the Ukrainian word "volia," meaning "will" and "freedom" simultaneously.

Ukraine. In 2014, they had volunteered to transport critical necessities to Ukrainian military units in the east of the country. Like many other volunteers, they would put together fundraising campaigns via social media, acquire the supplies, and deliver to the frontline equipment, first aid kits, food, and other essentials.

After 2014, the word "volunteer" in Ukraine came to denote any civilian who assists the military or others who were affected by the war. In 2014, Ukraine was unprepared for war, with only a small budget for the army and few supply chains. In February 2022, when the full-scale war began, the Ukrainian government, and later international aid as well, covered the main needs of the military. However, the support of volunteers was still crucial for the front, especially in the areas where the state was too slow or lacked finances, particularly given the fact that the army had increased threefold.[5]

***

Public transportation in the capital was disrupted. As a result, in the first days of the 2022 invasion, upon arriving in Kyiv Andriy and Anton volunteered as drivers. They took Kyivans wherever needed — commuters to train stations, medical workers to hospitals, service men and women to their units. They delivered food kits to the vulnerable and helped out wherever they could.

At that time, fighting had started in the capital's satellite towns, Irpin and Bucha, but it was still several kilometers from Kyiv. These two towns are separated from Kyiv by five kilometers of forest, and the Irpin River which flows between the forest and the town of Irpin. By 4 March, Russian troops had almost

---

5    When the full-scale war began in 2022, Ukraine directed 100% of the state budget for the military. International financial aid funded Ukraine's critical spending, such as healthcare and education, allowing the state to allocate all national taxes for the army. However, the Ukrainian military budget still could not catch up to the Russian budget. Russia had a ten-times bigger economy (and six-times larger population), primarily due to its oil and gas exports. Under these conditions, the role of volunteers was important. They supplied drones, cars, sniper rifles, night vision devices, and other niche weapons, as well as equipment easily obtainable on the open market.

completely occupied Bucha, which neighbored Irpin to the north. In Irpin, fighting continued with neither side able to establish full control.

Andriy and Anton learned about a humanitarian convoy that was heading to Irpin on 3 March — to deliver food and then evacuate people back to Kyiv. They decided to join it.

Irpin is a picturesque town, with homes nestling among pine and oak forests, and many trees preserved among the newly constructed, fashionable high-rises and townhouses. The town showcased the rapid development of the Ukrainian capital and its neighbors but with more harmonious urban planning. Irpin had many neighborhoods with detached houses, while the town center boasted elegant statues, illuminated fountains, and vibrant flower beds. All of this was now under bombardment.

On 3 March, Andriy and Anton — now part of the convoy — departed Kyiv, crossed the Irpin River, and reached the town. More than 65,000 people lived in Irpin before the war, many of whom were still in the town when fighting erupted beneath their windows. Suddenly, residents found themselves in the whirlwind of war, cut off from the outside world with barely any internet or mobile connection.

The convoy entered a part of Irpin that was still under Ukrainian control. "We looked around, some buildings were already damaged, but we were part of a convoy," says Andriy, at the time thinking "safety in numbers." "Other volunteers were coming to Irpin as well," he adds. "They weren't afraid, so we assumed we didn't need to be frightened either."

That day, even though under constant shelling, they gathered evacuees and returned to Kyiv intact. The next day, fighting broke out all around Irpin, and they were not able to repeat the trip. However, they tried to bring aid to Irpin and evacuate people again two days later, when the situation seemed a bit calmer. "The main mistake we made that day was believing that the drivers at the head of the convoy were aware of the worsening situation in Irpin and that everything was under control," says Anton.

The convoy took the same route as before, but this time it was more perilous. As they passed a Ukrainian checkpoint on the approach to Irpin, soldiers at the checkpoint were surprised to see them—a humanitarian convoy heading into real danger. "They were wide-eyed," says Andriy, "As if to say, 'Okay, bring your humanitarian aid and leave ASAP.'" The last checkpoint was already shelled. No one was left. Instead, there were bullet-riddled cars on the roadside with the word "Children" written on them. "We passed them as if in slow motion, sickened by the sight, but we had to drive on."

At the outskirts of Irpin, Ukrainian fighters pointed Javelins in the same direction the convoy was heading. "They were expecting an enemy," says Anton. Again, slow motion set in and time stalled, but Anton was able to make eye contact with one of the soldiers. By the look in his eyes, Anton understood what was ahead. "But the lead cars had already passed ... what should I do?" Anton considered for a split second, then kept driving after the others.

People were fleeing Irpin totally shocked. "You could hear shelling. A mother ran by, holding her baby pressed to her chest, squeezing him tightly," says Anton. "Still, somehow, it all felt normal. You start to understand how the human psyche works in extreme situations like that—it goes into denial and tries to pretend it isn't happening to you and that it can't be happening like this."

***

The convoy eventually arrived at the Irpin Bible Church on 1 Soborna Street. This new, spacious building had a new large concrete basement where Irpin residents, caught in the chaos of war, could stay. The church's caretaker, Andriy Ryzhov, told us that on some days there were 200–250 people in the shelter—among them were babies, children, and the elderly. Here people could find refuge, food, and a warm place to sleep. Much later, following Irpin's liberation, those whose homes had been destroyed by the Russian forces continued to receive help from the church while its staff and volunteers assisted in repairing bomb-damaged homes.

Anton and Andriy unloaded all the food they had brought with them and escorted four people to their car for evacuation—a couple, a two-year-old toddler and his grandma.

By then, the first part of their convoy had already picked up evacuees and departed from Irpin, heading towards the southern bridge in the nearby village of Stoyanka. Unexpectedly, a Russian tank appeared around a corner and shot at the front car. The vehicles behind them turned sharply and drove to another bridge on the Irpin side, Romanivskyi Bridge, only to find it had already been blown up. There was no other way to cross the river. Quickly, everyone abandoned their vehicles and headed under the bridge, crossing through the frigid, waist-deep water on foot. The connection between the front section of the convoy, and Anton and Andriy's rear part was severed. Neither group knew what was happening to the other.

A few minutes later, the back part of the convoy started driving, unaware of what was ahead. Suddenly, the massive bus that was driving first turned sharply. "Something was wrong because the bus driver would never turn like that on such a narrow road," Anton says. A car ahead also turned around. Anton stopped.

"What's up there?" he asked when the car slowed down passing by him.

"There's a tank."

"A Russian one?"

"No, a f***ing Italian one!"

The tank was parked a mere 400 meters away.

"That's it! The Irpin entrance is completely sealed off. We've been encircled," someone cried out in panic.

People started running back to the church. Meanwhile, Anton and Andriy were racing around the neighborhood looking for other ways out. At that moment, shelling whistled over their heads. Ukrainian military medics nearby, wearing bulletproof vests, instantly dropped to the ground and shouted: "Get down! Lie down!" Then, "Get to the shelter! Immediately!"

*All the way into Bucha, the roads were littered with burnt-out cars and dead passengers. Later, these vehicles were gathered and relocated to a spot near the road.*

*"A mother ran by, holding her baby pressed to her chest," says Anton. "Still, somehow, it all felt normal. You understand how the human psyche works in extreme situations — it pretends it isn't happening to you." Anton Senenko (left) and Andriy Piven.*

*Anton and Inna spent the time walking in circles around and around their Kyiv apartment. They heard explosions in the distance and decided to wake up their 18-month-old son Mark and leave. It was 24 February 2022. Illustrations by Nata Zakharchuk.*

*Hours passed. In a quiet corner, Andriy watched a video of his daughter over and over. All they could do was wait, not knowing what to expect – mentally preparing for every possible scenario.*

*"Andriy ran just like in a Hollywood action movie. And then I looked at the passengers. They sat there pale as death. 'That's the rescue?' they must have thought."*

*Andriy saw a young man lying on a street beneath a half-burnt tarpaulin. Drawing closer, he saw his legs, then pulled away because of the stench of charcoal-burnt flesh. He barely restrained himself from vomiting.*

*When Russia invaded in 2022, Yuriy Chornomorets, a theology professor from Kyiv, swapped his lecture hall for a sniper rifle.*

*"Everyone said goodbye to life, so actually it was quite easy. Only when it's all over do you realize that this thinking was complete madness." Yuriy Myronenko (right) and Andriy Kovaliov.*

***

In the church basement, Andriy went utterly silent.

"During the Maidan,"[6] he later told us, "there was also a tense atmosphere when Anton and I patrolled the streets together. Then I realized that everyone reacts differently to stressful situations. I fall completely silent. It's not a state of immobilization, rather it's a state of 'shutdown.' On the other hand, Anton is always cheerful and smiling in stressful situations. At first, I thought something was wrong with the guy, but I realized this was his defensive reaction."

The shelter gates were slammed shut so that the building would appear deserted and the Russians would not realize anyone was there. Anton was armed with a hunting rifle, but the medics advised him not to bring it into the building. When the thundering shelling paused, Anton dashed to a nearby storage shed to hide his rifle—but decided to keep the gun permit. "For some strange reason," he says, "I was still concerned that my car might get damaged. Then two hours later, a mortar shell hit the car and, well, I didn't have to worry about it anymore."

"We also ate." Together with military medics, he and Andriy shared borshch (beet soup). The medics were aware of the wrecked bridge and that the checkpoint and troops that were holding back the Russians had been overrun and killed. The medics' car, despite the fact it had huge red crosses painted on it, was targeted by Russians in armored personnel carriers. The Russians were now advancing further into Irpin, and it was unclear where the closest Ukrainian positions were and how far the enemy would advance. While still eating, the medics started discussing what they would do if the Kadyrovites—Russian paramilitary forces known for their brutality—broke into the basement.

"It was like a scene from a movie," says Anton. "You're sitting on your couch, eating, and a medic says, 'Well, if Kadyrovites get

---

6    Maidan—shortened name for Maidan Nezalezhnosti—Kyiv Independence Square, where the Revolution of Dignity took place in 2014, as well as the Orange Revolution in 2004. After that, the word Maidan came to denote a nationwide protest against the government.

in, we'll shoot them in the back with pistols, then use grenades.' I realized it was grave—it wasn't a movie, it wasn't a joke, and we didn't know what to say."

"The medics continued with their plans," adds Andriy. "One said, 'When the fighting stops in the morning, we'll grab weapons from the corpses and continue to fight' … he said it in such a numbed tone. We were unprepared for this scenario. Yesterday we were delivering sweet cheese in food kits, and today we'll be taking weapons from the killed and wounded soldiers and fighting in a town we know nothing about?"

The basement was dimly lit. Still, Andriy began searching the many nooks and crannies for hiding places. Meanwhile, Anton was looking for a way out.

"Take care of my sweetheart," Andriy messaged his relative.

Anton managed to catch a decent mobile signal and called his friend Yuriy, "I'm in a difficult situation. Take care of Inna and Mark." He barely got these words out, then realized his friend was shocked too. Next Anton messaged his wife Inna. "Be strong, and take care of Mark." Afterward, he managed to connect with a well-known volunteer and dropped their GPS coordinates. She promised to try to arrange an evacuation route.

Suddenly, one of the groups of people in the basement detected Russian soldiers through the tiny windows. Frightened, they pulled back. "Thank God they passed by, thinking the building was empty," Andriy says. The Russians were scouting around looking for Ukrainian soldiers. The next step was obvious—they would begin checking the buildings and looking for people. Knowledge of Russian soldiers' brutality towards those with a pro-Ukraine stance, particularly anyone aiding the army, had spread after the 2014 war.

Andriy and Anton sought out a fellow volunteer, Oksana, one of the convoy drivers, whom they describe as the "bravest driver" they had ever met. At first glance, they saw Oksana sitting seemingly still, legs crossed, "frozen," a calm expression on her face. Yet they could see she was trembling slightly.

She asked, "Texting apps deleted?"

"No," the two replied.

"Delete them, including Facebook and Viber," she said slowly and evenly, but her voice carried authority.

"Understood," they said in unison.

In minutes, their smartphones were erased of any traces that they had anything to do with supporting the Ukrainian army, or evacuating civilians, or with the shooting practice they took part in the previous week.

Oksana advised them to create a "cover story" about evacuating people for money. "Say people promised to pay $2,000 but still haven't paid."

Andriy thought, "How experienced she is. I would never have thought of that."

Anton was still unsure of what to do with his gun license. Oksana said, "Put it under your heel. You'll have time to throw it away. Things won't happen in a second."

Hours passed. In a quiet corner, Andriy watched a video of his daughter over and over. All they could do was wait, not knowing what to expect—mentally preparing for every possible scenario.

***

A barrage of shelling began. One mortar shell hit the church directly. Anton's imagination ran wild as he visualized the room on fire, thinking they would all perish, but it was only in his head. He shook himself back to normality, then he slipped from the basement up to the first floor, where he saw a Ukrainian soldier speaking with someone in the room. The door was knocked off its hinges. On the street, two tense soldiers with machine guns guarded the perimeter.

"It's the Russian soldiers," someone downstairs shouted in fear, not believing the Ukrainian army could have already pushed the Russians back.

The soldiers yelled, "We're Ukrainian soldiers—we've come to save you!"

A man ran up to Anton and started shaking him, shouting, "Anton, it's me!"

"Kostia?" Anton recognized the driver from the first leg of their convoy — the one that had left Irpin before the route was forced to shut. It turned out that the entire time they were looking for someone to help evacuate the back section of the column. They finally found several brave Marines who agreed to help.

When Anton recovered from his astonishment and recognized Kostia, he shouted over his shoulder to where people were still cowering in the basement, "They're our troops!"

The Marines were also shouting, "Which of the cars work? Take the women and children and leave! Get as many out as possible!" Then yelling into the basement, "Ukrainian Marines! Evacuate!"

In the chaos of the tumult, the military medics who had shared borshch with Anton came up to him.

"Friend, don't worry," they said. "Your car was hit pretty hard, but the engine should be okay."

Many in the basement still did not trust the evacuation. They were afraid of leaving what they thought was a safe place — to enter streets where they could hear explosions — but the clock was ticking and Russian troops were still close by.

Those few willing to leave hurried over to the convoy as the cars started their engines. A Marine yelled, "Go! Go!" Anton ran about looking for Andriy. He described this mad search as, "one of the most gut-wrenching moments of my life." At the final second, he spotted his friend who was still trying to convince the bus driver that this was the last chance for the ones still hiding to get out of this hell. But like those in the basement, the driver was too frightened to leave, let alone to start convincing people. Some volunteer drivers, including Oksana, took as many more as would come.

It was dark when they finally got out of Irpin. People's homes all around them were on fire. The town was engulfed in smoke. Anton was driving at 120–130 km/h to keep up with the Marines. For Anton, it felt as though these soldiers were true Titans. The destroyed Romanivskyi Bridge was clogged with abandoned vehicles, and the men realized that their whole group would have to cross the river under the bridge and on foot. They parked their cars on the riverbank and slid down under the bridge. They all tramped through the frigid water, in the dark, determined to reach Kyiv.

Finally arriving in the capital, the group was checked by the Ukrainian Security Service (SBU). Because of the newly enacted curfew, Anton and Andriy planned to spend the night in the metro station, but kind police officers drove them home.

***

"Friends, we don't have any more cars so we'll not be able to carry out humanitarian missions," Anton posted on Facebook that night. He and Andriy were suffering from an excruciating head-ache—after the shelling in Irpin, they both endured mild concussion that lasted for several days.

People messaged and messaged Anton that night pleading to evacuate their relatives from Irpin. By morning, his Facebook friends managed to find three cars for them.

At 8:30 am, Andriy and Anton departed for Irpin again. The two friends could not stop thinking about the people they had left behind; they had exchanged phone numbers with many of them. Then, while driving, they heard bad news—a mortar shell had exploded near Oksana, and her husband had sustained a serious injury to his thigh. "We had to turn a deaf ear to that. Our only thought was that we had to keep going," says Anton.

Approaching the destroyed bridge, they heard the distant sound of a machine gun firing. They were more cautious this time and decided to park further back. After they crossed the river on foot, they saw their old car was still on the river bank where they had left it. Damaged, but operable, unlike the cars they saw closer to Irpin which were burnt out. They set to work to fix it.

Anton ripped a piece of fence wire to tie the car's half-torn-off muffler. "Feeling guilty, I remember thinking, 'Well, I'll just take this little piece from a fence and return it when I can.'" In the days that followed, the men brought antifreeze, fuel, tires, and other items from Kyiv to repair their car. Every day they would drive in their new car from Kyiv to the destroyed bridge, leave it on the

Kyiv side of the bank, cross the river on foot, and switch to the damaged car that was trapped on the Irpin bank.

In effect, Irpin was under almost complete Russian occupation for only one day, 5 March. During that month, the Ukrainian military continued to push the Russians back but, generally speaking, there were always three zones in Irpin. Ukrainian troops controlled one part, Russians controlled the second, and the last was the gray zone. Sadly, Anton says, "Those volunteer drivers who went to Russian-controlled territory, including Bucha, are no longer alive."

Each time driving from Kyiv to Irpin, they enquired at the four checkpoints about the situation in the town.

At the first checkpoint, the territorial defense replied, "Oh dear, so much shelling, it's very dangerous there."

The second checkpoint was held by police, who said, "Put on your helmets and drive the next 10 kilometers fast."

At the third, they got more information. Marines told them how often Russians were shelling and where.

At the "zero" checkpoint, the one closest to the fighting zone, a soldier gave them the most precise information: how long ago the enemy strikes had occurred, how many Russians were killed, how many of Ukrainian soldiers were killed or wounded, and the actual streets where circumstances had changed.

Andriy and Anton also greeted every passerby they met as they drove, and slowed down to ask each driver heading out about the changing situation in Irpin. To protect themselves from possible shelling, they had donned body armor and helmets.

Mobile or internet connection in Irpin was jammed by Russians and damaged by shelling. To obtain at least a patchy connection, people in some of Irpin's streets had to climb to the upper floors, risking their lives. However, relatives constantly contacted Anton via social media, dropping the addresses where people, frequently without mobile and internet connection, awaited evacuation.

Andriy shows us a list of hundreds of addresses on his phone. Most of them are crossed out—they are the Irpin residents they managed to rescue. At first, many people refused to be rescued by strangers. To gain their trust, the men started asking relatives for personal details about those they wanted to be rescued.

The rescue from Irpin consisted of three parts: from Irpin to the Romanivskyi Bridge, crossing through the river under the destroyed bridge, and from there to Kyiv; then leaving Kyiv for Irpin and repeating the process. Andriy and Anton helped build a walkway out of planks over the river with other volunteers and the Armed Forces of Ukraine. It was a little easier then, because people no longer had to wade through the freezing water.

One time, the two friends carried an injured 20-year-old girl, Kateryna, across the river. She had moved from Crimea to Irpin after the Russian occupation of Crimea in 2014. Several days after the beginning of the Russian invasion in 2022, she had been transporting aid for civilians in her car, driving towards the town of Hostomel, which had also been captured by Russian troops. Her car was marked with huge red crosses and the inscription "Volunteers" but Russians shot at it anyway. Kateryna suffered bullet wounds to her leg and ribs. Andriy and Anton carried her under the Romanivskyi Bridge, and from there other volunteers drove her and others fleeing to Kyiv. Because of constant shelling by Russians, the cars and buses had to race off at high speed.

When people got to Kyiv, most of them broke down and cried, not believing they had escaped the horror of the bombardment. Some had abandoned their homes taking only a passport; others had dragged so many bags that it seemed to the drivers they had brought their entire lives.

Sadly, some evacuees were killed by Russian troops while escaping. On 7 March, near the Romanivskyi Bridge, a shell hit the car of a family that was trying to evacuate. "We saw children's bodies covered with white sheets. During our trips, no one who got into our car was sure they were safe," Andriy says.

Once, a missile landed near the shattered Romanivskyi Bridge, severely injuring a woman's spine, while Andriy and Anton were helping people across the river. "If you hear a projectile whistling, you fall; when it explodes, you get up, you run again," Andriy says.

Anton adds, four volunteers who were delivering food to Bucha—already occupied by the Russians—were shot dead. All the way into Bucha, the roads were littered with burnt-out cars and dead passengers. Later, Bucha would become infamous for the mass atrocities committed by Russians that took place there on roads, fields, streets, and in homes. The road killings took place in Irpin too. Once, the men saw a burnt-out car of volunteers with the Red Cross insignia on it. "The dead driver lay next to the car," Anton says.

***

Irpin changed for the worse day by day. But the worse it got, the less people were willing to leave.

Andriy and Anton went to pick up a family in a district of Irpin which had not suffered much from the shelling. But people did not want to go, saying, "You are just whipping up panic," although they could hear explosions only a few blocks away. Even those whose homes had already been shelled would sometimes reply, "Lightning doesn't strike twice in the same spot." Others were preparing food on fire pits, isolated in their backyards. Because they didn't see fighting in the neighboring districts, they thought they were still relatively safe.

Some people just refused to accept the war, as cruel and deadly as it was, imagining their yard was an island of stability within the hellfire. Then a few days later, in the same yard where they had said, "You are just whipping up panic," a woman was killed when a tank shelled her house.

In just a few days of siege, people aged by decades. Andriy recalls a man who lived in a garage after his house was destroyed by the Russians. He looked 65 but was only 32. He stayed there with his frostbitten legs until a tank fired on the garage and destroyed it too.

Andriy saw the young man lying on a street beneath a half-burnt tarpaulin. Drawing closer, he saw his legs, then pulled away because of the stench of charcoal-burnt flesh. He barely restrained himself from vomiting.

"Anton, I can't take him out."

Andriy explained to us, "I just couldn't do it. Physically, I felt sick. I knew I would have thrown up while driving." He was the only victim the men could not evacuate in their car.

Nonetheless, they promised him, "We'll definitely come back for you but we need to find a bigger car."

They found a Red Cross vehicle, "which traveled only where it was relatively safe," says Andriy. They approached it and saw "an obviously frightened driver." Luckily, they managed to persuade him to take the injured man.

The smells of war are something that Andriy and Anton cannot forget. After just a few days of war, a city without water and sewage turns into a waste zone. People have no choice but to leave excrement near their apartment building.

Several times a day, the two friends had to take cover under shellfire. "You can't be slack when it whistles—you need to drop to the floor," says Andriy. "Sometimes you're mistaken and the shell doesn't hit or it explodes far away. Sometimes you crumble like an old house, and your knees and arms get badly scraped and scuffed, but taking cover is a must."

***

In the last days of March, the Ukrainian army pushed the Russian troops back, and Andriy and Anton were able to reach the dwellings in Irpin they hadn't been able to get to earlier. Those addresses had been on their list for quite some time—especially the ones for the new residential complex, the Synerhiya, consisting of high-rise buildings.

"Anyone home?" they called out, walking down the stairs to the basement where they were to pick up a woman with two children.

Silence. Then someone cautiously asked, "Are you ours?"

It turned out there were dozens of people in that basement, not just three. They had sheltered there for 32 days since the occupation, while Russians lived in their apartments and looted the things they considered as being of value.

Andriy and Anton contacted other drivers. As they were taking people to cars, the two friends went to pick up an elderly couple. The couple was taking their time packing: the man was adamant he needed his blue insulating tape and a tape measure.

"They'd lost their sense of urgency due to a quiet period of no shelling," says Andriy. "It had rained, then stopped, and the sun came out. There was silence on the street and, although bombed out, the town seemed to be calm and quiet." He adds, "For us, it was perhaps the first time we walked in this area almost fully upright — before that, our shoulders were always hunched."

"It's a very difficult moment when evacuating people," says Andriy, "not to yell at them and say that people are dying and, by collecting things, you are taking time away from those who are also in line for evacuation. Get ready and leave — things don't matter. But it was very difficult to explain — all he was looking for was blue tape."

Not able to stand the stench any longer, Andriy decided to wait on the street. There, he saw two colleagues — volunteer drivers — who showed him another basement full of people. They started coming outside, inhaling the sweet smell of freedom. Andriy beckoned a woman to their car, then continued looking for other shelters where people might be hiding.

Suddenly, the Russians started firing shells. Andriy dropped down into a 10-centimeter layer of broken bricks and glass that lay on the asphalt. The shells above him flew to the house where Anton was.

"And at this time, I'm helping this grandfather who strolls leisurely out of his flat — with the blue tape and tape measure in hand. All good," Anton says, sarcastically.

As soon as Anton helped the old couple into the backseat, a shell crashed into a garage. Anton and the woman fell to the ground. The "blue-tape" couple struggled to get out of the car and drop down too. It was time to drive away. Anton managed to call Andriy on a walkie-talkie.

"Shelling! We have to leave!"

"Okay, go!" Andriy yelled, still lying on the asphalt, worrying that waiting for him would take too much time.

"I won't go without you! I'll pick you up near the burned-out gas station."

Andriy raced in army gear weighing 12 kilograms. Shells were exploding behind him. "He ran just like in a Hollywood action movie," Anton says. "And then I looked at the passengers. They sat there pale as death. 'That's the rescue?' they must have thought."

When they passed a few blocks, another volunteer driver stopped them asking where the people were that they had to pick up. He had not seen any and would not leave Irpin with an empty car despite the shelling.

On the last day of March, Ukrainian forces liberated neighboring Bucha. Andriy and Anton were among the first people to enter the tragically scarred town, which had been under Russian occupation for 28 days. They saw corpses lying everywhere on the street. Locals told them horror stories of Russian troops breaking into basements where they were hiding, and then tormenting them. Russians had executed the captured soldiers of the territorial defense and the security guards from a local enterprise. After de-occupation, volunteers found many people in basements dead.

"Shocking us was no easy feat," says Anton, "We had already met so many injured people and heard their stories. If the stories were extreme, we took these people to the police so they could be officially recorded. When you hear these kinds of accounts for the first or second time, you can't believe them, but after a while they become a conveyor belt of horrible stories that no sick imagination could invent — you become detached from them. One of our friends listened to all these stories in detail and documented everything. After that, she herself was traumatized and had to seek psychological therapy."

\*\*\*

Once the Kyiv region was liberated, Andriy and Anton had a difficult time re-adapting to city life and deciding what next steps to take. A few short days on, they started crowdfunding campaigns for Ukrainian soldiers in the east. Then they got behind the wheel again to supply the soldiers with vehicles.

Three months after the February invasion began, Anton said he "forced himself" to give lectures to students. "It all seems strange," he says. "I understand the troops returning from the front line. It's hard to return to a peaceful life." Anton admits that the most difficult thing for him was not seeing his wife and son for months.

"War teaches us not to put off living. It's amazing to see how often people waste their lives," Anton says as we walk to the Kontraktova metro station in Kyiv in May 2022. "The Ukrainian military won back time for us. It was impossible to plan our lives even a minute ahead. Plans to meet next Thursday were bizarre because you didn't know if you would be alive next Thursday. In every battle, our military buys us minutes. Now that my wife and son are very far away, I understand how many moments I could have had but lost. Hug your wife, son or daughter, do not put it off."

Even after the Russian defeat in the Battle of Kyiv, Andriy and Anton did not consider the situation in Kyiv safe enough, and even had gas masks prepared because, Anton says, "You can expect anything from the Russians."

"My Facebook feed is now full of obituaries," Andriy adds sadly. "You truly understand that more and more people are dying. We must continue preparing for hostilities. We need to deal with it more dispassionately, in a balanced way, appreciating every resource — whether a liter of fuel or a thermal imager."

In 2014, when corrupt President Yanukovych fled Ukraine, people at the Maidan Square in Kyiv placed candles in memory of the Heavenly Hundred, the protesters killed by snipers during the revolution. At the same time, they were rejoicing that it was all over. That day, when patrolling the streets, Andriy and Anton had shared the same thought, "It's only the beginning."

As it turned out, it really was.

# Put Life on Hold and Fight

When Russia invaded Ukraine in 2022, Western media and politicians were highly pessimistic about Kyiv's fate. International headlines stated that Russia was about to seize Kyiv in three days, while experts judged Ukraine as having no chance to win against the second-largest army in the world.

Ukraine's military was aided, in no small way, by the Territorial Defense Forces — mostly volunteer civilians with little-to-no formal training but with an iron will to protect their homes against foreign aggression. The territorial defense proved crucial in the defense of the cities of Sumy, Chernihiv, Kharkiv, and other regions, and especially in the battle for the heart of Ukraine — Kyiv.

The 2022 Battle of Kyiv shows that even in today's highly technological wars, the outcome greatly depends on how local people respond.

\*\*\*

In 2014, when fighting started in the east of Ukraine, Kyivan Vladyslav Stepanenko was studying electronics at the Kyiv Polytechnic University. Once a week, he attended special military classes offered to university students through the state program of military education. The course allowed students to obtain a junior officer rank but was low-level and, offering only a few days of field training, was too theoretical. So, after a year he realized, "If we are sent into hot spots, we might survive perhaps a week or so." Unlike most of his peers, Vladyslav started looking for alternative programs, and in 2015 he enrolled in a free, month-long training program offered by the NGO Ukrainian Legion. He decided to become a member afterward and regularly engage in military exercises. Alongside him were hundreds of Kyivans who had witnessed Russia's military aggression in the east of Ukraine, and were keen to gain military skills. Veterans who had fought in Donetsk and Luhansk regions became instructors in the Legion and passed on their experience to others.

"In eight years, from 2014 to 2022, changes in the army were tangible. While Soviet-style commanders had instructed their soldiers to 'skip some tasks' because 'the main thing was to survive,' the new generation of Ukrainian commanders — those with war experience since 2014 — were saying, 'We are accomplishing the task and saving lives.'" People from organizations like the Ukrainian Legion were drivers of these changes, also prompting gradual yet comprehensive reforms in state norms.

***

For years, experienced Ukrainian commanders as well as military NGOs like the Ukrainian Legion, were promoting the creation of the territorial defense, lobbying the state to change the existing law for procurement and management for these units. The idea behind territorial defense is that local people regularly participate in military training so that when their village or city is attacked, they are prepared and already organized in local battalions to fight, thus enhancing the regular army.

The Territorial Defense Forces originated from local self-defense volunteer units, formed in 2014 throughout Ukraine, and existed in semi-organized forms registered with the Ministry of Defense. In January 2022, only two months before Russia's full-scale invasion, the new law made the territorial defense a separate branch of the Armed Forces of Ukraine with a regulated structure and proper funding. Within the first month after the law was passed, 10,000 new volunteers enlisted in the territorial defense forces throughout the country, even though not all training centers were ready.

Kyiv's 112th Territorial Defense Brigade was formed in 2017, allowing civilians who were already training in NGOs to be enlisted as part of the national defense preparation. One of their ten-day training exercises took place in 2021 — a year before the full-scale invasion — on the northern outskirts of Kyiv. The National Guard, National Police, and a few Armed Forces units played the role of the "attackers," while the territorial defense units acted as the "defenders," practicing protection techniques and counter-sabotage strategies.

Positions established for this training were maintained afterwards and during the actual attack of 2022 were quickly prepared for defense of the capital.

\*\*\*

Vladyslav recounts how, in the spring of 2021, the territorial defense reservists were put on high alert. The first signs of Russia's full-scale attack against Ukraine — Russia's troop build-up around Ukraine and the construction of the controversial pipeline Nord Stream II — were both raising questions. Experts cautioned that the threat of a new Russian invasion could be linked with the new pipeline, which would allow Russia to sell gas directly to Europe bypassing Ukraine's gas transport system. Thus, Russia could conduct war with Ukraine without loss of income from one of its main gas export routes.

Still, many people, as well as political elites, did not believe a full-scale war was possible. Just one month before the invasion, President Volodymyr Zelenskyy infamously attempted to soothe citizens, by talking about weekend barbecues and the approaching spring holidays. When the invasion — forecast to start on 18 February — did not happen, people started to joke about it.

Meanwhile, reservists were already preparing. Vladyslav shows us a scar on his hand — "a memento" from unloading weapons in Kyiv's 112th brigade as work got underway. He tells us how several weeks before the war, a group of activists who self-organized through Facebook initiated a public inspection of bomb shelters. "Yet Ukraine is very diverse," he says. "Even if a family member is undergoing military training, this doesn't guarantee that all family members will take it seriously."

\*\*\*

On the evening of 23 February 2022, Vladyslav could not contact his chief of staff, so he was not surprised when his chief called very early the following morning:

"Vlad, everything's fine, wait for further instructions."

Vladyslav found his chief's words odd but thought there was nothing out of the ordinary. Next, he turned on the TV. A children's cartoon was playing, but on the rolling news at the bottom of screen, in huge letters, were the words:

"WAR HAS BEGUN IN UKRAINE."

\*\*\*

Members of one of Kyiv's territorial defense's six battalions had gathered in a predetermined place by 8 am. There were just 30 of them. Among them was Officer Yuriy Myronenko, Deputy Chief of Staff of the 129th battalion. In civilian life, he held senior management positions in major financial institutions and provided expertise in an analytical think tank that focused on reforms in Ukraine. Three years earlier he had joined Kyiv's defense and regularly upgraded his training, but like most of his peers, he had no experience in real combat.

In the village of Novi Petrivtsi, on the northern border of Kyiv, fighting had already begun. The next morning, a Russian armored vehicle entered Obolon, Kyiv's northernmost district on the western bank of the Dnipro River. Yuriy's battalion, which by that time had grown to almost 100 people as a result of a significant uptake of volunteers, neutralized the vehicle within 15 minutes. Still, everyone knew that to stop more Russians approaching Kyiv, many more people would be needed.

"Only the incredibly quick military decisions taken by the commander of our battalion, the commander of Kyiv's 112th Territorial Defense Brigade, Oleksandr Pavliy, and the Ministry of Defense, saved the situation," Yuriy tells us two months later in Kyiv. On that second day of the Russian invasion, his defense battalion received a large number of weapons, and in a few hours, his battalion of less than 100 grew to 650. By evening, the number had increased to 800. On the third day, there were already 1,200 people.

The situation was similar in other battalions, not only in Kyiv but throughout Ukraine. In the headquarters of one, Vladyslav was dealing with the influx of newcomers, enlisting them in ranks. Some of them, like the members of the Ukrainian Legion, had already collected all the things they needed into backpacks, and "at the first call — and some even without a call — went to their military units," says Vladyslav. "Others had undergone little to no military training. The newcomers who came to enlist were of all ages and professions and often from the same family. They included brothers, parents and sons, young couples. The basics of how to use weapons correctly and safely were taught right there at the recruitment point," Vladyslav says.

"Under such conditions, you learn three times faster," adds Yuriy. "You know how to shoot from an NLAW (lightweight, shoulder-held anti-tank missile) in as little as seven minutes of training. You quickly learn how to use a machine gun, and instantly — almost instinctively — how to dig trenches and maneuver. Usually, it takes years to learn all this but we learned everything in a month."

Some people came to headquarters and said, "I can't shoot, but I want to be useful." These volunteers were assigned to enlisting or other practical tasks behind battle lines. "People used to pay bribes to escape the army, and now they're doing everything to join," Vladyslav says.

On the second day of the invasion, more than 700 people crammed together to enlist in Yuriy's battalion. "The crowd was huge, and it took me 20 minutes to persuade people to disperse and wait. This was the first time we met so many people willing to join the military at the same time, in one place. Such overwhelming feelings are impossible to forget."

*\*\**

Each battalion was divided into groups of 50 to 100 people and dispatched to key positions: some in Kyiv, Irpin, Bucha, and Moshchun, all within a five-kilometer radius of Kyiv. Others were placing mines under the Hostomel highway to cut off the Russians. At Hostomel airfield, where Russians made their first landing attempt, the territorial defense and other units were fighting alongside the Ukrainian National Guard.

"The fact that we battalion officers knew each other and understood who was responsible for what helped us to quickly get down to work," says Yuriy. "This is what allowed some units to grow tenfold. The battalions had organizational core groups consisting of 10 to 20 people."

This model of an organizational core guiding newcomers worked well with other battalions too. About 95% of personnel joined Kyiv's 112th Territorial Defense Brigade within the first days of the full-scale war. But the other 5% who joined before the invasion, like Yuriy, knew how things worked and could organize others. The battalion officers were allowed to make their own military decisions on the ground, without waiting for orders from above.

"We could do whatever we wanted," says Yuriy. "We understood how many Russians were coming and we could decide where to strengthen our positions. It all moved very fast, because in the first few hours, we had to stop the lead Russian troops and show them that there were many troops in Kyiv. But we weren't even creating an illusion, because, indeed, a huge number of people took up arms. For me, 24, 25, and 26 February were like one day, and only two weeks later, from the logs of hostilities, did I realize that then we didn't sleep, didn't eat, and indeed lived through it as if it was one day."

The situation was tense everywhere Yuriy's battalion was fighting, but it was especially daunting in the village of Moshchun, just five kilometers from Kyiv. "Every hour we waited for the Russians to attack," says Yuriy. "Everything was on a knife's edge. We had a hair-raising feeling for about four days, and everyone said goodbye to life, so actually it was quite easy. Only when it's all over do you realize that this thinking was complete madness ... everyone has children and families. But, at that time, all of us were in a state of mind that a single person by themselves can't have. We all united, and together we kept a cool head."

***

Kyiv was under siege, getting used to the sounds of explosions. Civilians were living not knowing what the next hour would bring. Likewise, in the headquarters of Vladyslav's battalion, he had a feeling that at any moment, if the Russians approached, he would have to stop working on logistics, enlistment, or weapons-training and grab all weapons and fight. For the first four days, Vladyslav continually wore a helmet, until finally he took it off. As fate would have it, ten minutes later the outer wall collapsed from heavy shelling, and large chunks fell on his head, leaving yet another "memento" war scar. Things did not get better for him. A few days later, he was diagnosed with bilateral pneumonia. Still, he did not stop his efforts and continued working on logistics, even while in hospital.

Meanwhile, many Kyivans were assisting the military. Hanging the national Ukrainian blue-and-yellow flag out of a window or on the street was enough to signal that this was a depot accepting donations for food, equipment, and anything else needed by the military.

"I didn't see a difference between military and non-military people at that time," says Yuriy. "We were all in one camp. For example, many civilians cooked for us in school kitchens. Overall, I never felt such strong emotions, even during the revolution in 2014. Then, there wasn't the same constant danger ... not the overwhelming enemy forces that we saw during the siege of Kyiv every day. I realized that I didn't understand people at all. Those I counted on didn't help, and vice versa. In such times, people become completely different. But we all understood that the top command wasn't going to give up, and this was one of the things that kept up our morale."

\*\*\*

Initially, Kyiv defenders were afraid they would not be able to overcome such a multitude of Russian troops.

"They would come in, we would kill them, and then they would kill us. There were so many of them," Yuriy says.

But things began to change. The last four days before the Russians retreated, the Ukrainian armed forces fought them off with all their might. They threw everything they had at them. A barrage of heavy artillery never stopped blasting from the Ukrainian side. On the fifth day, the Russians retreated.

When it was finally quiet on the city outskirts, Yuriy says the 112th defenders felt even more anxious, simply because it seemed surreal.

Closer to the end of March, when Russian troops were pushed further away from Kyiv, Yuriy sensed exhaustion for the first time since the invasion began. He worked for two hours; then fell into a deep sleep. When he talked about the experience with other officers, they said they had felt the same.

"Everyone told me to record my memories, but there was never any time," says Yuriy, telling us his story. "Thankfully, I managed to recall it all."

We met up with Yuriy in Kyiv two months after the expulsion of the Russians at the opening of the exhibition "Invasion. Kyiv Shot" in the National Museum of History of Ukraine. The atmosphere was celebratory, yet tinged with sadness, because of the losses Ukraine continued to suffer in the war and the awareness that winning a battle does not mean winning the war. The exhibition was to be opened by Commander Oleksandr Pavliy, Kyiv's 112th Territorial Defense Brigade, but he could not join because he was attending the funeral of soldiers from his unit.

"Today, I was at two funerals," Yuriy says. "Both of the killed had defended the Obolon district from day one. I see so many funerals of soldiers every day that I can't count them anymore. We can't say that we are used to it. We try to attend funerals to meet with the families of the killed, to see their mothers, children."

The name of the exhibition in Ukrainian is Navala, translated into English as "Invasion," which does not quite carry the same connotation. Navala means a huge and savage group that attacks en masse with no warning, destroying everything on their way. The Ukrainian word particularly suits the situation in 2022, when the Russian assault, with its superiority in manpower and equipment, attempted to overwhelm Ukrainian forces. In some places, like on the outskirts of Kyiv, Russian columns stretched for 60 kilometers.

"The Russians surely assaulted Kyiv thinking we had no defense — not enough weapons and too small a military force. But instead, armed thousands showed up. It was a huge surprise and — to put it mildly — a disappointment for the Russians," says Press Officer of Kyiv's 112th Territorial Defense Brigade Andriy Kovaliov. He is confident that it would have been enough for the Russians to simply break into Kyiv and sow panic, no matter in which district, "All battles were difficult, but the hardest was the battle for Kyiv."

Most of the 112th brigade personnel who took part in the defense of Kyiv went on to fight on the front line in the east of the country, while many of the wounded soldiers were treated in hospitals.

\*\*\*

In the first two days of the war, 21,000 rifles were distributed to volunteers who had joined Kyiv's Territorial Defense Forces, many of whom had never held a weapon.[7] This radical decision led to some chaos and mistakes, but also achieved remarkable results. At one point, members of Kyiv's territorial defense mistakenly detained the Ukrainian Minister of Energy, knocking him over and

---

7    Ukrainian Minister of Defense Oleksiy Reznikov said about this in an interview with Ukrinform (https://www.ukrinform.ua/rubric-polytics/3756451-oleksij-reznikov-ministr-oboroni-ukraini.html).

pressing his face to the asphalt. At another time, while searching for saboteurs, territorial defense members unknowingly killed their own by friendly fire. On the other hand, the rapid response to the threat led to notable successes. Pensioner Valentyn Didkovskyi, a resident of Bucha who signed up for the territorial defense and was given a grenade launcher, pitched it from his backyard and hit a Russian fuel truck in a column that included four tanks. Quickly taking cover, Valentyn transmitted coordinates to professional soldiers who were able to shell the column within minutes.[8]

Self-organized groups were also involved in providing provisions to the army, which had tripled in size within a few months. Vladyslav once asked a soldier who had returned from his position in Kyiv, what he needed. The soldier made a list for himself and his unit, and Vladyslav found everything. Word caught on, and civilians came forward to help. Soon people were calling Vladyslav, saying, "We're bringing you a whole truckload of goods," or "We're bringing half a traincar of food." Vladyslav still does not know how some people knew about him. "I think we are winning the battles because there are volunteers in Ukraine: not only now, but since 2014 and all the years in between."

Vladyslav talks about both sides of the coin: "Ukrainians have their positive and negative traits. On the negative side, many people like to put things off until the last minute. We are still digging ourselves out of what we could've done — but didn't do — before the 2022 invasion. On the positive side, out of nowhere heroism can surface. I once asked a commander what heroism is, and he told me, 'Heroism is where some people in positions simply give up, but others step in.' In the case of volunteers — if we didn't have any food, and they brought it — they are heroes. Someone didn't do their job somewhere, so somebody else had to."

However, during this time in Ukrainian history, aside from acts of heroism, certain crucial work at a structural level was carried out in advance. "I would like to praise those people who developed the Territorial Defense Law. Where would we be if there

---

8    Volodymyr Didkovskyi's story was published by Ukrinform on 8 November 2022 (https://youtu.be/MMMoTr_1bQI?si=ZY02ldY9NMMKU0sU).

hadn't been such a legal framework? People would come, and what to do with them?" Yuriy says, recalling the first days of the invasion when a mass of volunteers arrived at territorial defense recruitment.

In his historical essays, the Ukrainian historian Ivan Lysiak-Rudnytsky (1919–1984) noted two wings of Ukrainian political thought: first, the left-leaning, represented in particular by Mykhailo Drahomanov, who valued decentralization and self-organization; and second, the conservatism of Vyacheslav Lypynsky, who believed that the revolutionary spirit of negation lacked the urge for constructive solutions, and the spirit of self-organization lacked hierarchy, verticality and law.

The affinity for decentralization and the spirit of the liberation struggle, along with strong criticism of authorities, remained defining elements in the political landscape of Ukraine at the beginning of the 21st century.

Yet it seems that the success in repelling the Russian attack on Kyiv in 2022 was attributable not only to self-organized enthusiasts — volunteers ready for self-sacrifice and acts of heroism — but also to those who had been systematically preparing for the war since 2014: for example by creating new national-level institutions such as the Territorial Defense Forces.

***

Two months after victory in the Battle of Kyiv, the city is far from being the vibrant metropolis it once was. The city's metro works, but trains run less frequently. Cafes are opening up, but are adjusting their hours to stay in line with the daily curfew. And, although a few central areas are quite full, most of the previously overcrowded streets are half empty. Traffic in the city has declined by nearly half. "I always wanted Kyiv to be less congested, but now I'm more cautious about my desires," is a comment often heard. Yet, it is a great joy to be in Kyiv, realizing that all of this might have been lost.

In May 2022, Vladyslav took charge of a mortar platoon which was waiting for weapons to arrive before leaving for the front line.

As he was preparing to head east, a video ad he helped to create weeks before the 2022 invasion was playing in the carriages of the Kyiv metro. It calls on Kyivans to join Kyiv's 112th Territorial Defense Brigade.

As we breathe the May air in Kyiv, Vladyslav rejoices that more people have begun to speak Ukrainian following Russia's attack. After the 2022 invasion, the Russian language in Kyiv was not heard as often as before the war. Surveys show that in Ukraine almost half of Russian speakers switched to Ukrainian, dropping the number of Russian speakers to a mere 13%, compared to 26% before the war and 42% in the 1990s when Ukraine gained independence from the USSR and from three centuries of Russian oppression.[9]

Vladyslav's parents switched from their native language of Ukrainian to Russian when they moved to the city from their rural home. Like many in Ukraine, they were victims of an aggressive Russification policy during the Soviet era. As a child, Vladyslav was puzzled as to why his grandparents, whom he visited in their village, spoke Ukrainian, while his parents spoke Russian at home. His grandparents inspired him to switch to Ukrainian years before the start of war in 2022, "Maybe someone from my environment will make the same choice," Vladyslav used to think. And it happened. His parents began to speak to him in Ukrainian.

---

9    The data is based on a Rating Group poll and the 2001 census (https://euromai danpress.com/2022/09/17/russias-war-is-speeding-up-the-ukrainization-of-ukraine/).

# Sniper-Theologian

On a sunny May afternoon in Kyiv, on the edge of the vast and forested Holosiyivskyi Park, three men are casually aiming a huge black sniper rifle at an old brick tower, dominating the skyline. The men, two of them in Ukrainian military uniform, are surrounded by thick oak trees that are hundreds of years old. These oaks may have witnessed battles during the 17th-century Cossack (Kozak) Era when Ukraine was a de facto independent, militarized state, wary of the constant danger of incursion, either by Polish landlords or the Russian Tsar's army. The three armed men standing here at ease resemble those formidable Cossack warriors, but instead of sabers, they hold 21st-century rifles.

Two of the men are soldiers from the Aidar Battalion. The third, wearing a gray T-shirt with the print of a blue-and-yellow flag and shadow figures of soldiers, is Yuriy Chornomorets, a theology professor who, when Russia attacked Ukraine in 2022, swapped his lecture hall for a sniper rifle.

"What a beautiful place," we greet Yuriy and the soldiers, entering the yard of the small block of flats on the edge of the park where he lives.

"The huge tower in the center of the park is good to test sights," Yuriy replies. He holds a Barrett M107—a weapon that can strike from a distance of two kilometers. In Yuriy's words, "the fear of politicians."

His and the soldiers' cheerful mood reflects the recent victory in the Battle of Kyiv, a fight that protected this park and the home to which Yuriy now invites us. His apartment is an eclectic mix of antique-style furniture and paintings, alongside military supplies—a mountain of canned goods, tents, sleeping bags, foam pads, boxes of ammunition, and five sniper rifles. The soldiers gather up some of these supplies to take to the front line and leave us alone with Yuriy.

"Did you buy rifles before the war, or once it started?"

"Oh, that's a nice story," says Yuriy. "My wife teased me that if I buy a weapon, the war will start. But it would have started anyway."

***

Three decades ago, when things were still peaceful, Yuriy's grandfather taught him to shoot. At first, he gave him lessons at a 100-meter shooting range at school and later at professional ranges. "You should do nothing, but be prepared to do everything," he told his grandson.

Yuriy trained for years, but eventually gave it up to immerse himself in the study and instruction of philosophy and theology. In 2022, it became evident that Russia was about to invade Ukraine on a full scale. Exactly a month before the February invasion, Yuriy's acquaintance, a Ukrainian colonel, called him to say that military personnel had received weapons. For Yuriy, that meant impending war.

"Have you taken your children out of Kyiv?" Yuriy asked.

"They're already in western Ukraine."

Yuriy called Pavlo Haidai, the founder of the cultural organization Between the Ears (Mizh Vukhamy), which funds the translation of philosophical works into Ukrainian. Pavlo too had already been preparing for the war and helped Yuriy quickly acquire several rifles when weapons outlets in Kyiv were sold out.

"Aristotle's Metaphysics, together with Ibn Sina, served as a support for my rifle," Yuriy tells us, taking two thick volumes, translated by Mizh Vukhamy, from the table that is cluttered with boxes of cartridges and other rifle equipment—from sights to mufflers.

***

In the first days of the full-scale invasion, Yuriy went to enroll in the Territorial Defense Forces of Kyiv's Holosiyivskyi District, taking his sniper rifle with him. Upon seeing the rifle, the commanders enlisted him in a group of experienced Aidar Battalion fighters instead of an ordinary infantry unit. Most of the soldiers of this battalion—created as a volunteer formation in 2014—were primarily fighting in the east. However, a few of them were in Kyiv and started fighting near their homes in the capital.

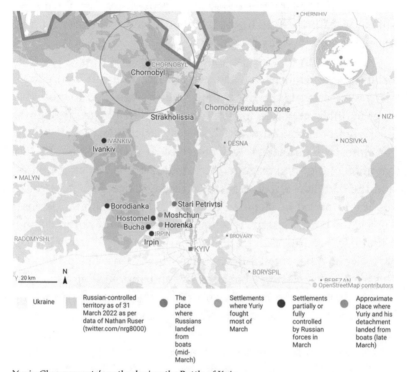

Yuriy Chornomorets's paths during the Battle of Kyiv.

Weeks before the invasion, Russian saboteur groups entered Ukraine. Yuriy's detachment's first success was capturing one of the groups that was approaching Kyiv from Obukhiv, a satellite town to the south. These saboteurs were from the so-called Luhansk People's Republic—the proxy republic created by Russia in 2014, in an occupied part of Ukraine's easternmost Luhansk region. Some of them could speak Ukrainian and pretended to bring aid. However, images of bridges and military positions on their tablets revealed them as Russian mercenaries.

*** 

In early March, Yuriy's detachment was redeployed near Horenka, a village five kilometers west of Kyiv on the Irpin River. The river and several places nearby became Kyiv's northwestern shield. Many bridges along the river had already been blown up as a tactic to stop Russian troops.

Yuriy's unit took up positions on the river's bank. Kyiv was behind them, while ahead, across the water, more and more Russians were assembling. Every day, the Russians tried to cross the river in different places, intending to pour into a huge forest girding Kyiv from the northwest. This forest, stretching along the river for almost 20 kilometers, was protected at that time only by the battalion of the 72nd Brigade, the battalion of the National Guard, and the battalion of "others," as Yuriy says. The "others," which his unit belonged to, included volunteers of the Territorial Defense Forces, the border guards who had retreated from Chornobyl; the Ukrainian Security Service (SBU), as Yuriy says, "driving cool SUVs"; and other small military units. This defense line prevented Russians from crossing Irpin en masse and approaching Kyiv.

At that time, the Russian army did not have enough drones to use on a tactical level, and it was easier for Ukrainian troops to trick them.

"The first line of trenches would be left empty," Yuriy says, recalling one of the tactics his unit used. "Why?" he asks rhetorically. "The Russians had no idea that there was nobody there — they shelled the trench around the clock. Although we had orders to go to the first line, we convinced everyone that we should stay in the second line. Only when the Russians floated a pontoon across Irpin did we jump to the first line to repel them." Another life-preserving approach was to avoid the crossroads that Russians regularly and heavily shelled. After two soldiers from Yuriy's platoon had been killed by artillery at a crossroads, the priority became choosing alternative routes.

Because the Ukrainian army had far fewer drones than it would have later, the snipers' first role was reconnaissance.[10] While observing the terrain from high locations—hills or rooftops—Yuriy watched Russian troop movements across the Irpin River and their landing attempts.

One time he reported to his comrades about suspicious movements that might be a sabotage group and should be checked. It was obvious to Yuriy that the soldiers were poorly coordinated. He spotted them landing in a factory on Horenka's edge, behind Yuriy's positions, where they found themselves trapped under Ukrainian fire. The Russians set the warehouses on fire, but heavy chemical smoke blew back to their positions, instead of at the Ukrainians. The Russians then bombed the house opposite the factory, which they mistook for a Ukrainian position—but it was a pony stable. For days, the ponies kept running around Yuriy's detachment looking for grass to graze on.

Yuriy worked near Horenka, always keeping his light Remington sniper rifle close by. "Up to 400 meters means 100% death for the Moscovite. If the distance is further, you need to aim well."

For several nights, the terrain was illuminated by moonlight: Yuriy and his fellow snipers saw Russians clearly, even without thermal imaging. They were looking for "fat" targets, e.g., colonels or other commanders, to sow panic among the Russian military. "It was easy to detect them," he says. "Just look for the people brandishing their arms and shouting a lot."

---

10   Since 2014, the Ukrainian army has been procuring drones of operational significance with a range of dozens of kilometers. At the same time, the state at first overlooked inexpensive tactical drones. These inexpensive drones were supplied by volunteers en masse in 2022, including a civilian Mavic drone and later various forms of FPV drones as strike drones. Since 2023, within the project Army of Drones, the state has paid considerable attention to this weapon, purchasing dozens, and later hundreds of thousands of tactical drones, and establishing separate drone companies at each brigade. On 6 February 2024, Ukraine's President Volodymyr Zelenskyy signed the decree establishing the Unmanned Systems Forces as a separate branch of the army.

\*\*\*

Yuriy says that Russians were fighting as a huge block, trying to adjust the entire block for any given situation, while Ukrainian forces relied more on small groups and personal initiative. The Russians deployed lengthy military convoys for the Kyiv offensive, up to 64 kilometers long. They attacked with huge numbers in the hope that they could break through Ukrainian defenses. However, the "blitzkrieg" failed, and their long columns worked against them, as they became increasingly vulnerable to retaliatory attacks. During the battle for Kyiv, Ukrainian snipers attacked Russian troops, not only from the front, but also from the sides, while the convoys were slow and cumbersome in their long, single-file formations.

Initially, Russian convoys were protected by multiple military units on both sides of the central convoy. Later, Russians began using singular, solid lines, with three columns advancing in parallel—one as the main, and the other two protecting on either flank. In response, Ukrainians started using small groups of soldiers; for example, two grenade launchers, two snipers, and one machine gunner. "These small groups," says Yuriy, "crept towards the guarding column, edging through it, and said, 'Good evening, we are from Ukraine.'"

"And then came the most phenomenal moment ..." Yuriy tells us about the most extreme case a friend of his experienced in Yasnohorodka, at the outermost Russian position southwest of Kyiv. "Exactly 34 shots and 34 corpses. Goodbye."

In the southern Kherson region, Russians rapidly advanced nearly 200 kilometers due to the lack of Ukrainian troops in this section of the front. The first months of the war were also particularly challenging for snipers here, mainly due to the flat, steppe terrain. While in forested areas, a sniper mainly crawls—sometimes as far as five kilometers at a time—to find a good position, this was impossible on the steppe. In the Kherson region, snipers mostly worked "as the Americans do." They found good spots along the front line and from a high structure, or a hill, made only one shot and then quickly escaped by car. Yuriy says they had large losses of equipment in the south because the Russians knew that after a sniper took a shot, a car would be waiting behind, and their insane shelling would begin. A Russian Orlan drone flying overhead might not spot the snipers but would home in on the car.

Once, a sniper was killed because he used a rangefinder. "Such a trifle—his rangefinder ray—which is invisible to the human eye but visible to the tank, was detected," Yuriy says. "A Russian tank shot directly and killed him instantly. He was a great guy. But he didn't have the—so to speak—passion for hunting. Why measure with a rangefinder? I always say not to use a rangefinder unless critically needed. You have to first think about how not to reveal yourself."

He tells us that some snipers were killed because they went to a position without a balaclava or at least a face cover. "Only on PR photos will you see a sniper's rifle that is not masked or their hands without gloves." In real-life combat, these simple items make the difference between life and death.

*** 

The massive chaotic shelling and frontal attacks across the town of Irpin and the Irpin River failed the Russians. They found themselves stuck and had to try other spots to break through the Ukrainian defenses towards Kyiv. Deploying more reserves, the Russians eventually managed to cross the river farther north, near the village of Moshchun.

In addition, Russian sabotage groups from the Dnipro Reservoir attacked Ukrainian troops from the rear as a distraction maneuver. The Dnipro Reservoir stretches 70 kilometers from the Ukrainian border with Belarus to Kyiv and is 10 kilometers wide. Russian troops used several boats to land on the reservoir's bank between Stari Petrivtsi and Novi Petrivtsi, just 10 kilometers north of Kyiv and five kilometers from Moshchun.

The front line shifted south, even closer to Kyiv, to a forested plain with lakes and swamps between the Irpin River and the Dnipro Reservoir. This became the next defining spot in the Battle of Kyiv. Russian troops occupied the largest part of Moshchun in mid-March and were about to move farther, using this last village before Kyiv as their foothold. Ukrainian reserves were deployed to the village—among them Yuriy's platoon.

"Picturesque," says Yuriy about this place. His position was near the Moshchun lakes, created by several dams on the small Moshchunka River that flows into the Irpin. It was a beautiful spot, not one you would associate with war. A huge cottage, where deer foraged peacefully, was close to Yuriy's position. However, the fighting and heavy Russian shelling almost completely destroyed Moshchun, leaving no undamaged houses. It was in this area that the famous Ukrainian photographer Maks Levin was killed on 13 March while documenting the consequences of Russian military aggression.

Meanwhile, Ukrainian troops had blown up the Kozarovytska Dam at the mouth of the Irpin River that flows into the Dnipro Reservoir. It increased the water level in the Irpin, as well as in neighboring swamps, springs, and lakes, creating additional obstacles for the Russians.

According to Vyacheslav Hrul[11], acting commander of the 134th Battalion of the 114th Brigade of the Territorial Defense Forces, a few soldiers walked 400 meters, carrying by hand one ton of explosives—50 boxes, each 25 kilograms—to the dam in several trips. Vyacheslav, together with others, carried these boxes at night, under Russian shelling, keeping a distance of 20 meters between each other in case a Russian projectile should hit one of them. In that event, only one would be lost and the others would be far enough away to be saved. They were lucky and everyone survived, while the blown-up dam further disrupted the Russian assault on Kyiv.

"Maintaining this outpost was a daunting task. After all, Moshchun could have become a gateway for the enemy en route to the capital," Ukraine's Commander-in-Chief Valeriy Zaluzhnyi later said about this battle. "However, our soldiers showed

---

11    Vyacheslav Hrul told his story on the Brave Hearts talk show on the 1+1 TV channel (https://youtu.be/lcq5DgonSTA).

miracles of military skill. Under the feet of the invaders, not only land burned, but also water. Ukrainian defenders blew up bridges and pontoon crossings, preventing the enemy from advancing. They held Moshchun. And this protected Kyiv."[12]

Yuriy says holding these northwestern gates to Kyiv was indeed on a knife edge. "One day Russians took a long time to decide where to land the pontoon. Then, under the stealth of night, they landed right in front of us and began to cross the Moshchunka River. We had a guy, Liam, who experienced a military encirclement by Russians several times in 2014 in the Donetsk region and barely survived. And now he says, 'It's the end for us, 15 minutes of battle.'"

But just at that moment, a Ukrainian MLRS Grad fired 16 missiles. "Boom! Boom! Boom! and that was the end for the Russians. We didn't even have to shoot," Yuriy says. "Yet, we started wondering why the MLRS didn't target the pontoon, because usually they do."

Suddenly, they heard the rumble of a tank column. This time, Liam said, "five minutes of battle." But it turned out that these were Ukrainian tanks from the 72nd Brigade. They passed by Yuriy's unit from the flank and rapidly crossed the water, past that Russian pontoon, and advanced farther. "In no time, the northern part of the forest was liberated," Yuriy says.

His platoon didn't expect this surprise Ukrainian operation. Volunteer units, like Yuriy's, were fighting alongside the territorial defense, conducting supportive tasks and holding the line, while more complicated moves were conducted either by regular brigades or special forces. Yuriy's infantry unit had few casualties because of the fire support from the 72nd Brigade, which together with territorial defense protected the most difficult direction from Kyiv — northwest. Yuriy praises the brigade, and especially its artillery gunners as being, "highly professional, hitting the target with every shell."

---

12    The General Staff of the Armed Forces of Ukraine shared this statement on 10 April 2022 (https://www.facebook.com/watch/?v=376799087641852).

"The Russians were shelling five to six times more, but chaotically, covering huge squares, not specific sections. The Ukrainian artillery was waiting, determining Russian coordinates ... waiting ... and then Boom! Boom! Goodbye! They could see the Russians relocating tanks—Boom! Boom! again, and five tanks are burning. The Russians began shelling everything around them—the entire front line from every barrel they had. They were in a firing frenzy because they lost five tanks and had to take revenge."

"The efficiency of the territorial defense and other volunteer battalions largely depended on how well the regular units formed the core," Yuriy says. For instance, his friends from the volunteer Carpathian Sich Battalion advanced successfully with the 92nd Brigade north of Kharkiv. However, there were other brigades with a limit of 30 shells per day that failed to support infantry.

Since the core of regular units near Kyiv was highly professional, newcomers to the army, who were holding a machine gun for the first time, could quickly join the actual fight. Yuriy says a variety of people fought alongside his unit. "There were students who lived nearby, and together they enrolled in the territorial defense. Everyone thought they were cry-babies, but they turned out to be monsters, no worse than the SBU. They had common sense, determination, and no fear. When the shelling and the chaos of the battle starts, if you're afraid, you're already dead. Not being afraid is the key. Just keep to that and hope to be lucky."

Some Ukrainian soldiers walked kilometers through enemy territory to bring ammunition to encircled troops. "They just loaded backpacks and walked. Yes, there were losses, but there were also those who made it all the way, and came back alive and well. We could have quietly crept all the way to Moscow through the enemy's rear if we had such a task," Yuriy says half-seriously. "I think this solution is long overdue—to go, shoot, and return. Because it has all dragged on for too long. He sometimes comes out of his bunker, and a Barrett could shoot him, even at 2.5 kilometers," he adds about Putin.

Yuriy explains that at the front, the best snipers belong to different categories. The first is those who took formal courses, trained for a long time, and are highly professional. The second is those who served in the army or somewhere in private security, and thus earned a sniper qualification. The third is professional hunters who shoot without calculations, but as they learned to do on the hunt. Many women are snipers and work with a variety of weapons, including those considered semi-sniper, and have high results. In one case, Yuriy helped a husband and wife who were a sniper team.

"Snipers have a great impact, not only because they inflict losses on the enemy but also for psychological reasons. The enemy knows, 'Snipers are out there, so we need to hide and can't go forward.' They call for tanks to arrive and help them. Psychosis and fear set in. If you put out 1,000 good snipers who shoot steadily, you can quickly push the enemy into the trenches."

\*\*\*

"Russians came here by boats, so why can't we go to them by boats?" Liam asked after the liberation of Moshchun and the platoon's rotation to the rear. He proposed to conduct a sabotage attack in the Chornobyl exclusion zone, which Russian troops had occupied. "I know several people who live near the exclusion zone," he added.

Liam, Yuriy and nine other men received a boat and sailed to the north of the Dnipro Reservoir to sabotage the Russians' rear. After the victory in Moshchun on 21 March, the tide of the Kyiv battle had started turning in the Ukrainians' favor, and an additional push could force the Russians to retreat.

Liam and his men were not alone when they sailed. There were other groups, including fighters of the volunteer Carpathian Sich Battalion and several foreign volunteers from the International Legion. Five Americans, one Briton, and one Lithuanian joined in. They landed first in the area north of Kyiv. Yuriy's unit followed. "Look, the gangsters have arrived. When will the regular army come?" international legionnaires joked upon seeing volunteers of the territorial defense with different types of uniforms and equipment.

The American fighters were well-equipped, Yuriy tells us, with their own sniper rifles and machine guns — one of them even had a Stinger. For a short time, early in the war, anyone could bring any type of weapon across the international border.

"It turned out the Americans we met at the Chornobyl zone were all Trumpists," Yuriy says. "And when you tell them that Grandpa Biden also seems to be a conservative with balls, they say it's not the same. They have an ultra-Republican worldview according to which there are 'points of evil' that should be fought. They saw there was a problem here and that help was needed, and so they came. The British soldier knew how to work on everything from sniper rifles to Stingers. He looked very young but had been fighting since the 1991 Desert Storm."

For Yuriy, the inconvenience of working with these international fighters was that they did not ask for help. "They drag around boxes with machine gun ammunition themselves. They might collapse under the weight, but won't ask for help. You have to offer to help. Usually, we in Ukraine just say, 'Hey, help,' when boxes need to be carried. But once you've offered them help, they're glad to receive it."

During the Battle of Kyiv, Yuriy met more fighters from other countries. One Georgian said he fought everywhere against the Russians wherever there was a war. Sadly, during the Battle of Kyiv, he was killed in action. Another international fighter, a Latvian, came with his own weapons. Yuriy met several more international fighters, "All wonderful people and highly professional."

Yuriy's detachment approached the Chornobyl exclusion zone through an abandoned village. They had a scout with them who had a tablet and could communicate with the General Staff to coordinate the mission, but his connection was jammed. Luckily in the Sukholuchchia village, they were able to connect from the second floor. "Locals from the village hosted us, and we were able to hide in their houses. Russians had many observation posts and fortifications in the area, but they couldn't guard every corner, especially when they started retreating from Kyiv under Ukrainian pressure," says Yuriy. "The village people had a habit of burning a lot of firewood, so it was hotter than a sauna. I have heart problems, and it was difficult to sleep there."

His group proposed to blow up one of the bridges near Chornobyl to cut the escape routes for Russians. They prepared explosives and drew up a plan, but before they reached the bridge the next morning, most of the Russian troops had hastily retreated. Yuriy's group found the location of Russian Iskanders that had shelled Kyiv, as well as secret Russian documents. These they passed on to counterintelligence, "We came to the sad realization that if a brigade had been deployed to build a defense line along the Teteriv River[13] and if bridges had been blown up before the Russian attack, the horrors of Bucha and Irpin would never have occurred. Russians could have taken the Hostomel airport near Kyiv by landing troops, at most, but we could have quickly killed them there."

While military commanders mostly did prepare their personnel for the upcoming invasion and were on high alert, this was not the case with the country generally. President Volodymyr Zelenskyy was praised for his firm stance at the beginning of the invasion, but at the same time was criticized for his failure to declare martial law earlier and deploy brigades along the northern and southern borders in advance.

***

For the Chornobyl mission, logistical support provided Yuriy's unit with only 12 cans of stewed meat and a bunch of sweets, half of which were honey. It took time to arrange proper supplies for thousands of newcomers to territorial defense. Yuriy called his friend Valeriy Fedoranych for help. Valeriy lived in Ukraine's westernmost region, Zakarpattia and was able to load a truck with three tons of food, as well as sleeping bags. After the

---

13   Teteriv River flows 40 kilometers south of the Belarusian-Ukrainian border, roughly halfway from Belarus to Kyiv. However, Russian troops managed to quickly pass the river in the first days of the war and were stopped only near Kyiv.

Battle of Kyiv, half of the supplies remained, and Yuriy's platoon gave them to special operations forces near Kharkiv.

Yuriy saw this help as an example of the implementation of a religious doctrine. "Valeriy is Protestant and when they cook their local stew, the whole family gathers to can it. This is a Protestant ethic — you must serve those in need. When there is a war, and soldiers need help, they provide it. If you are a real fighter, you'll eat an entire can — if you're a 'cry-baby,' you'll only eat half," he says, smiling.

Earlier, while fighting near Horenka, there were no hot food supplies, only dry rations in limited quantities. Yuriy's unit cooked for itself whenever it could. Once, in a pause between fighting, he and a few other soldiers went to a nearby village. Only 15 people had stayed in their homes near the front line, but there were a lot of abandoned chickens. The soldiers decided to cook two buckets of chicken soup for their frontline section. "Everyone thought that I'm a professor and don't know how to do anything — how to cook from real, not supermarket, chickens. They were wrong," Yuriy tells us the story, as he brings us a hot pot of soup filled with meat. "We had lunch recently," we say. "Is this lunch? Just a snack," Yuriy replies, smiling.

\*\*\*

After a month of intensive fighting and a week in the Chornobyl zone, Yuriy started to feel ill because of his heart disease, and (likely) radiation impact. His group headed to Kharkiv, while he went to Kyiv to procure necessary supplies. He bought Blaser and Barrett sniper rifles, and other weapons that could be purchased at military stores. In this way, he found himself working as a volunteer, helping the military by fundraising and purchasing equipment.

His first order to fill was for snipers fighting near Zaporizhzhia. The bullets cost UAH 500,000 ($17,000), but his friends and Facebook followers managed to raise the sum in three days. Another sniper called, also asking for sniper bullets. Yuriy's volunteer activity skyrocketed. After two years, as of May 2024 he had purchased 295 sniper rifles, 255 optical sights, 218 mufflers, 45 thermal sights, 30 cars for sniper groups, and other add-ons. He also managed to obtain over 290,000 ammunition rounds. In total, he was able to collect millions of dollars that were donated by Ukrainians, foreign donors, and several major sponsors.

"You go to the Ibis military shop. They tell you they've only got ten pieces left of this type of cartridge. I say it's for my nephew on the front line. A long silence and then they say 'OK.' So we get a bunch of ammunition. Next time, we come with a partner and the Ibis manager asks, 'Whose nephew is that for?' and we say, 'Both of ours.'" The manager laughs but sells the ammunition. "Well, there really is a nephew we got the ammunition for. He's fighting in Azov," Yuriy says. When he started filling requests, there was a huge deficit of weapons in shops, but later the situation somewhat stabilized, and shop owners would give him generous discounts, to help as much as they could.

"One of our sabotage groups that included a sniper was almost surrounded during a mission, but they got out successfully. The sniper called me, 'I have 27 rounds left and need at least 100. Take my salary, just bring the cartridges.'" Yuriy went to Ibis, asking for 500 rounds. The shop only had 330. He took all of them and bought 600 more in another store. He loaded up the car, put packs of medicine, bulletproof vests and thermal imagers on top of the boxes, and went to Sloviansk. He delivered the aid to Kulchytskyi's battalion, where "cool guys, top-level professionals were serving." They grabbed those cartridges like children grab candy. "We thought 100 rounds would come," a soldier said. Instead, there were almost 100 boxes. Yuriy asked them what they had and what they did not have. He returned another time with the camouflage equipment snipers had asked for.

Local tailor companies and other random people quickly learned how to sew ghillie suits from special types of thread to resemble grass or leaves common to each type of environment. This included camouflage for a rifle, the head, the face, and clothing. And, of course, tactical gloves with openings for fingers. Snipers need to have a light touch on the trigger.

Two of Yuriy's friends owned a construction company and used to play paintball as a team-building exercise. Just before the war, they procured weapons and created an entire platoon from their employees. One time they called Yuriy, "Get us a Stugna." They had a man who could shoot from this Ukrainian-produced anti-tank guided missile system.

"They think I can procure anything, but I actually can't," Yuriy says. He could only find weapons available in the civilian market. This included a range of sniper and other rifles—all of which could be purchased after passing tests on psychological health. Only short-barreled weapons were banned for purchase in Ukraine and, obviously, heavy equipment. However, after the Russians were pushed back from Ukraine's north, some people managed to store captured or abandoned Russian tanks and IFVs in garages. Later, all of this equipment was retrieved by police. A popular video showed a farmer towing a tank with his tractor. These comedy episodes provided humor at a very dark time, uplifting spirits.

*** 

As a theologian, Yuriy Chornomorets studied the theological underpinnings of Russia's Orthodox Church. He traveled throughout Russia, and in the process acquired a deep understanding of Russian society, culture, and ideology. In May 2022, he shared some of his thoughts as to why Russia started the full-scale invasion and why the West failed to see it would happen.

### The foundations of the Russian political regime and ideology

The civil religion that has evolved in Russia preaches that Russia is ostensibly some kind of special territory of good, and it now wages a battle against the "rotten West." Any means are justified because Russian ideologists have already proclaimed they are fighting "the last battle."

At the beginning of the full-scale war, it was thought that — seeing great losses — Russians would go to the streets and start protesting. But we have underestimated one strange principle that exists in Russia. They know that what pours out from the TV is a lie. However, they will still stubbornly hold on to this lie because it is their worldview, even though it is contrary to the real world. A person will cling to this lie as much as possible and hate everyone and everything precisely because it contradicts this lie. This is not even an ideology but a kind of civil religion, and there is only a very small group of Russians who do not believe in it.

We are dealing with this kind of "Manichaeism," which opposes itself to the whole of culture and the whole of civilization. It says, "You are too materialistic there, so we will kill you." Russia says that the West is consumerist and that it has lost its ideological foundations. And maybe that's true. But what do you do in Russia? You are engaged in super consumption and feed the people with ideas about a special mission, which is not there. You do not keep any of your promises. If you are idealistic, be like Mahatma Gandhi — without violence. The idea that Russia is supposedly some kind of special territory of good is a very destructive idea.

The Georgian philosopher Merab Mamardashvili looked at this Russian nationalism with horror and warned that when they expressed the idea of the "last battle," they would say that any means would be acceptable, and Russian people would accept the idea. Because Russian society is like jelly, without civil society and self-organization. Indeed, Russian ultra-nationalist Alexander Dugin and other people are coming and saying, "We have the last battle." And then the authorities are ready to lie about Georgia, lie about Ukraine, or any other country, commit immoral acts — and believe that they will not be punished.

What we see from 2012 to 2021 is that Russian state propaganda and even the Russian Orthodox Church have instilled the ideology of fascism, sharing all those features that Umberto Eco describes, including even the cult of machismo. Macho Putin flew everywhere, walked with bears, showed off his naked torso on a horse, and so on.

Our problem is that we read little of Hitler's wartime speeches. If we studied those speeches, we would know that not only were "the Jews" to blame for everything but with them, "world democracy" and "the rotten West." All of this is what Putin and Kirill, the Patriarch of Moscow, are saying today. Almost verbatim. They are stubborn—they know that fascism is based on lies, but they continue to profess it.

I traveled to Russia. Such incredible natural resources—they could be living better than in Saudi Arabia, receiving immediately after birth $100,000 in your account. However, in Russia, most of all, I disliked the complete savagery I saw. For example, people who reside around the monastery Optina Pustyn, where lots of tourists come, live from the proceeds of these tourists and, at the same time, tell me how they hate Optina Pustyn. I then thought, "Guys, what are you drinking? This Optina Pustyn feeds you, you have to pray for it. And you sit as if before the new 1917[14] and think, 'when will we finally set it on fire.'" To make such an attitude and worldview possible, it is necessary to keep the population at a low level of education and to have very strong collectivism and infantilism.

---

14    When the Bolsheviks ordered to "steal the stolen" from the bourgeoisie, which led to massive economic destruction and famine.

*A woman with a blue and yellow bouquet enters the cathedral. Such two-color bouquets are brought for a soldier's funeral. While waiting, she approaches the portraits of service members killed in the war.*

*Flags are placed by each grave, creating the impression of a large powerful army, but the painful sense of lost souls who have passed much too early prevails. The Field of Mars.*

*While strolling through Chernihiv's downtown, it is easy to forget about the war. Many streets are completely cleaned up, in sharp contrast to the very same downtown just a few weeks before. However, the outskirts tell a different story. There are streets where every building has suffered damage or been destroyed by Russian shelling. Chernihiv's outskirts and La Pizza Espresso on Victory Avenue which fed 22,000 people during the siege.*

*"Democracy is less effective at war. But we have to persevere, and I think we need to work on explaining and educating people that we will only win together or lose together," says Ukrainian MP Inna Sovsun.*

*In the improvised headquarters in the restaurant's basement, new work is in full swing. Six people, including the owner of La Pizza Espresso Oleh Bibikov, work diligently on many small but urgent initiatives.*

*Among the rye fields, where grain ears had already sprouted, some projectiles which had fallen from a Kamaz truck were still there. Nonetheless, Andriy from Lukashivka was determined to complete sowing.*

*The first internally displaced persons who arrived in Novovolynsk were from Kyiv. "They came to the town council saying: 'I am an IT specialist. I am an accountant. I have a car. I can do this and that. Tell me how to help,'" deputy mayor Yuliya Lefter recalls.*

### Russian Orthodox Church and Russian chauvinism

The very existence of Ukraine is "unacceptable" for Russian Orthodox Church Patriarch Kirill. The branch of Russian Orthodox in Ukraine began a systematic information war against Ukraine, saying the voting of communities for the transition to the Kyiv Church is "persecution."[15]

Patriarch Kirill of the Russian Orthodox Church has not just taken a servile position regarding the state, but one in which it repeats in full everything the state says. Former Patriarch Alexei, who died in 2008, distinguished between Ukrainians, Belarusians, and Russians, but Patriarch Kirill began saying in 2015 that Ukrainians, Belarusians, and Moldovans were not just part of the Russian world, but sub-ethnic groups in the Russian nation. And the very existence of Ukraine for Kirill is an act of genocide because it is allegedly the division of the great Russian people. Very strange ideas.

At first, the position of the central apparatus of the Moscow Patriarchate Church in Ukraine was that we live in Ukraine. The Russians tried to influence this, but 95% of their instructions were ignored. However, when Metropolitan Onufriy was elected to lead the Moscow Patriarchate Church in Ukraine, he agreed to the pro-Russian development.

From that moment on, they began a systematic information war against Ukraine. They started to oppose Ukraine in the OSCE, saying that Ukraine oppresses them. It was very funny. They come to the OSCE and say that we have a mass violation of the rights of

---

15    After 1991, three major churches were active in Ukraine. The Ukrainian Greek-Catholic church was subordinated to Rome. The Ukrainian Orthodox Church was independent and recognized by other world Orthodox churches in 2019. The Ukrainian Orthodox Church of the Moscow Patriarchate, despite its name as "Ukrainian," was subordinated to Moscow. After the Russian invasion in 2014 and especially after the Ukrainian Church was recognized worldwide in 2019, worshippers massively switched from the Moscow Patriarchate to the Ukrainian Church. The state stood aside religious matters for a long time, and after the 2022 invasion decided to terminate lease agreements on historical state-owned churches with the Moscow Patriarchate, and transfer them to the Ukrainian Church. Russia called it, allegedly, "persecution," although major churches with architectural significance were owned by the state or municipalities from the very beginning.

the Moscow Patriarchate in Ukraine. Excuse me, what is the violation? The community gathered and voted for the transition to the Kyiv Church. In the village of Ptyche, for example, all but eight people voted for the transition from the Moscow Patriarchate to the Kyiv Patriarchate, and this was called persecution. In every such case, Russians shouted that they were being persecuted. And then, when the Ukrainian Church of the Kyiv Patriarchate received tomos (recognition) from Bartholomew, Patriarch of Constantinople, they turned against the whole world of Orthodoxy, saying only Moscow Orthodoxy is right.

**Two trajectories of the Russian future**

The Russians are not hopeless, but they must abandon these dreams that they will build something distinct and that they condemn Western individualism and the rule of law because they want to live "by the laws of higher love." And for the sake of these "laws of higher love," they tortured millions of people in the 20th century.

The bottom line is — just forget about the laws of higher love. Start from the rule of law. Then, even if America may not appear in Russia, Canada will for sure, and Russians will live normally without this eternal heroism, emotional pressure and idiocy. But if they continue to preach savagery for a long time, they will soon simply become a territory of Muslim states. By 2050, every second person in Russia may be Muslim. And they will not be able to do anything about this. They cannot say, "Do not give birth to children, dear Muslims," or "Russian women: give birth to ten children."

Once, many thought that the Germans would never become "normal." But they changed (some even too much, not being able to fight anyone). It was also once thought that Poles and Ukrainians would never reconcile — but they did.

With the Russians as well, now we see barbarism, but if they manage to press the stop button, there will still be a chance that this glacier of idiocy will melt. Although, of course, we will live with them, even if peacefully, still at a distance. There will be no friendship, admiration for the "great Russian culture," and colonial attitude to imperialism anymore. We will always remember that there was a battle between freedom and fascism, and they were on the side of fascism.

## Russians' motivation to go to war

Putin talks about an aggressive NATO and the time it takes for a missile to fly from the Kharkiv region to Moscow, but, in fact, from Finland it is two minutes faster. So why wage war, then? For some reason, they are not very worried about NATO's aggressive actions on the territory of Finland. It is already clear to everyone that the only reason for the war is that Ukrainians are a separate people, not a part of Russia.

The only goal of the war is to destroy Ukrainians as a nation. They hate us because we do not want to be like them. And why should we be like them? We have never agreed that freedom should be given to the authorities. For Russians, it is in the secular doctrine that Führer Putin decides everything, as well as in the church doctrine, where they believe that free will is dangerous. It is better to give freedom of will to the church authorities, and they will decide what is canonical.

During the fight, we saw that Russians are incapable of creative personal action. Instead, they destroy everything. Some pets were running up the hill, while Russians were stuck in the factory where they landed. And they shot these animals. Why? "Because we can," as they say. You're surrounded in that factory, so better save the ammunition and turn on your brains … I think it's a war between civilization and barbarism, absurd barbarism.

You know, an alcoholic hates being an alcoholic, he hates other alcoholics, but most of all, he hates those who do not want to drink with him and those who do not drink at all. And here it is the same.

## Why evil is rarely stopped in time

The sooner complete military aid reaches Ukraine, the faster the war will end, with fewer human losses in Ukraine and fewer economic problems for the West. Some in the West have a very primitive position that because it is said, not to kill or that violence is bad, it immediately follows that it is not necessary to protect our children. It is clear that if someone insulted you at work, forgive and do not kill this person. There is obviously no need to be angry and expand the circle of violence. But when we have a war between nations, when they are determined to destroy us, it no longer works. Defensive war is always justified, and the Pope knows that too.

President Biden once wrote, and I like the idea, that we should not just restrain Russia, but actively oppose it. Russia cannot be forgiven when it crosses the red lines every time. Hitler came to power in 1933, and in 1935 he violated the demilitarization of the Rhineland and introduced troops there. If the West had then intervened in this situation, and under the Treaty of Versailles could have intervened, they would have lost 1,000 soldiers in 1935, but would have removed Hitler from power. Yes, they would be condemned for losing these people, but they would have suppressed the evil at its root. If they had intervened in 1937, they would have lost 5,000. If, in early 1939, they would have lost even more and would still be condemned because no one would have known about the concentration camps and the mass murder of Jews yet.

There were articles saying that the war has dragged on and, whatever it means, Ukrainians "should be realistic." So, if the West did not want the war to drag on and avoid greater economic losses, then Ukrainians had to liberate the entire territory of Ukraine as soon as possible. The solution to all economic problems lies in the rapid restoration of Ukraine's territorial integrity, so, please, more sanctions and more weapons. And don't worry, the fate of Europe is decided here in the steppes of the southeast of Ukraine, as it has always been. We are the shield of Europe. We will stop these newest of barbarians and put an end to this here.

## Pacifists lack imagination

When proposing to "end the war" by surrendering, people lack the imagination to put their child in the place of the victim who was raped or suffered under occupation.

The first $5,000 for this Barrett sniper rifle (while saying these words, Yuriy shows one of his own rifles standing next to the wall) was given by Protestants who were pacifists before the war. They used to say that we had to reconcile with the DNR and LNR (unrecognized proxy "republics" that Russia created in the occupied parts of Ukraine's eastern regions in 2014) to find a compromise. They said that we should love our enemies. They even said that if there is rape, you still have to be patient because our ancestors were once savages, but then, through the generations, they became civilized. They preached all this about patience, and then I asked what they would do if there was violence against their children. And they immediately backtracked saying this was only their ideal position.

Then the Pope said that we must put up with it at any cost. It is clear that he has no children and that he cannot imagine what he would do if his daughter had been raped in Bucha. People do not have the imagination to put their children in the place of this victim of war. And this is where humanity begins. Treat others not even how you want to be treated but how you want your children to be treated.

Suddenly, when the war began, those pacifists called and said: "Yuriy, we are donating the first $5,000 for a Barrett. Aim well." I told them that they were pacifists. They said, "Yes, and we are still pacifists now. And you are also a pacifist. We know, and we're giving you money for a sniper rifle."

"Great idea," I said.

# A Message from Occupation

such problematic, such frightful poems,
full of anger,
so politically incorrect
no beauty in these poems,
no aesthetic at all
the metaphors withered and fell to pieces
before they could bloom
the metaphors buried
in children's playgrounds
under hastily raised crosses
frozen
in unnatural poses
by the gates of houses,
covered in dust

— Yuliya Musakovska, "such problematic,
such frightful poems" (excerpt),
translated from the Ukrainian by Timothy Snyder

In 2014, Russia occupied parts of Ukraine's eastern Donetsk and Luhansk regions. The invasion was portrayed by Russia as a proclamation by local separatists, who then unilaterally renamed the regions the Luhansk People's Republic and the Donetsk People's Republic. The so-called republics, unrecognized internationally, were puppet statelets controlled by Russia until openly annexed by it in 2022.

In Rubizhne, located in the northern area of the Luhansk region, the first fighting broke out in May 2014. But by July, the Ukrainian armed forces had fully liberated Rubizhne, as well as other towns nearby, like Lysychansk and Sievierodonetsk. The 50,000 Rubizhne residents lived a calm life for the next eight years, despite being located just 35 kilometers from the territories occupied by Russia and the front line. Despite the 2015 Minsk ceasefire agreements, which failed to completely stop hostilities, an average of 20 Ukrainian soldiers were killed each month on the front from 2016 to 2021.

\*\*\*

On the night of 24 February 2022, Sofiya[16] was sleeping peacefully in her Kyiv apartment until 5:30 am, when she was awoken by a phone call from her mother.

"Child, the war has begun." Her mother was calling from Rubizhne, the town where Sofiya was born and lived most of her life.

"It can't be true!"

Sofiya began scrolling through the news while reaching out to her contacts — her work connected her with colleagues in many cities across Ukraine. As she made her calls, their voices echoed a sad reality. Her friends — from northern Chernihiv, eastern Kharkiv and Sumy, central Irpin and Hostomel, and western Krasyliv — were affected by the war. "My world," Sofiya says, reflecting back, "was split into the 'before' and 'after.'"

Later that day, Sofiya and her husband fled the capital, heading for a small village near Kyiv. She looked up at the Motherland monument and at the Ukrainian flag and wept, "I'll definitely come back to you."

In the village, missiles flew over their small house every night. They taped blankets over the windows and spent the nights with their pets, sheltering behind two walls, as citizens had been advised to do. "Each time, we would listen for where a projectile was flying," says Sofiya. "I prayed it wouldn't hit our home. In my mind, I talked with my grandfather who had died many years before, and I asked him for protection. After panic attacks, when it was finally quiet and I was able to return to my senses, I would text my mother, sister, and friends."

A few days later, on 8 March, Sofiya abruptly lost contact with her mother and sister, who were still in Rubizhne. Breaking through Ukraine's northeastern border and the previous front line to the south, the Russians were advancing closer and closer toward the town, shelling it constantly. Power lines were destroyed and cut off, mobile connection was disrupted. There were no water or

---

16   The names in this story have been changed at the interviewee's request for safety reasons.

food supplies in the town. Sofiya kept sending texts to contact her family, hoping every minute to hear back from them. Meanwhile, her friends were trying to contact her.

"We are blocked! The house is on fire! Save us!" Sofiya's classmate, Nadiya, wrote in a text message on the evening of 9 March. Nadiya lived in a district where there was still some mobile connection. In an attempt to help her friend, Sofiya started calling all the support services she could think of and was able to help rescue the family. Black from smoke and covered in dust from crushed concrete, Nadiya, her husband and son were miraculously saved.

On 11 March, Sofiya received another tragic message — her friend's in-laws had been shot by Russian forces while driving from Rubizhne to Kreminna only a few kilometers to the north. Minutes before, the couple had been bringing food from a nearby village to Rubizhne, which had been cut off from supplies. The woman died immediately, but her husband was able to call his son and say his last words. He spoke with his son until his heart stopped. Months after their murder, their bodies could still not be found.[17]

Sofiya kept messaging her mother, sister, and aunt. Each text included, "I know you are alive ..." "evacuation from ..." and "I love you." She felt disappointed after her phone conversations with her relatives and friends in Russia, "They are blind. They said that Russia is saving us from Nazis and doing good deeds. They still don't believe me."

For a long while, Sofiya didn't hear from her mother, sister, or aunt. It seemed an eternity. Then one day, her sister sent her a short message, "I put our mother on the bus."

---

17    In the first ten months of the 2022 Russian invasion, 415 civilian deaths were recorded in the Luhansk region alone, as reported by the regional head, Serhiy Haidai. A significant portion of these deaths resulted from Russian shelling, but many people were also killed at close range with firearms, and some endured months of torture in Russian detention facilities. According to the UN Human Rights Monitoring Mission in Ukraine, more than 10,500 civilians were killed and 19,875 injured from February 2022 to February 2024 in Ukraine. This number includes 587 killed children. However, this number of civilian casualties is significantly undercounted in cities that were occupied after the intensive fighting at the start of the full-scale war in 2022 — such as Mariupol where it was impossible to determine and verify the exact number.

Sofiya says, "I was trembling in bed for three long hours. I begged heaven for my mother to get here safely." Together with many other people from Rubizhne, Sofiya's mother was rescued by an evacuation bus that had been organized by Ukrainian authorities.

They were able to escape through a humanitarian corridor to a town nearby. Sofiya says, "I knew it was still dangerous in that town." She found a local taxi number and asked them to pick up her mother and take her to the train station. From there, her mother was able to reach Dnipro, and finally took a train to reach her daughter in Kyiv, on 16 March. "I cried as I ran along the platform. I inhaled the scent of her hair and cried," says Sofiya.

Her mother told her with tears in her eyes that when she and other people from Rubizhne had run to the evacuation bus, on the streets they had seen bodies of those killed—men, women, and children, with their bags and belongings strewn around them. Burned houses were all around; others were still on fire: in Rubizhne, they had to drink water with residue of ashes to survive. Despite all this, Sofiya's sister and aunt decided to stay in their homes. Sofiya says, "Every day, I asked the universe to keep them alive."

A friend of Sofiya's mother, an "educator with a big heart," just a few days earlier had gone to get water from the Yuzhna district of Rubizhne, but did not return. She had been killed by Russian shelling. No one could retrieve her remains because of the increasing danger in Rubizhne, and she lay at the place of her death for weeks.

On 29 March, Russians reached the town center of Rubizhne where another of Sofiya's friends, Solomiya, and her two children lived. With gravel in their faces, they first crawled, then ran to the remaining Ukrainian-controlled territory on the outskirts of the town. They were lucky to escape Russian shelling and managed to reach an evacuation bus that brought them to a safer place.

On 5 April, a poisonous pink smoke appeared over Rubizhne—Russian forces had hit a tank containing nitric acid. Severe poisoning can lead to pulmonary edema and loss of vision. Every day, Sofiya scrolled through numerous Telegram and Viber chats where people caught in the throes of war continued to seek their family and friends. On one, she saw a video of apartment buildings neighboring her mother's that had "collapsed like dominoes." Next to them stood the kindergarten Sofiya had attended as a child, but now, in the yard where children had once played, stood six new crosses with the date "05.04.2022" and the names of those buried there. Not only in Rubizhne, but across all areas of Ukraine affected by Russian occupation, stand crosses made from whatever crude materials are at hand. Owing to the never-ending shelling and the fear of capture at any moment by Russian troops, people were unable to properly bury their dead relatives and neighbors.

During weeks of street fighting and shelling in Rubizhne, the flat where Sofiya's mother lived was badly damaged. In her sister's flat, windows were blown out. Her aunt's once-charming house, surrounded by a pretty fence, had been hit by shells and completely destroyed. The seeds Sofiya's mother had bought to plant at their cottage were strewn about, never to be planted.

"24 February 2022 — that day I lost many things. I lost a part of myself and found a new one," Sofiya says. "This new part of me is strong and able to search for cars and cargo, and to raise funds for humanitarian aid for people from my family's hometown. I have found new friends. People completely unknown to me gave me things and helped with reposts and retweets. Only faith in our country and in myself keeps me going, as well as knowing that each of us has a great heart and willpower."

At the beginning of April 2022 Sofiya said, "I know I will return home to Rubizhne, go to my mother's kitchen, and be able to make coffee for us. I will be able to hug my sister and aunt and make cherry pies. I know that my husband and I will return to Kyiv, to our apartment with roses in the kitchen, where before the war we were happy. We will get our lives back. Everyone."

Sofiya's first dream soon came true — she was able to return to Kyiv. But after two and a half years of war, Rubizhne remains under Russian occupation, unreachable beyond the front line.

# Blue and Yellow, Black and Red

Our tomorrow is there, behind our backs.
And our children, parents, and families are there.
And those we lost "on the shield" as brothers
They, too, are behind our backs.

— Antytila band, "Fortress Bakhmut," the song was released in 2023[18]

In May 2022, the war was barely visible in Lviv, the largest city in the west of Ukraine, almost 1,000 kilometers from the front line. Shops and offices were bustling as usual, but this peaceful façade was a very thin curtain, torn apart more and more every day by the shrieking sirens of alerts and the endless processions of coffins arriving from the front.

When a convoy of two, three, or more vehicles bringing those killed in action enters the city, all vehicles in the opposite lane pause for a moment of silence. Relatives, friends, and (when possible) close comrades of the fallen soldier are part of the convoy. Flagpoles from the convoy vehicles fly a state blue and yellow flag and a historical red and black flag—the latter was used by the Ukrainian insurgency against Soviets and Nazis from 1941. It has acquired new symbolism since Russia's war against Ukraine in 2014: yellow and blue colors, when doused in blood, turn red and black. This is why this flag is now regarded as the ancillary flag of wartime Ukraine.

When a killed soldier hails from a village, residents honor the procession on their knees, holding candles and forming an unbroken chain of lights on the road. Once the procession has passed,

---

18    The band Antytila has been one of the most popular pop-rock bands in Ukraine since the early 2010s. When Russia launched its full-scale war against Ukraine, three members of Antytila, including frontman Taras Topolia, joined the Territorial Defense Forces. Their music video "Fortress Bakhmut" (Fortetsia Bakhmut), released in February 2023, was filmed on location in the frontline town of Bakhmut during fighting. Additionally, Antytila collaborated with English singer-songwriter Ed Sheeran on a remix of his song "2step," with profits from the music video being donated to humanitarian aid efforts in Ukraine. The band has also been actively volunteering, providing aid and support to the military, and donating proceeds from its concerts.

they follow to the village church. This is what occurs all over Ukraine every day.

In the city of Lviv, many of these somber processions arrive at the Cathedral of Saints Peter and Paul, which has now become known simply as the Garrison Cathedral. Built in 1610–1630, the cathedral has stood for centuries in the city's historical center, among the stone and brick buildings from olden days. Entering, one senses the bonds linking this place to those who fell on the front: numerous portraits of downed soldiers hang in tribute along these walls, and the flags of Ukrainian military units stand in a straight line. In the first three months of the 2022 full-scale war, 70 Ukrainian defenders were buried by chaplains from this cathedral. As of 2024, the number had grown to hundreds.

\*\*\*

At the cathedral's entrance stands a man of modest height, his face clean-shaven, betraying no hint of being more than in his early forties. He wears a simple black robe. Father Andriy Sidanych, one of 14 chaplains of the Garrison Cathedral, is waiting for two more deceased to arrive. Like other chaplains, he rotates between service in the cathedral and the front line, where he provides solace and support to the soldiers of brigades originating from Lviv. Father Andriy is informal—his manner is gentle and reassuring as he mixes with people, even in the midst of all the pain wrought by war.

A soldier humbly approaches while we are talking with Father Andriy.

"Excuse me," he says urgently. "Could you tell me where it's possible to get things in the cathedral?"

"Yes. What do you need?"

"First of all, I need good boots."

"Which unit are you from?"

"125th."

"Aren't you from the part that has already left for the front?"

"In the process."

"Wait a minute. I'll call a colleague who is on shift, he'll help you."

The chaplains of the Garrison Cathedral have been providing aid to soldiers since the beginning of the war in 2014. At the beginning of the 2022 invasion, in the first three months alone, they delivered to the front over 30 off-road vehicles, body armor, first aid kits, and much more badly needed equipment, including some basic items such as quality boots that the army could not provide instantly in the necessary amount to the hundreds of thousands newly mobilized.

In 2014, Father Andriy became friends with many young men studying at the military academy. Among other activities together, they would go hiking in the Carpathians. After Russia attacked in 2022, most of these young officers went to the front.

"The most painful thing," Father Andriy tells us, "is moments when we perform a wedding, and then a few days later we have a funeral for the very same soldier who has been killed at the front."

A soldier, Mykyta Yarovyi, had his wedding here recently. In just three days, he returned to the cathedral in a coffin.

As we spoke with Father Andriy, people began to assemble for another funeral service.

***

A young woman with a blue and yellow bouquet enters the cathedral. These days, such two-color bouquets are brought for a soldier's funeral. While waiting, she approaches the portraits of service members killed in the war.

On the opposite side of the cathedral rests an old casket bearing the solemn inscription Memento Mori (Remember You Must Die). This simple phrase reminds visitors to look beyond their material comforts. At present, the Latin phrase echoes poignantly with the heavy toll paid by young soldiers on the front line.

This old cathedral was once part of Lviv's fortification walls. Shortly before the war started in 2014, it became the main center of the Lviv military chaplaincy. Over the years, the chaplains have placed about 20 flags of Ukrainian military units in a row that now separates the sanctuary from the nave. During spring, the mid-day sun's rays cast their sheen directly onto these flags.

On the left side stands a huge 3-meter cross made of birch log. It survived massive shelling by Smerch MLRS in Pobieda village in the Luhansk region in 2014. Soldiers of Lviv's 80th brigade brought it here together with small fragments of military vehicles that were targeted by the shelling. These fragments, as well as pieces of destroyed equipment and munitions, are placed beneath the cross, still smelling of rust, smoke and gunpowder—"smells of the war." Andriy says, "Soldiers feel it is not natural for humans to kill … but there is a duty to protect. The evil that attacks us should be stopped. Otherwise the consequences will be even worse."

Above the cross, paper doves hanging from fine threads suspended from the ceiling sway gently. Children fashioned these doves a few years ago, and they will remain here until victory, when peace returns to the country. Several pictures of children whose fathers have died in the war since 2014 are on the side wall of the cathedral. These are only a fraction of a much larger photo series displayed at Kyiv's Boryspil international airport.

*** 

Like most Lviv cathedrals and churches, the Garrison Cathedral was closed shortly after the USSR's occupation of the city at the onset of the Second World War. In 1939–1941, Soviet secret police executed thousands of Ukrainian intellectuals, political figures, and members of the underground resistance in Ukraine's west. The local Polish population also suffered executions, and many were later deported from the USSR to communist Poland. In 1946, the authorities of the USSR forced Jesuits serving in the cathedral to abandon it and turned the building into a storage depository for books. At least 2.1 million books were stored here, ironically helping to preserve the cathedral walls by absorbing dampness.

After the 1991 declaration of independence, 140 KAMAZ trucks were needed to remove the books. The Garrison Cathedral was only reopened in 2011, with restoration still ongoing on 24 February 2022. Just three months earlier, artisans were able to unveil the restored facade. At the moment the full-scale invasion began, paint was still drying on the recently restored ancient ceiling frescoes and the scaffolding was still there to continue the restoration of the next few meters of frescoes. The years-long painstaking work was interrupted by Russia's invasion and instead of restoring the cathedral's most valuable sculptures, iconography, and art pieces, these priceless works had to be hastily wrapped in thick layers of foam rubber to protect them from possible airstrikes.

The condition of the Garrison Cathedral at the time of the invasion was reflective of Ukraine as a nation. The restoration of the cathedral was only a tiny part of the rectification of Ukraine's history, which was critically undermined during the destructive Soviet period. Research of the thousands of the nation's archival records and the investigation of Russian imperial and Soviet crimes had been in full swing since the beginning of Ukraine's Independence. New museums were being opened, such as those honoring victims of Ukraine's greatest national tragedies: Holodomor, Stalin's genocide by starvation in 1932–1933; as well as the Baturyn massacre, committed by Tsar Peter I in 1708. Ukraine introduced numerous political reforms after the 2014 Revolution of Dignity, but only had time to complete part of them, such as financial decentralization, which allowed local communities to quickly renovate major public infrastructure, or digitalization of most state services.[19]

---

19  In the 2010s, the state created numerous new institutions to support Ukrainian culture, such as the Ukrainian Cultural Foundation, the Ukrainian Institute of National Memory, Ukrainian Book Institute, and the Ukrainian State Film Agency, let alone supporting countless local and private initiatives striving to revive and research lost heritage. Key completed political reforms included decentralization and a series of anti-corruption reforms, which encompassed the creation of the unprecedented Prozorro online system. Prozorro and related services ensured the transparency of state procurement, as well as full disclosure regarding politicians' and their relatives' property and income. The newly created High Anti-Corruption Court has been successfully working since 2019, considering cases of top corruption that were investigated by another new institution, the NABU (National Anti-Corruption Bureau). The uncompleted reform of lower courts remained the main shortcoming of the political system, when Russia attacked Ukraine in 2022. The military, police, and other prior Soviet-style institutions were also being transformed by new laws.

Significant evidence of other Russian and Soviet crimes was only in the process of discovery when the full-scale war started. To mention just a few examples, as late as 2019 a previously unknown mass grave of 19 victims executed by the NKVD[20] was exhumed in the Ukrainian town of Dubno, near a former Soviet prison. Previously, 400 skeletal remains had been found there. In 2018, 78 such remains, riddled with bullet holes, were found in 24 pits near a former prison of the NKVD. As recently as 2021, the city of Odesa started excavating a huge mass grave encompassing five hectares of filled-in trenches. Thousands of victims were expected to be found there. Archival data revealed at least 8,000 NKVD executions had taken place near Odesa in the late 1930s.[21] Most of the remains will never be identified to allow for proper burials.

If the Russian invasion in 2022 had succeeded, Ukrainians would have lost the chance to uncover past crimes and commemorate those who were tortured. The war, therefore, was not only about territory, but for the past and future of Ukrainians as a nation. To complete the research and investigation into past Russian and Soviet crimes, Ukraine has had to secure not only territories but to gain more time. Each new day, month and year was bought by the lives of the country's fighters. The coffins of those killed in action continued to arrive.

***

Several dozen people have gathered near the Garrison Cathedral as two military vehicles arrive. Young soldiers, still students of the military academy, are removing coffins. The procession begins with a soldier carrying a wooden cross. Two more soldiers carry portraits of the dead, several others carry Ukrainian flags.

---

20  The NKVD was the precursor to the KGB, an equally notorious state secret police used to terrorize and execute "enemies" of the Soviet regime.
21  The three cases mentioned here were described in the following Radio Svoboda (RFE/RL) publications:
https://u.radiosuvoboda.org/a/odisha-nix-reprecie-roscopki/31424356.html
https://o.radiosvoboda.org/a/news-drohobich-78-zartov-nkvs/31358574.ht
ml; https://www.radiosvoboda.org/a/29973842.html

The coffins will not be opened in the cathedral — the bodies are too mutilated. A military band follows the procession, playing somber music dedicated to those who have given their lives for their country. Before entering the cathedral, Father Andriy offers a few words of commemoration. A soldier in a military, pixelated uniform is wiping away tears. He is holding blue and yellow flowers. The wife of the killed soldier, also in uniform, leans over her husband's casket, tears in her eyes. She too is serving in the army. Another soldier reaches out with her hand in silent condolence.

The fallen Senior Sergeant Oleksandr Moyisenko and his wife, both in their early forties, served side by side in the same unit. Oleksandr was killed while they were fighting the enemy. The other man, Sergeant Serhiy Turpetko, was killed in battle a few days earlier. Before the funeral service, which will be held for both of them at the same time, people gently lay flowers around the caskets. After the service inside the cathedral, the military students carry the caskets on their shoulders back through the doors. The band begins to play the funeral requiem. At this point, many more people succumb to tears.

"Buses are available for those who wish to attend at the Lychakiv cemetery. Please come," a friend of the family beckons to the mourners.

Six municipal buses await, as the cemetery is several kilometers away. In the bus, some soldiers discuss the situation on the battlefield. They speak about the types of weapons they have received or expect to receive soon.

Starting with the Russian military aggression in the east of Ukraine in 2014, many killed soldiers from Lviv have been buried at the Lychakiv cemetery, not far from the historical graves of the renowned Ukrainian writer Ivan Franko (1856–1916), artist Ivan Trush (1869–1941), opera singer Solomiya Krushelnytska (1872–1952), and other acclaimed Ukrainians. However, within a few weeks of the 2022 full-scale invasion, the remaining cemetery plots were filled. Next to it was a vast field which, at first glance, seemed empty, covered by grass. In fact, it was also a cemetery — one arising from Ukraine's painful and complicated history. This stretch of land is now known as the Field of Mars.

Initially, it was a military cemetery for over 4,700 soldiers of the Austro-Hungarian army and allies who died in the First World War. They were Austrians, Germans, Ukrainians, Poles, and fighters from other nations. When the Soviets occupied Lviv during the Second World War, they exhumed the graves. Instead, over 1,000 Soviet and NKVD soldiers were buried in the middle of the field in a single mass trench along a narrow pathway marked by meager grave plates. During the excavations in 2023–2024, archeologists discovered that many of the soldiers were chaotically thrown into the pits. In 2024, their remains were reburied in a specially designated area at the other new Lviv cemetery.

After Ukraine's Independence in 1991, the remains of the victims of Russian terror were also moved to the right side of this Field of Mars. In the 1990s, 390 victims of Bolshevik terror from the Zamarstiniv prison in Lviv were re-entombed in three crypts, with small stone crosses marking the site. Several commanders and soldiers of the UPA (Ukrainian Insurgent Army), who fought against both the Nazis and the Soviets in 1942–1945, were also buried at the edge of this field. After WWII, the UPA was still active, although the war had ended for most of the world in 1945. The Soviets were not able to stop the last of the insurgents until the 1950s, when they finally and cruelly weeded out the last remaining resistance members.

The largest part of the Field of Mars remained mostly empty, with the old gravesites on the edge of the field, low and barely visible. Between March and May 2022, 40 new graves with tall flags studded the field. By June 2024, the number had grown to 750. A blue and yellow flag, and a red and black flag, are placed by each grave, creating the impression of a large powerful army, but the painful sense of lost souls who have passed much too early prevails.

In February 2024, marking two years of full-scale war, Ukrainian President Volodymyr Zelenskyy—for the first time—revealed that since February 2022, 31,000 Ukrainian serving military personnel had been killed in action. The figure, however, included only identified and confirmed cases, without numerous missing soldiers. In the middle of 2024, most Ukrainian villages had one, two or sometimes more soldiers killed in action. Driving across Ukraine, one can spot flags in rural cemeteries here and there, while every big city has its own "Field of Mars" sprinkled with flags. United in a symbolic countrywide net, these countless flags form a collective monument to those who sacrificed their lives for freedom.

*** 

Two burial pits have been dug for the fallen soldiers honored today at the Garrison Cathedral. Before entering the cemetery, the band plays the funeral march one more time. Ukrainian flags which cover the coffins are then presented to the soldiers' families.

Once the coffins are lowered, Father Andriy offers a final prayer. He then "seals" the grave by dropping the first four handfuls of soil. The undertakers start shoveling the excavated earth back into the graves. They work quickly, while everyone remains silent. The scraping of shovels and the thump of soil falling onto the coffins seems louder than any military band. The undertakers complete their task and place a cross in the ground to mark the gravesites. They tell the mourners to lay the deceased's portrait and flowers on the mound.

Gradually, one by one, people withdraw. Finally, only the soldier's wife in military uniform remains in front of her husband's portrait. She does not move. Her friend reaches out her own arm: only then does she gently rise.

***

Nearly 100 Ukrainian soldiers who died from 2014 to early March 2022 are buried inside the old Lychakiv Cemetery. An older couple and a teenage girl are cleaning candle holders at one of the graves that dates from the first month of full-scale war.

"Now they are so clean you can bring them into the house," the couple stands silent while the girl speaks incessantly as if trying to console them. We approach warily and ask if they can share something about their son, Taras Didukh.

"What is there to say?" the mother says sadly.

In a sad voice, she starts to tell her son's story. "He first studied at the Lviv Military Lyceum of the Heroes of Kruty. Then he graduated from the Odesa Academy, where he studied for four years. He really wanted to be a paratrooper, he didn't want to be in another military unit. Immediately after the academy, he went to the war in Donbas."[22]

Before 2022, her son served on the contact line in Shyrokyne and then in Stanytsia Luhanska. He had signed a contract for five years and was a platoon commander. Weeks before the full-scale war started in February 2022, his unit was rotated to the Shyrokyi Lan training site in the south. There they encountered the new invasion. He died in the Kherson region near Nova Kakhovka, by the village of Shylova Balka, two months before our conversation. He was only 22 years old.

"We don't know exactly how he died. They said that artillery immersed their column from above and he was hit by shrapnel at the back of his head ... damage to the main vessels. He called us on the first day of the new invasion on 24 February; after that he just wrote. He said that everything was fine."

"There are a lot of boys from the 80th brigade here ... this whole row," his mother says, looking over the line of graves. "What more is there to say? There are no words. It is impossible to accept it. I still do not believe that it is so. He was my only son."

We are all still for a while. "Are you his sister?" we ask the girl.

"A girlfriend," she replies.

---

22   Donbas—an abbreviation of "Donets Coal Basin," referring to the mining area in the east of Ukraine, near the Siverskyi Donetsk River, encompassing parts of the contemporary Donetsk and Luhansk regions. The term later came to generally signify these two easternmost regions of Ukraine.

# Godforsaken Villages

For nearly a month in March 2022, Russian forces attempted to capture Ukraine's northernmost city, Chernihiv, which would allow them to redirect all their efforts towards Kyiv. Chernihiv was besieged on all sides — all but two villages around the city were occupied. These sparsely populated settlements amid forests became epicenters of suffering. Russian troops looted, raped, and held villagers hostage. A month of terror ravaged the quiet villages where previously little had occurred.

*** 

Two months after the liberation of the region from the Russian onslaught, the war is still palpable everywhere. The Chernihiv region borders Russia, and a checkpoint is set up every 10 kilometers, significantly more than around the capital. The Ukrainian military thoroughly inspects documents and vehicles of people passing through. Destroyed and damaged houses, the smell of burned-out military vehicles, recently shelled civilian cars, remnants of projectiles are commonplace — they all speak of fierce fighting in the region not long ago.

The village of Yahidne lies next to the Kyiv highway, just 10 kilometers south of Chernihiv. Taking the Yahidne turnoff, we saw piles of debris from shattered agricultural storehouses, charred or badly damaged by shelling. These ruins contrasted starkly with the greenery of spring vegetation bursting forth under the sun's warm rays. Near the old farm, its yard covered with shattered glass and rusty remnants of burned vehicles, four men were cleaning something.

"Russians entered the village on 3 March, and for several days fighting was ongoing," one of the men told us. "They were afraid to come at first while our forces were here. And then their air force hit a roadblock and a tank. Afterward, the Russians started moving further in the Chernihiv direction towards Ivanivka."

The man told us that he was born here in Yahidne, and before the war he had worked at the local school—the very site of infamous Russian atrocities. "I turned on the boiler at the school just as the Russians arrived, and then I stayed in the school basement. I sat there together with all of Yahidne's residents."

When we asked if he had heard of any cases of Russian torture, he replied, "I saw it … and I experienced it myself."

"Can you tell us about it?" we asked.

"No. It's disgusting. I don't want to remember. My son served earlier in the armed forces, his uniform was found. Then they beat us. It's good that at least one decent person was among them, and we lived."

"Money was taken from almost everyone, they even tore out the floor looking for things. What were they looking for there?" he said as he turned back to his work.

The village seemed almost empty and abandoned. After a while, we came across an elderly woman working alone in a garden.

\*\*\*

On the edge of Yahidne, nestled near the forest, stood Tamara Matiukha's cottage. She and her husband built the cottage with their own hands many years earlier. "Neither my parents nor my husband's parents helped us, we built it from scratch," Tamara says, her voice tinged both with pride and sorrow. The couple toiled from the first light of dawn until the long shadows of dusk. Over many years of living under the Soviet Union, when goods were always scarce, Tamara, like many others, developed the habit of getting what she could and storing it. She lovingly selected soft linens and cozy blankets, items that evoke a sense of home comfort, intending them as future gifts for her children and grandchildren. "Our pensions are modest," she mused, "but I could leave something for them. I could leave them the house."

Peaceful forests wrapped around the back and the side of the house. On 3 March 2022, from the depths of these woods, Russian military machinery—tanks, ZIL trucks, and mortars—were getting ready to enter the village. "They swarmed like locusts. The sight of so many—it was sheer terror," says Tamara. The elderly couple, both in their seventies, took refuge in the basement in their yard. They heard loud explosions: during a fierce fighting, her house was hit and reduced to ashes, with nothing left standing but a dingy old stove amid the rubble. Their house was the first to burn down in the village. That day, Russian forces occupied Yahidne.

Under the muzzle of machine guns, Russian troops forcibly took Tamara and her husband to the school basement. The Russians drove all of the more than 350 residents of Yahidne who had not fled the village into those cramped and filthy basement rooms. Even those who had fled the besieged city of Chernihiv, believing they would be safer in the small village, ended up in the basement. The Russians also threw Tamara's daughter with her six-year-old son and eleven-year-old daughter into the basement.

At first, they all feared that the Russian soldiers would gun them down. The Russians took away everybody's phones, warning, "If we find a phone, we will shoot every third person." Tamara and her family handed over their phones, but the shrewd ones buried theirs in the sand. Some of the young managed to relay a message to the Ukrainian forces in Chernihiv, "Every inhabitant of Yahidne has been driven into the school's basement."

Clearly, the school basement was unsuitable for habitation. Water oozed from the ceiling and the walls. It was dank, wet, and cold. In the largest room, over 150 people were squeezed in, each with less than a square meter of space. Among them were the disabled, the immobile, and the sick. Armed Russians were stationed on the floor above, turning it into their headquarters, while confining 367 people below. Among the hostages were 77 children, including infants.

Due to the lack of ventilation, the air in the basement was unbreathable. Gasping for air, the captives pleaded with the soldiers to let them see their medic. As soon as the doctor entered the basement, he felt nauseous. After that, the Russian soldiers allowed their prisoners to knock out a few bricks in the wall to let some fresh air in.

Each morning at 7 am, the captives were released to queue for the toilet. Anyone caught savoring the outside air a moment too long was met with harsh shouting from the guards. With the slightest infraction, the Russians fired bullets over their heads, sending them back to the basement. Throughout the day, they had no other choice but to use a bucket in front of everyone. The indignities did not stop there. When someone asked for toilet paper, the Russians mockingly handed them school textbooks—but only those in Ukrainian history, literature and language.

People were starving. Russians gave them tiny portions from their military rations—one for several persons. A portion consisted of a small piece of dried bread and one teaspoon of spread for the whole day. Later the Russians "increased" portions to 200 grams of lean porridge, again for the whole day.

Tamara and her daughter would give almost all of their measly portion to their children. Many others did the same. The 11-year-old girl understood there was no more food, but her six-year-old brother would implore plaintively after each meal, "Grandma, I'm still hungry, I haven't had enough."

"It was horrible that the child was starving, and you couldn't give him anything," Tamara says, tears welling up in her eyes.

The youngest child in the basement was only two months old. With little air to breathe, no food and no diapers, the baby cried incessantly. No matter how hard the mother tried to soothe her, the baby's screams pierced the air. One day, the Russians summoned Valeriy Polhuy, a representative of Yahidne from the local municipal council, to come upstairs.

"What do you need?" a soldier asked.

"We have no baby food. There are little children, but we have nothing to feed them. They need diapers, hygiene wipes," Valeriy replied.

The soldier said he would bring these few items but demanded an exchange. He ordered Valeriy to find two people to be interviewed for the media—one for the Russian media, saying how desirable it was to live among the Russians, emphasizing how well they were being cared for and how happy they were to welcome the Russians. The other interview would be meant for the Ukrainian president, asking him to surrender.

Conditions for those with health issues were especially dire. There was hardly any water. Among the sick was Tamara, who suffers from diabetes. She needs to drink three liters of water a day. Instead, she was allotted a mere three sips. "I would draw it into my mouth, then moisten, then swallow, and that's all."

People asked the Russians to let them bring food from their own homes, but the soldiers ignored their pleas for three weeks. Meanwhile, people knew that the soldiers were looting their homes. Some troops had arrived wearing cheap knee-high rubber boots, but after a while, they were wearing the footwear of the village men. "Sneakers, trainers — white, black, green, or red. They strutted around the village in them," Tamara says with disdain.

By the end of March, Ukrainian forces were making progress towards the occupied village. It was beginning to dawn on the Russians that they were under a threat. Only then did they permit a few captives to prepare food for all over fire pits in the schoolyard. Tamara's daughter lived nearby. She and a neighbor rushed to the home to get food for the others. The Russians barred their way and instead handed them two sacks of potatoes. As soon as the women moved away from the house, gunshots rang out over their heads, forcing them to run.

The cherished potatoes were cooked over the fire and each child got two. "They ate those unpeeled potatoes as if they were chocolate," Tamara says with a sad chuckle.

"Grandma, I would like to eat more potatoes," said her grandson.

"Baby, there is no more."

"When we get out, grandma, you will boil us potatoes, and I will eat so, so much potato."

Ten people died in the basement of Yahidne school. For a long time, the bodies remained among the living, gradually decaying. Later, Russian troops allowed villagers to remove and bury them.

Tamara believes that about 20 Russians stationed in the school were from an elite Russian unit, possibly special forces, who were commanding other soldiers and had given the order to confine people in the school basement. They were well-dressed, robust, and muscular. At the same time, it appeared that other soldiers stationed in the village were likely from Tuva, a remote region bordering Mongolia.

"Give us women," the drunken Tuvan soldiers would say when they peered into the basement. Tamara says that the "elite" soldiers would hold them back.

Amid the terror and cruelty in the basement, a few soldiers wanted to show themselves as being benevolent. One in particular would come up to Tamara's grandson, pet him on his head, give him a piece of chocolate or a tiny juice box, and say, "I have three boys like him. As soon as the war is over, I'll request a demobilization. I will not stay any longer."

"Did he survive until his release or not?" Tamara says with scorn. "Good or bad, may none of them return home. I curse them."

The day on which the Russians finally retreated came unexpectedly. At 7 am on the morning of 30 March, the soldiers opened the door and let people out to the toilet. After that, they herded them back into the basement and barricaded the door — something they hadn't done before.

Not long after, the imprisoned people heard loud shouting and rumbling. The soldiers upstairs were scrambling to and fro, the engines were roaring, vehicles were heading in every direction. Tamara says, "We huddled together thinking, 'This is the end.'" Then, by midday, it fell silent. Some men in the basement managed to push open the doors. Stepping out, they found the school and its yard deserted. Those who had managed to hide their phones from the Russians immediately called contacts in the Ukrainian military in Chernihiv.

"Don't disperse," came the reply. "Who knows who is wandering around the village. Wait until someone comes to you." Another night passed in the school. The next day, 31 March, Ukrainian soldiers arrived. People embraced them, wept with joy and relief.

They imagined the next moments to be sheer heaven: to enter your own home, to take a shower or bath, to eat at your own table, to collapse into your own warm bed. But this was not to be. Instead of homes, some found only ruins. For those whose homes were still standing, they discovered their rooms pilfered and dirty, their kitchens filthy, and their refrigerators empty. While the Russians starved the locals, they fested on their captives' meat, cheese and vegetables. Those villagers who kept livestock found their pigs shot and their chickens strangled; they found carcasses that the Russians had left behind after eating them. Some soldiers even ate the dogs.

Tamara's granddaughter was emaciated and so traumatized that her mother immediately took the children out of the village. Tamara and her husband stayed in their daughter's house which had survived. Soon volunteers from all over Ukraine started arriving. "Without them, it would have been very difficult," says Tamara. "We hope for victory … we believe there will be victory."

*** 

Of the villages around Chernihiv, only in Yahidne, where the Russians had created their headquarters, were all the people forced into a single basement. In the surrounding villages occupied by the Russians, people hid in their own homes and basements while the Russian soldiers roamed through the village.

Roman Movhan, a volunteer from Chernihiv who was among the first to bring aid to the liberated villages, recalls the story of his friends from Viktorivka, the village south of Yahidne that was also under occupation.

Their family was at home when they heard the entrance door bursting open.

"Is anyone alive? If not, we'll open fire all over the house," Russian soldiers yelled.

The family came out of hiding.

"Do you have any weapons or relatives from the military? Show the documents," Russians commanded.

"We have no weapons, and neither do we have relatives."

"Do you have vodka?"

"Yes."

"Hand it over!"

They gave some of what they had.

"Is there something to eat?"

"Yes."

"Give it!"

Roman says, "Surely, you understand – if you were forced to kneel under a machine gun, then no matter what kind of patriot you are, you will hand over food or vodka or anything."

After shoving down the food and guzzling all the vodka, the troops told the family, "We're leaving, but we will come back – if not us, then others from our unit. If the gate or doors are closed, you are corpses – we will shoot you without question."

They opened the door and sat in the house. At night, other Russian troops came:

"Is anybody alive?"

And again, they asked for alcohol and food. The next day, still more came.

"We have already given everything," the man said, his voice trembling.

The Russians left, without incident. This family's house was not robbed, possibly because they were home, unlike their neighbors' house, who had left the village before occupation.

Yuriy Mykolayovych, 55, from Lukashivka, north of Yahidne, told us a similar story. One day, a drunken officer came to him and started shooting in the air.

"If I find anything, you are a dead man," he shouted. "What do you have in your cellar?!"

Yuriy showed him that there was nothing but potatoes and fodder for the animals. The entire time, the soldier pointed his machine gun at Yuriy. Then he heard the barking of a dog. When he realized it was a German shepherd, he took the dog. But on the second day, she returned to her home out of instinct. The soldier came again and grabbed her, as she tried to pull away barking viciously.

"I asked why he needed it, and he said he had dreamed of having a shepherd for two years. He took the dog, and that was that, we never saw her again," Yuriy says sadly.

Sometimes people were beaten just for "living too well." Once Russian soldiers, likely from a remote eastern region, saw a big henhouse with some storage facilities and tiny windows. They first checked the house, then dragged out the family. They pointed at the henhouse, and asked:

"Who lives in that house?"

"It's not a house, it's a henhouse."

"Do you think we're stupid?!" a soldier shouted, "Open it!"

The owner opened it, but no soldier ventured forward. Instead, a soldier threw in a live grenade. When things settled, a group of soldiers ran inside with machine guns cocked and saw chickens. Afterward, the entire family was beaten for "putting chickens in a house." Another local man told Roman that once the Russians took his power charger and beat him until he "agreed" with them that it was a surreptitious model of a NATO phone.

Locals say that when some Russian soldiers from a remote eastern region lived in the village of Lukashivka, they ate chickens without cleaning their feathers: hey took a chicken, cut through the feathers, turned its skin inside out, fried it on the fire, and ate it.

Russian soldiers were roaming the village streets looking for women and young girls, so people started hiding them. Locals said that in Ivanivka drunken Russians gang-raped a woman and murdered her husband. Many of these stories remain untold by the victims, but some have been verified. The Prosecutor's Office of the Chernihiv region reported that in one of the region's villages, Russian officers tried to rape a 16-year-old girl.[23] 39-year-old Nataliya Yatsiuk told a similar story to journalists[24] — two Russian soldiers tried to rape her but Nataliya managed to lock the basement door after one of them. Her husband grabbed the other soldier's gun and the soldier ran away. After the incident, the family managed to hide in a quiet corner of the village until the end of the occupation.

---

23 The Prosecutor's Office of the Chernihiv region reported this on 29 July 2022 (https://chrg.gp.gov.ua/ua/news.html?_m=publications&_c=view&_t=rec& id=317067).

24 Ukrainian publication Texty reported this case on 4 April 2022 (https://texty. org.ua/articles/112163/ily-ydesh-s-namy-yly-strelyaem-detej-yak-rosijski-so ldaty-teroryzuvaly-simyu-na-chernihivshyni/).

No one can know how many such monstrosities by Russians took place in occupied territory.

\*\*\*

Seven kilometers to the northeast of Yahidne lies the village of Lukashivka. When the Soviet Union collapsed and people were allowed to own their property, Anna and her husband started their own farm. The Ukrainian state assigned to every former collective farm worker a plot of land, but many people decided to sell theirs immediately for much-needed funds. By 2022, Anna's farm had grown from one horse and one cow to 120 cows. The couple farmed 400 hectares of land. This land included their own, together with some plots they rented from others. When Anna's husband died in 2020, their children and their families continued the business.

At the time when the inhabitants of Yahidne were being herded into the school basement, Lukashivka had not yet been captured by the Russian forces. In the early days of March 2022, Anna's family was helping the Ukrainian military nearby. In particular, they offered them places to sleep in their well-kept barn and brought them food.

Soon thereafter the farm was destroyed by Russian invaders. "On 7 March," says Anna's son-in-law Andriy, "we were hit by Russian Grad rockets for the first time." Soon after that, the Russian forces continued shelling with tanks, advancing closer towards Chernihiv, just 12 kilometers away. They shot at the vegetable storehouses and the granaries. Dozens of cows died from shrapnel wounds. Others were wounded and lay on the fields helpless.

In early June 2022, traces of battle were all around the farm: several destroyed armored personnel carriers and wrecked cars belonging both to the Ukrainian military and the Russian invaders.

In Lukashivka, hardly a house can be found that is not severely damaged, if not completely destroyed. On 9 March, the village was seized by Russian forces. From there and the neighboring village of Ivanivka, the Russians shelled Chernihiv and its suburbs.

Not far from Anna's farm which they had destroyed, the Russians discovered Ukrainian self-propelled guns, and realized the farmers had housed the defense forces on their farm. They started checking the documents of the farmers' families. When they got to Anna's son, they took him out to the fields for questioning. They shot over his head, cut his leg and tendons, and knocked out his teeth. The Russians demanded the family reveal where the Ukrainian soldiers were. Anna's son was not the only one who suffered this barbarity: other young men from villages were also cruelly interrogated, while some were forced to walk through live minefields.

Russian soldiers locked Anna and her family in their cellar, not allowing them to go out for three days. During this time, all the wounded cows and calves died pitifully. "Wherever cows were hit, there they lay. Some were injured and still alive but could only lie there, waiting for death. Calves were lost too," Anna says. Half of their farm was destroyed. When Russian forces were finally expelled on 30 March, Anna found only 63 cows alive out of 120. She says they do not know what to do with the business they had been building up for years. Once freed, they could still not sell milk because there was no electricity in the village. Thus, the milk was wasted. Andriy is a little more optimistic. That same spring he began the planting season in their fields that were formerly places of battle. De-miners had destroyed the most dangerous projectiles there. Yet deeper explosives might still be in the field, making it challenging to sew crops. Among the rye fields, where grain ears had already sprouted, some projectiles which had fallen from a Kamaz truck were still there. Nonetheless, many Ukrainian farmers were determined to complete sowing in the spring and to plan the fall harvest.

Near the field stood an almost completely burnt-out military vehicle. Yet two Ukrainian soldiers were unscrewing parts from it. Due to the lack of parts, many pieces were taken from the battlefield, including from Russian equipment: in 2022 Ukraine and Russia were still relying on a lot of similar equipment from the Soviet era.

Several destroyed Russian Kamaz trucks still stood near the storage site. The granary pocked with holes from artillery fire stood with a tattered roof, and inside the remaining stored wheat was beginning to sprout.

# The Route to Life

Aiming for Kyiv, by the eighth day of the full-scale invasion, the Russians had almost completely encircled the northern city of Chernihiv, located 70 kilometers from the Russian border. At that time significantly more than half of the city's pre-war population of 285,000 still remained in their homes, according to data from local authorities. Had Ukrainian troops yielded just one more village to the south, the Russians would have completely encircled Chernihiv.

\*\*\*

To get out of the nearly encircled city, residents had to cross the 200-meter-wide Desna River, which borders Chernihiv from the south and is surrounded by numerous swamps. There are only three bridges from Chernihiv that cross the Desna.

The first bridge, on the city's southwestern ring road near Shestovytsia village, was blown up by Ukrainian forces while retreating in the first days of the Battle of Chernihiv. The remnants of the bridge fell under Russian control on 28 February. Due to its destruction, the Russians were not able to advance further across the Desna immediately. However, a few days later they managed to construct a pontoon crossing, and then entered villages south of the city on 3 March, including Yahidne, almost completing Chernihiv's encirclement. They cut the main Kyiv highway, further complicating any escape. From this moment on, to flee the city became a risky and dangerous choice.

From the newly occupied area, Russian fire could now easily reach the second bridge from Chernihiv, located at the beginning of the Kyiv highway, just six kilometers to the north of the Russian positions. Some people attempted to cross this bridge and navigate off the Russian occupied highway onto rural roads at their own peril. On 9 March, a Russian tank fired at a car with Diana Yemelianova's family inside. They were near the Kolychivka village trying to escape. Seeing a tank, her husband Oleksandr floored the gas pedal, desperate to outrun the danger, but the fire of the tank was too dense. The car sputtered to a stop just 200 meters away. Oleksandr shouted to everyone to get out, but his 15-year-old brother Maksym could not. His lifeless body lay on the back seat, his eyes rolled back, blood trickling from his mouth, and a gaping three-centimeter wound in his chest. Diana's mother was also wounded and could not walk any further. "I love you very, very much!" were her last words. Only the couple survived, having crawled three kilometers through the marshes.[25]

*The Battle of Chernihiv: initial stages. Russians almost completely encircled Chernihiv on 3 March 2022. Source: Wikimedia Commons.*

On 23 March, Russians bombed and completely destroyed the second bridge, cutting the way for vehicles altogether.

The last remaining bridge was pedestrian and although a little further from Russian positions, it was still under shelling. In the last days of March, it too was badly damaged.

After 3 March, the only way from the encircled city was through a narrow bottleneck, where at every point the Russian positions lurked less than five kilometers away. Their mortar and

25  This story was recorded by Olha Onyshchenko for Suspilne Chernihiv (https://suspilne.media/chernihiv/222059-tri-kilometri-piski-z-prostrelenou -nogou-cernigivka-pri-viizdi-z-cernigova-potrapila-pid-obstril/).

artillery fire had a range long enough to blanket the entire area. Dangerously close to the Russian troops, tens of thousands of the Chernihiv population managed to escape the siege through this bottleneck, using secret rural roads. Many people risked their lives to help others on the way. They used their own cars to help the escape and quickly organized hidden overnight shelters for those fleeing.

\*\*\*

One group of volunteers, consisting of just 12 people, eventually evacuated thousands out of the besieged Chernihiv, while delivering essential supplies to the city on their return trips. "Terrible things happened, but we were able to save many," Oleksandr Momot tells us. A local entrepreneur and single father of a 14-year-old son, he was among the first to patrol streets with the local territorial defense, and soon joined the urgent evacuation efforts. Like many other members of the volunteer group, he lost three cars to Russian bombardment while helping people escape.

Roman Movchan, another member of the group who worked on energy efficiency for the Chernihiv city council knew the necessity of self-organizing evacuation from his own experience. As Russian troops advanced, he had to find a way to save his parents from Kolychivka, bordering the south of the city. Roman evacuated his parents and, because local authorities had abandoned Kolychivka, he started evacuating others.

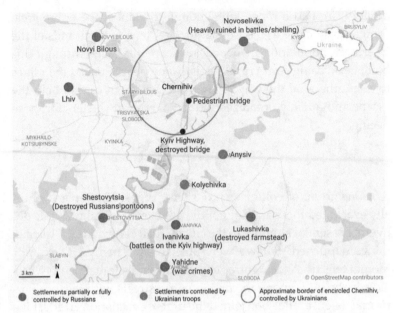

*Destroyed and damaged bridges from Chernihiv and the beginning of the Route to Life.*

Many maps from the first days of the 2022 Russian invasion showed that the Russians occupied almost the entire Chernihiv and Sumy regions. However, locals saw that Russians were moving mainly by highways, occupying villages along the way. Yet, they left large parts of territories and small roads in between uncontrolled. Thus, the volunteers were able to drive undetected 200 kilometers between Chernihiv and Kyiv many times—with Russian troops on both sides of their escape routes.

"We were not the first to devise this strategy," Roman says. "In fact, we borrowed this tactic from the Ukrainian military, who also bypassed Russians by using rural roads from all sides."

Chernihiv residents conveyed information about the hidden evacuation route person-to-person. Having crossed the river, they walked nearly a kilometer through the swampy valley to reach volunteer cars waiting near the Anysiv and Yenkiv villages. They did all of this under constant threat of Russian fire that was able to reach the escapees who were still close to the city and killed dozens of innocent civilians.

Yevheniy, another volunteer from the group of 12, tells us that he saw 11 people killed in two days. According to Ukraine's emergency service, the Russian military killed 100 civilians in the Chernihiv region in the first 19 days of the invasion. This number did not include occupied villages where many more victims were later discovered.

"I saw many injured people, and I too was attacked." While Yevheniy was crossing the pedestrian bridge from Chernihiv with another volunteer, Maksym, Russian forces suddenly opened fire and started shelling the bridge. The men dropped to the floor and lay there in the middle of the bridge for over 20 minutes, wondering what would happen next. Yevheniy could feel the bridge quivering and shuddering after the impact of every shell — tremors resonating through his core. As soon as it seemed safe to get up, they continued helping people and bringing supplies, although the bridge was pockmarked by shrapnel and full of large shell holes.

Yevheniy tells us that during March, while evacuating civilians and wounded soldiers, he lost four cars to Russian shelling. "There was no fear," he says, "because we had no other choice. After seeing mothers with children running across the field and shells falling all around them, literally running for their lives, how can you allow yourself to be scared? We had to save them, as well as grandmothers and grandfathers."

***

Cars were waiting at the meeting place and evacuees were packed into vehicles and set off to continue their perilous journey. "We had a big blue cargo van but the axle broke — people were being transported like sardines, piled on top of each other to get out," Roman says about the first days.

There is no exact count, but volunteers say nearly 75,000 people escaped from Chernihiv via the hidden routes, mainly by volunteers' cars. Those evacuated by Roman's group were taken to a kindergarten in one of the villages. The building was concealed among forests and had been converted into a layover base. Four local women managed the kindergarten, providing meals and caring for evacuees. People would rest there for a few hours or a night and then move on. Before the war, few people had any reason to visit this remote village. But it was now bursting at its seams, with hundreds at a time sleeping on the kindergarten floor.

Some of the Chernihivans remained in these quiet villages along the forested Desna banks, hiding from Russians and waiting for Chernihiv to be liberated. Others moved further, leaving the Chernihiv region altogether through dangerous battle zones.

After delivering safety-seekers to Kyiv, the drivers would turn back and bring much-needed supplies to those left behind. Chernihiv desperately needed food during the siege. Some bakeries were willing to help deliver bread to the region from as far away as Volyn, 700 kilometers to the west. However, due to fighting, trains could only make deliveries as far as Kyiv. Volunteers picked them up from there and took them further. Roman's team alone delivered eight tons of bread. Another priority was medical assistance. Everywhere there was a need for medication to control chronic conditions such as asthma, diabetes, epilepsy, and others.

***

In mid-March, the SBU (Security Service of Ukraine) contacted volunteers and told them to "shut the project down," because evacuation routes were visible by satellite. Russian drones could pick up areas of cars which were abandoned by people after they ran out of fuel, break down, or simply be left in villages where people stayed.

The volunteer group quickly decided to hide all vehicles so that the evacuation could continue. This was not a simple task, since there was little foliage at that time of year. Abandoned facilities helped. In one case, a half-finished school building hid close to 100 cars. The Desna and its swamps concealed rural roads, making Russians oblivious to the scope of the evacuation just a few kilometers away.

An enormous number of cars were also backed up on the Chernihiv bank of the Desna. After the bridges were destroyed, people had to leave their vehicles before crossing the river, either by the pedestrian bridge or boat—after the pedestrian bridge was badly damaged the group of volunteers had to rely on boats. Yet, boats did not guarantee safe passage either, given that the Desna's main river stream was exceptionally wide during spring flooding, washing over surrounding valleys and tree groves, just a few kilometers from Russian troops.

\*\*\*

Due to fighting and complicated supply, none of the gas stations worked in the north of the region. Finding fuel to continue the evacuation was one of the most difficult tasks for drivers.

"Everyone on our team ran out of money while trying to purchase fuel," Roman says. We had to ask people willing to help buy fuel in the west of Ukraine and bring it to Chernihiv or nearby. Many pitched in wherever they could. However, drivers occasionally had to purchase fuel at extortionate prices from black market vendors who suddenly popped up at the time of the shortage. If a liter of diesel cost UAH 40 ($1.3) in the west of Ukraine at the time, Roman paid up to UAH 250 ($8.3) near Chernihiv.

"I was building a house before the war," Roman says. "I still had loan money, so I invested them for fuel and volunteer aid. We helped the military in any way we could, including purchasing thermal clothing and sleeping bags for soldiers of Ukraine's Main Intelligence Directorate (GUR), who guarded our bank of the Desna. Our entire team ran out of money, but so many generous people were willing to help."

Unfortunately, not all volunteer drivers survived. On 30 March, Russian mortar shelling hit five cars in the same spot and they all burst into flames. Two drivers burned alive right next to their car, including 19-year-old Anastasiya Tahirova, who was transporting food to the city.

\*\*\*

The Ukrainian troops' strong resistance never allowed the Russian troops to break the defense of Chernihiv or cut the narrow evacuation route. GUR commandos and Special Operations Forces (SOF) used Javelins and drones to protect the Desna River north of the evacuation route, preventing Russians from crossing. The enemy failed to deploy a pontoon in the area, and their attempts were thwarted by GUR and SOF who sent Russian vehicles to the bottom of the Desna and swamps. High water levels were on the Ukrainian side. At the same time, regular troops engaged in combat in the villages south of the evacuation route, halting the Russian advance from the other side and preventing total encirclement.

Before joining the evacuation team, Oleksandr patrolled the route together with local territorial defense troops. From time to time, the territorial defense shared dinner with GUR and SOF fighters. Oleksandr says these soldiers from special forces were "just like machines. They called each other G1 and G2. They had so many Javelins—I'd never seen such an accumulation of weapons. I'm extremely grateful to them," Oleksandr explains.

At the same time, while the military was holding back the Russian onslaught, some Ukrainian traitors gave away their positions. Roman says they later discovered that a father and son team of traitors from Kolychivka had leaked information to the Russians, which then allowed the enemy to aim their fire on the local cultural center where soldiers were at the time. The treason did not bring a decisive success and Ukrainian troops were able to hold the front line in the village, while the traitors were caught by the villagers and arrested.

\*\*\*

Seven hours after the Russians were pushed back from the villages south of Chernihiv, Roman, Oleksandr and other volunteers drove to them to deliver bread and medical aid. No areas had yet been de-mined and there were corpses everywhere—Russian soldiers, Ukrainian soldiers and civilians. There were many anti-tank mines. "We just hoped they shouldn't blow up if we hit them with our car, but we didn't put that to the test," Roman says.

Two months after the liberation of Chernihiv, villages and roads used for evacuation were still littered with rusting car frames. Many dozens of civilian cars, destroyed and burned by enemy shelling, stood on the roadsides, emitting the stench of rust and soot—the smell of a battlefield. Destroyed Russian and Ukrainian equipment was also on the roadsides and in fields, grass growing around them and from every hole in the equipment's remnants. In Ivanivka village, Russians marked every house gates with their notorious "Z" symbols, as if to compensate symbolically for their failure to advance further and cut the route to life. Rocket frames were protruding from the concrete, while badly damaged buildings and completely destroyed streets stood frozen in time.

Not far away, just outside Lukashivka village, a burned SUV stood on the roadside. Next to it towered a newly erected cross crafted from recently cut timber in memory of victims killed there.

***

On the hill in Anysiv, one has a beautiful view of Chernihiv across the Desna. It is the first village on the route of life where people boarded volunteer vehicles after crossing the river. Had the Russians taken this hill, they would not only have cut off the road but also gained the best positions with a direct line of sight to Chernihiv; their artillery could easily have leveled the city center.

After the liberation of the entire region, a small chapel was built on this hill by Ruslan Martsinkiv, the mayor of Ivano-Frankivsk city 600 kilometers to the west of Chernihiv, who came to the region during active hostilities to assist volunteers when they initiated the evacuation route. His car came under Russian shelling but he survived. The chapel was built as a token of gratitude and is also a testament to the incredible evacuation effort during the Russian siege, as well as to the hidden route that saved thousands.

"What did we feel? Nothing, whatsoever," Roman says, reflecting on their volunteer mission. "It needed to be done, and that's that. At the time, we didn't consider why, and we didn't discuss big ideas. Nor did we ask ourselves, 'At what cost, at what risk?' No one thought about it. It just had to be done."

Telling his story, Roman speaks quietly, his gaze introspective. Hardened by almost two months of horrors, it seems that nothing can astound him anymore.

Oleksandr says that while walking through liberated Chernihiv, a stranger would occasionally approach him and say, "Thank you so much, because if it wasn't for you, I might not be alive." Oleksandr is happy to be back with his 14-year-old son who he has raised alone since the age of six. "Now I teach him how to clean a machine gun in the evening. We have to be ready for anything, just in case."

# Restaurant in the Warzone

Studying to be a chef in a small town in central Ukraine, Oleh Bibikov dreamed of opening his own chain of restaurants, and often shared his grand designs with school friends. His classmates sometimes mocked him, saying it was too ambitious a dream for someone from a small village in the Kropyvnytskyi region—and not from a wealthy family. But Oleh was serious. Since his childhood, he had dreamed of this alone, often spending hours watching cooking shows. After finishing his studies and full of determination, he moved 500 kilometers north to more than 1,000-year-old city of Chernihiv, the administrative center of the same-named region.

Oleh started with a small kiosk near a bus stop. In due time, even before turning 25, he and two friends, a massage therapist and a lawyer—neither of whom was wealthy but both hard-working—got together and opened their first restaurant, which would eventually become the La Pizza Espresso chain. Soon after, they launched another. Then just before the 2022 Russian invasion, they were on the brink of opening a third.

"I was never afraid of work," says Oleh, as we sit in the pleasant ambiance of his restaurant on central Victory Avenue. Creatively designed, it is full of greenery and natural light. It is easy to forget that just a few weeks ago this city was under Russian siege, with bombs dropped by enemy aviation. But today, we order pizza al pesto and a shrimp salad. The full menu is available to customers, despite all bridges to Chernihiv having been destroyed and supplies being significantly disrupted. "These are just nuances of our reality," he says. "Yes, supplies are compromised, but can the restaurant do without something like iceberg lettuce?"

Through the window, we can see pedestrians and the streets. The bombed-out Hotel Ukrayina is well within view—its third, fourth, and fifth floors are destroyed. While the Russians besieged the city, this restaurant was transformed into an oasis of hope for thousands, and when food became scarce, it became a lifesaver.

***

According to local authorities, at least 130,000 Chernihivans stayed in the city throughout the entire 36-day siege, while Russian forces almost daily dropped air bombs and fired shells. Although their attacks completely destroyed several suburban districts, many did not leave their homes. Some people simply could not leave, including the elderly, the sick, or those taking care of them. Others were afraid to travel along the dangerous routes or simply didn't want to part with homes. Many decided to stay and help the trapped residents and the military.

People prepared for the city's inevitable blockade, filling up on fuel and clearing grocery stores of food. Within a few days, most stores in the city were empty and closed because regular supplies were cut off. If the siege continued, the prospect of famine could become a real threat.

In Ukraine, the memory of famine remains very much alive. The 1932–1933 Holodomor (murder by starvation) was a genocide by artificial famine orchestrated by Joseph Stalin. Communist authorities deliberately and forcibly seized all food and livestock from villagers. The Holodomor remains one of the most tragic chapters of the 20th century. According to moderate estimates, 4.5 million died from hunger in just one year. The ravage did not pass without leaving its mark. A modern-day grocery market study shows that people in those regions of Ukraine that were part of the USSR at the time of the Holodomor suffered a generational trauma. To this day, people in these regions buy food in large quantities to stock up on essentials like flour, sugar, and biscuits. Some elderly people still keep large stocks – at least of crackers – stored in their attics or basements.

From the first days of the full-scale war, Oleh and his business partner Ihor opened the doors of their restaurant, located in the Chernihiv downtown area, and 150 volunteers stood side by side with them helping to prepare food. Among the volunteers were the restaurant's staff and their acquaintances, as well as city residents willing to help. Soon there were more than 300 people, and since there was not enough space for all of them in the restaurant, they used a 2,000-square-meter kindergarten that was right behind them, even though it was still under construction.

"Perhaps we were the only Ukrainian region that fed its military with salmon sandwiches and shrimp," Oleh smiles. The restaurant's food stocks, originally meant for customers, were repurposed in emergency sustenance kits. Initially, the restaurant fed soldiers, rescuers, and hospital workers. But as the number of kitchen volunteers increased and the need for food in the city grew more acute, they distributed food kits and hot meals to 22,000 city residents regularly. Some were able to go to the restaurant for meals; for others, deliveries were made. A few volunteers worked in an improvised call center, with each person responsible for a part of the city to organize deliveries.

Throughout March 2022, the familiar clamor and clangs of restaurant kitchens were deafened by explosions outside the windows. "No one gave up, and was not going to give up," says Oleh. "Everyone kept going non-stop. Russians bombed here in the early days of the war, exactly at the time volunteers were making 2,000 cabbage rolls for the military." Another time, eight tons of mackerel were brought to the restaurant. "'Swish Swish Swish.' We were marinating fish in buckets so that the drivers could take it away. We had everything you could want here," Oleh says.

The volunteers used 160 tons of sugar in large sacks to cover the windows, ensuring that nothing in the restaurant would be blown away during the bombardment. However, on 12 March, "everything in the restaurant was turned upside down" when a Russian missile hit the central Hotel Ukrayina, just 200 meters from the restaurant. Plates, food, and everything else that was on the shelves crashed to the floor. All the volunteers stopped for a couple of minutes to clear everything up, then got back to work. They knew that thousands were depending on the food they were preparing.

During Chernihiv's siege, volunteers at La Pizza Espresso made tens of thousands of pizzas and sandwiches, five tons of cheesecake, and tons of other meals. In addition, they delivered tons and tons of oil, butter, sugar, corn and more, all in sizable food packages, to city residents. The work was so intense that the restaurant chef Iryna — Oleh calls her a "woman of steel" — burned her hands so badly that it took months for the wounds to heal.

Alongside the shortage of food supplies, the city suffered from a lack of water and electricity due to disrupted infrastructure. Under Russian shelling, the restaurant owners and volunteers brought three power generators to the city, each worth $30,000. One of them had been donated by another young entrepreneur, Yura Stakhiv who, as Oleh says, "deserves a lot of medals" for his contributions to the city.

To have much-needed water, they drilled a well in the backyard of the restaurant right in the city center. A huge drill-rig drove into Chernihiv early on 23 March and drilled the well, but could not leave the city: that same day the last standing bridge to Chernihiv was blown up. "They blew up the bridge, and we knew that we wouldn't be able to leave the city. But it didn't particularly affect us," says Oleh. His group remained dedicated to the choice they had made: stay with Chernihiv residents.

***

La Pizza Espresso managed to feed thousands but it was not the only initiative. In one city warehouse, a couple, their daughter and her husband, as well as a few neighbors and friends, were packing food and hygiene kits. Meanwhile, their 9-year-old son was jumping up and down on a trampoline. He got used to playing while explosions boomed outside.

"I understood that there would be a war," says 41-year-old Dmytro Tkachenko, a professional bobsledder. "It's just that we didn't want to believe until the last moment that it would be on such a scale. Everyone wants to hope for the best. When the war began, there was no time for such thoughts," he adds. "The volunteer movement got underway."

City authorities in Chernihiv ordered the opening of abandoned warehouses, supermarkets and other businesses for the use of volunteers. Dmytro's family operated one of these, day and night. "During the siege, everyone came to understand the value of bread and water," he says. Believing that the bridges would be blown up and Chernihiv would be cut off, in the first days of war the family filled their warehouse with food and other necessities. Dmytro's many contacts in the international sports industry proved to be of great help.

Dmytro's small team fed about 1,000 people every day. They determined which people needed the basic things, and supplied these people first. In particular, many disabled people were stranded in their homes and not able to get assistance. Hygiene products and diapers were in high demand.

Most Chernihiv bakeries had run out of flour. Dmytro's team gave 10 tons of their stocked flour to one of them, Bulochka bakery. It baked 1,500 loaves of bread each day, which were then delivered to the most needy.

Dmytro had a functioning water well in his house, which he shared with others after the central water supply was cut. The family worked ceaselessly even though mortars and howitzers exploded constantly. "I was calm," Dmytro says. "Well, if the projectile hits, then I'll pass into eternity. If it does not hit, it's good, and I will continue working."

At one point when Dmytro's young son was playing on the trampoline, some drivers walked into the warehouse transporting humanitarian aid. Just then a shell exploded in a neighboring district with a particularly loud sound. The boom frightened them, and they dropped their boxes right there and quickly ran off.

"Dad, why did they run away?" the boy asked.

Dmytro's team had settled into a paradoxical tranquility. However, in March, in the middle of the day a Russian shell exploded so closely that the warehouse was seriously damaged.

The family and all volunteers got out of the building, and saw it engulfed in flames. The houses all around were on fire too. "It's only a miracle that we weren't hit directly," Dmytro says. The family used fire extinguishers to fight the flames, and thankfully they and firefighters were able to save the warehouse and supplies. The very next day, they returned to work in the warehouse to continue delivering food, despite the road now being strewn with rubble.

Once, when Dmytro was driving in the city center, a Russian mine exploded just 15 meters away. His car was damaged, but he was mostly unharmed, having only suffered a mild concussion. Another time, having arrived at the next house for delivery, Dmytro found there was no house anymore. It had been completely destroyed, with only two fresh graves dug in the yard. A son had buried his parents, who had been killed by the shelling, right there. He had no other choice because there was no possibility to get to the cemetery. "You look at all this and do everything you can to help people at least a little," says Dmytro.

\*\*\*

In hard work, facing survival conditions, emotions often take a back seat. "At first, I didn't feel any emotions at all," Oleh tells us. "It was on 5 April, when I burst into tears, at a soldier's funeral when his mother came forward to mourn her son." By early April, the Russian troops were finally pushed back from the Chernihiv region, leaving behind pain and devastation.

Oleh wears a traditional Ukrainian embroidered shirt almost every day now. He is leading us through the numerous rooms of the unfinished kindergarten where his team of volunteers had stored food. They needed to help those villages which were gradually recovering from Russian occupation.

One of the rooms is filled with hundreds of bags of hazelnuts and peanuts. Another is full of vegetables, and yet another stores just sugar. Even before entering each room, the scent is so strong that a visitor can guess what's inside. It is almost like stepping into a museum dedicated to the smells of food.

"It seems like there's so much," says Oleh, "but it'll go quickly." He adds that the supplies with a long shelf-life will stay untouched because everyone is wary of another siege.

When La Pizza Espresso's story became famous, many charity organizations, including the World Central Kitchen, decided to support it. But logistical issues sometimes posed a problem. "Once we were given 200 tons of flour. That's a lot. But now it had to be packaged into 5-kilogram bags and delivered to people. A 5-kilogram package costs 12 hryvnias ($0.32 cents). To pack 200 tons this is a considerable sum ($12,000) because a huge number of packages is needed. The same happened with 100 tons of pasta, which people also needed because the food situation was very critical."

"That's why, as a volunteer, often you don't get home until midnight, falling off your feet, but you can't actually fall asleep because you keep going over and over what happened during the day," says Oleh.

In the months following the liberation of the Chernihiv region, the restaurant delivered more than 1 million food packages to people from 190 villages who had suffered under Russian occupation. Volunteers put together hundreds of grocery bags, about 10 kilograms each, composed of the restaurant's supplies and donated food. The packaging of grocery sets did not stop for a single day.

"There are people who have lost everything — lost all their savings — and no longer have a job. How will these people live?" Oleh asks with concern. "Some say: let the authorities deal with it. But the authorities also have important work to do. They need to restart the thermal power plant, repair power lines, and repair gas and water pipes."

While strolling through Chernihiv's downtown in early June 2022, it is easy to forget about the war. Many streets seem to be completely cleaned up, in sharp contrast to the very same downtown just a few weeks before. Families are eating ice cream, kids are blowing soap bubbles. However, the outskirts of the city tell a different story. There are streets in Chernihiv where every building has suffered damage or been destroyed by Russian shelling.

La Pizza Espresso's team were among the first to help people in the most damaged districts of the city and nearby villages repair homes that had been damaged or destroyed by Russian shelling. A total of 200 people from all over Ukraine came to Chernihiv to help the growing team Oleh had organized. For a month, people of different backgrounds — among them teachers, musicians, lawyers, and judges — patched roofs and windows, and rebuilt rooms and entire walls. But as time passed, in the summer of 2022 only 20 people from this group remained to continue rebuilding damaged houses. "Everyone has their own families and jobs, and they can't help us all the time. These 200 worked here for about a month, and they deserve great respect for that alone. Soon it will be autumn, cold and damp. People without houses will get sick if they are not helped now," Oleh says.

Even after liberation, the threat to people's lives has persisted. The Chernihiv region's forests have been left full of mines and other explosive devices. Without help, people and children from low-income families had no choice but to do improvised "life demining" to clear areas for firewood needed for winter. "Everyone understands there will be no gas this winter and no coal," Oleh says. To save lives, his team gathered firewood for people.

As we leave the restaurant, we meet 25-year-old Ihor, one of Oleh's two business partners. He says, "Those who left the city during the Russian occupation, and then returned, don't understand this at all. I'm disappointed that they're doing nothing here. They don't understand how necessary it is to help those who sat in fear in basements and lost their homes. But we will keep going."

In the improvised headquarters in the restaurant's basement, new work is in full swing. Six people work diligently on many small but urgent initiatives. One is a special mosquito net for soldiers. This year, the Desna River's unprecedented flooding has swelled the mosquito population in the forested Chernihiv region, where Ukrainian soldiers guard borders, checkpoints and critical infrastructure around the clock. Oleh's team has devised head nets akin to those worn by beekeepers, to provide at least some protection from the pests.

All Oleh's savings during the nine years of work since he was 16 were used up on the 2022 volunteers for Chernihiv. Although the third La Pizza Espresso restaurant was already built pre-siege, there was no money left: neither to open it, nor to pay new staff.

"It's difficult to work now," Oleh admits. "You talk endlessly with donors, travel, show them results, count on them for something—then maybe you get something, but many times you don't. You sit on roofs, drag slate, boards and tarpaulin. Then you drive to a pick-up site and you return carrying heavy sacks of flour and sugar. For example, firewood. It's not cheap and needs to be wrapped in large batches. And the car needs to be fixed to move them. Today the mechanic handed me a list of almost $1,000 for what needs to be fixed in the car. And that's how it is all the time."

Oleh answers the phone and listens to the next request. Each time he hears about the suffering that has touched so many people around him, he knows that they are much worse than his own.

\*\*\*

While we are talking with Oleh, a cheerful, middle-aged man with glasses and a beard approaches him. Oleh introduces us to Father Roman, a priest in the Ukrainian Orthodox Church, who has come to the restaurant for food packages to deliver them to one of the region's remote villages near the border with Russia.

In the village, only 300 people lived before the Russian invasion. Three months later, there remain only 50. In these remote villages, few young people lived even before the war, and since then there are practically none. "In these villages, in the middle of forests, people live off whatever they collect and can sell. Now even that is gone because everything is covered in mines," says Father Roman. "But sometimes what you bring to people is not as important as having come to them — personal communication is so essential."

Farther Roman serves in one of Chernihiv's oldest, most beautiful cathedrals, St. Catherine's Cathedral. It was built in the Ukrainian Baroque style at the turn of the 18th century to honor the memory of the Ukrainian Cossacks of the Chernihiv Regiment, who under the command of Cossack Colonel Yakiv Lyzohub stormed the Turkish fortress of Azov in 1696. Together with his brother Semen, Yakiv funded the church's construction. It was originally built as a defense structure — its walls are about three meters thick — and it stood intact for 300 years. Then in 2022, Russian shelling broke its windows but fortunately did not cause serious damage.

While all the churches in Chernihiv were closed, St. Catherine's Cathedral remained open every day during the siege. It wasn't long before people started looking to the cathedral for help, "Some needed medicine, some needed food, some just sought comfort. I wanted to help everyone," Father Roman says. At first, he brought whatever he had at home, but soon Oleh helped to organize a volunteer group. Now Father Roman's church helps the volunteer initiative with building materials. "Sometimes people think that humanitarian aid has already been sent to the Chernihiv region," Oleh says, "that people in Chernihiv already have enough. But in fact it's still very little when you compare it to the scale of destruction. The war is no longer here, but the consequences — restoring everything — requires colossal resources."

Beyond the physical transformations in Chernihiv since 2015 — new bicycle paths and lush parks — Father Roman tells us he has observed subtler shifts, largely in the societal fabric that has manifested since the transformative 2014 Revolution of Dignity. "The most rewarding thing is that new people are stepping up to defend Ukraine in the aftermath of the revolution. The national consciousness is now awakening, despite decades of Soviet repression, famine, and the extermination of Ukrainians."

# Border with Empire

...war shortens the distance
from person to person, from birth to death,
from what we never wished for—
to what it turned out we were capable of
...
the world got blown up into pre- and post-war
along the uneven fold of the "no war" sign,
which you'll toss in the nearest trash,
on your way home from the protest, Russian poet,
war kills with the hands of the indifferent
and even the hands of idle sympathizers.

—Halyna Kruk, "No War" (excerpts), translated from the Ukrainian
by Amelia Glaser and Yuliya Ilchuk

In the beginning of Russia's full-scale war against Ukraine, many still believed it was "Putin's War," rather than a Russian national effort against Ukraine, and cherished the hope that Russians would massively protest against the war and against their President Vladimir Putin. It soon became evident that many Russians were, instead, ready to join the army for the conquest of Ukraine, both through compulsory mobilization or paid contract. A few sporadic protests soon after the Russian invasion were quickly dispersed by police without much resistance.

Ukraine's Commander-in-Chief (2021–2024) Valeriy Zaluzhnyi, after almost two years of war, admitted[26] that it was his miscalculation to assume Russia would stop fighting after losing 150,000 soldiers. In any other country, such casualties would have stopped a war. But not in Russia, where human life is cheap and where Putin's reference point is the Second World War, in which the USSR sacrificed millions as cannon fodder.

Kharkiv, the second-largest Ukrainian city located just 30 kilometers from the Russian border, is connected to the Russian city Belgorod by a short highway. In Kharkiv, Russians and Ukrainians

---

26  Ukraine's Commander-in-Chief Valeriy Zaluzhnyi wrote about this in his article for the Economist (https://www.economist.com/europe/2023/11/01/ukraines-commander-in-chief-on-the-breakthrough-he-needs-to-beat-russia).

encountered one another more frequently than in most other regions of Ukraine. However, this did not mean that Kharkiv eagerly awaited the arrival of Russian troops, as Putin had hoped. Historically, the Kharkiv region was settled by Ukrainian Cossacks. In the 18th century, the prominent Ukrainian philosopher Hryhoriy Skovoroda, who in his works had emphasized the importance of self-knowledge and authentic living, worked here most of his life. In the early 20th century, the city became a Ukrainian literary center. Subsequently, in what became known as the Executed Renaissance, the Soviet authorities executed hundreds of Ukrainian writers who even slightly disagreed with the Soviet ideology and Russian supremacy in the early 1930s. The Kharkiv region suffered greatly from the Holodomor and was heavily Russified in the subsequent years, yet it never lost its Ukrainian roots. Since the late 1990s, one of Ukraine's most renowned contemporary writers, Serhiy Zhadan, has lived and worked here. During the full-scale invasion he was actively supporting the city and its defenders by delivering various material aid and weapons as well as conducting large fundraising campaigns during his concerts. In 2024, he joined the military.

Many Kharkiv residents joined the Armed Forces of Ukraine to fight in the east between 2014 and 2022, and in 2022 many of them resumed their service to defend the city. Oleksiy, callsign Tiger, was 28 years old when he joined the army in 2014 and fought until 2016. When Russia launched its full-scale invasion in 2022, he quit his position as a top manager in a large construction company in Kharkiv and took up arms again to defend his home. "Unfortunately, journalists often make it appear that our enemy is weak, but it's untrue," he told us in 2023 after the successful Ukrainian Kharkiv counteroffensive. "First, Russians have a lot of weapons; and second, a lot of people. At the beginning of the war, 145 million people lived in Russia. Ok, now 250,000 fewer, but this is still a lot."

\*\*\*

Pavlo lived in the Kharkiv region for most of his life, most recently looking after horses at an equine rehabilitation center.

However, years before the war he worked in Russia for some time. "Russia is very similar to Orwell's '1984,'" Pavlo tells us. He believes the dystopian novel by George Orwell, published in 1949, reflects today's Russia, where the state is constantly at war and the vast majority of the population is brainwashed and live in perpetual fear—ready to support any state decision in its fight against imagined enemies.

Pavlo says, "Their state television propagandist Vladimir Solovyov first said, 'Hmm, Ukraine, we can conquer it in a blink of an eye.' But afterward, he said, 'We are at war with Europe's second strongest army, after our own.' And no one notices this contradiction."

"Ukraine must be wiped off the face of the earth," a Russian once told Pavlo, years before 2022.

"What exactly did Ukraine do to you?" Pavlo asked. "The fact that your government can't provide proper services for you and robs you are your problems ... We live freely, choose our president and future, and do not interfere in your internal affairs."

Pavlo tells us that many of the Russians he has met shared similar hostile views towards Ukraine. "Perhaps because the hatred towards Ukraine and the West was cultivated in Russia long before the war." At best, other Russians told Pavlo they "maintain neutrality," and do not get involved in political affairs. Independent polls prove that most Russians passively support their government's policy to wage war against Ukraine, while a smaller part are ready to participate themselves.[27]

"Only after they're personally affected, only when they go to a store and the price is three times higher, only then will they begin to think a bit. If some people in Russia even go to protest, they end up detained and simply cease to exist. Nobody will ever know where they are, and nobody will take revenge. State TV will report nothing ever happened and everyone will believe it, or at least pretend to. In Ukraine, during the Euromaidan Revolution in 2014,

---

27 One of the examples is the poll conducted by the Laboratory of Public Sociology (Laboratoria publichnoi sotsiologii) in autumn-winter 2022 (https://www.svoboda.org/a/strah-porazheniya-ili-podderzhka-pochemu-rossiyane-vybirayut-voynu/32407202.html).

only about 1,000 people came out at first. They were beaten by police, and in response 5,000 more came, then 50,000, and 500,000."

***

Pavlo spent the first week of the war near the village of Karavan, working at the equine-assisted rehabilitation center. The center was three kilometers north of Kharkiv, towards the border with Russia. With a deafening roar, Russian MLRS rockets, ballistic and cruise missiles would fly over his head towards Kharkiv day and night. He saw smoke rising over Kharkiv and the satellite city of Derhachi.

"Russian shelling never stopped for more than 30 or 40 minutes at a time," says Pavlo. "Why were they bombing residential areas? Savagery and absurdity. And why fire at the Feldman Zoo, or Central Park, or street markets such as the largest, Barabashovo?"

Russian shelling hit the Feldman Ecopark on the Kharkiv northern outskirts on the very first day of the invasion. In the next few days, the ecopark suffered numerous aerial attacks, which killed and wounded animals. Several park workers were also wounded and killed while feeding animals and evacuating them. On 7 March, having advanced close to the park on the city's ring road, Russian troops shot two employees. Their bodies, riddled with bullets, were discovered later in April hidden in the toilet facility.[28]

At the time, the front line was only 10 kilometers from the Karavan stable. All his co-workers had left, and Pavlo was alone feeding horses and exercising them daily. They were terrified by the constant explosions, and every time he tried to soothe them. All of this was not part of his job but he could not abandon them to suffering.

---

28   The detailed story of Feldman Ecopark, including the case of shot workers of the park was published by the Ukrainian outlet Bihus.info (https://bihus.info /mavpy-vmyraly-vid-rozryvu-serczya-yak-rosiyany-znyshhyly-unikalnyj-fel dman-ecopark-pid-harkovom/).

Pavlo tells us that at one time he drove from Karavan to an ATB supermarket in Kharkiv to buy food. People were standing in a long queue when shells began to fall and explode nearby. Pavlo was not wounded, but Kharkiv, the city with a pre-war population of 1.4 million, had already suffered one of the highest casualties yet inflicted. In just the first three weeks of the war, 500 civilians were killed by Russian shelling. This number, according to Ukraine's emergency services, did not include victims that were found later. Higher casualties were only registered in Mariupol, the port city in southeastern Ukraine encircled by Russian troops in the first days of the war. During the three-month siege of Mariupol, entire districts of high-rise buildings were razed to the ground by Russian bombing, and more than 20,000 civilians are believed to have been killed, although the exact number is impossible to calculate.

Pavlo used to communicate mostly in Russian: however, after the Russians attacked in 2022 he switched completely to Ukrainian. He dismisses the alleged oppression of Russian speakers in Ukraine which Putin rationalized to justify his so-called "Special Military Operation" in February 2022. "That was absolutely made up. Article 10 of the Constitution of Ukraine protects all languages spoken by national minorities. And the fact that a person living in Ukraine should know the state language is obvious."

The other myth invented by Russia is the so-called "brotherhood" between the Ukrainian and Russian nations. Despite popular notions of similarity, the Ukrainian and Russian languages are significantly different. Ukrainians can understand Belarusians and Poles, however, when Pavlo tried to speak in Ukrainian to Russians, "They don't get half of what you're talking about ... We have never been brotherly peoples, and after this, we definitely never will be ... There is no other way out of the war than a military victory for Ukraine. Neither can we hope for any internal opposition within Russia."

Like many Ukrainians, Pavlo learned early on about the atrocities committed by Russian soldiers. "When entering villages, Russians destroy everything out of envy, because they have never seen people living in villages comfortably." People from Russian rural areas, especially national minorities whose home countries had been colonized by Russia in the past, were disproportionately represented in the Russian army's lower ranks.

Pavlo had acquaintances from Russia, and in the first weeks of the war he spoke with them about the fighting, shelling, and war crimes that Russian soldiers were committing. "It's easier for them to believe it's all fake and nothing like that ever happened."

Another of these acquaintances said, "Well, let it all end, and then everything will be fine," as if all Russian killing and aggression could be erased from memory in a single day, as it is in TV propaganda.

"Things will not go back to normal again," Pavlo says.

***

As the fighting moved closer to Kharkiv, on 3 March Pavlo returned to his home village of Pasiky, 60 kilometers south. There was no fighting nearby, but it did not turn out to be safe. The village was located near a highway, a railway, and a railway station, and the Russians might have thought that there were some important targets.

On the night of 8 March, Pavlo was fast asleep in his house on the edge of the village, when suddenly he heard an explosion just meters away. A structural beam collapsed on him, but he was able to get out as the old oak house was quickly engulfed in flames. Pavlo raced away, dressed only in sweatpants and a light top, but luckily he managed to grab his jacket with his passport inside. Every other valuable, including his mobile and bank cards, was burned.

Pavlo could not see what hit the house. He thinks Russians must have shot a missile or rocket into the village, where the blast wave and shrapnel set his house on fire. In shock, he started walking toward Kharkiv, hoping to stop a passing car. The temperature was -18°C. Luckily, two cars stopped on the way, each taking him a few kilometers closer to the city. There were barely any cars on the road as he got closer to the city. He had to complete his trek on foot with the onset of frostbite in his feet.

Upon reaching Kharkiv, Pavlo passed by his military enlistment office, but it was no longer there—it had burned out. By now, he could not feel his toes at all, nor did he realize how damaged they were. Limping the rest of the way to the railway station, he was fortunate to find a train evacuating people to the west of Ukraine where it was safer.

The train kept stopping and turning off its lights to try to conceal itself from Russian shelling. Pavlo's meager clothing and passport was all he had left. Being hit by the house beam had left huge bruising on his face which was turning a deep purple as it spread across his face. People moved away from him. Thinking he was a looter, a woman asked the conductor to check his documents.

After reaching a hospital Lviv, he learned he had second-degree frostbite in his feet. He had to spend several days in the hospital recovering, but fortunately none of his toes had to be amputated. Showing his passport, he was able to withdraw some money from his bank account, and bought a new mobile. "Volunteers helped a lot," he says. "I was really surprised by how people welcomed me. They provided me with temporary shelter at a school. I hope to go and defend the country soon, to repay our so-called 'brother-liberators.'"

"Putin started this absurd war, just destroying our cities and sending Russia further and further back in time," says Pavlo. "They've got a huge land mass—just use it and develop it. Instead, they're making up fairy tales about a threat from NATO, they talk about NATO attacking. If NATO really wanted to attack, now is a perfect time. But it would be good if Japan remembered the Kuril Islands, which were taken by Russia, if Georgia mentioned Ossetia and Abkhazia, and if Moldova and Azerbaijan took back their territories, which were also stolen by Russia."

As soon as his condition improved and he could walk normally, Pavlo went to the military enlistment office to register. In the first weeks of the full-scale war, queues appeared near military enlistment offices around Ukraine. Many came after receiving a call from the military to enlist, while even more, like Pavlo, just showed up.

Officers enlisted Pavlo in the National Guard where he had to pass through training before going to the front.

Pavlo says with confidence, "Victory will be ours, because we are defending our land, and Russians don't know why they came here. We simply have no other options."

# Defiant Existence

In 1883, during the reign of Tsar Nicholas I in the Russian Empire, a decree was issued with the title, "On Additional Rules for the Resettlement of Peasants with Little Land to Areas with Abundant Land." Families were uprooted from their homes and, under guard, relocated hundreds of kilometers from their ancestral lands. In this way, the empire sought to more densely populate its new territories, especially those in the south of Ukraine formerly known as the "Wild Field," where Ukrainian Cossacks had lived under self-governance from the 16th to the 18th centuries.

Among many others from across Ukraine, under this law several dozen families were forcibly resettled 700 kilometers away to the village of Bohoyavlenka from the northern Chernihiv region. However, not far from the village, these families lost their way. Local authorities allowed them to establish a new village between what are now the cities of Mariupol and Donetsk. In this area where there was no forest, the settlers erected makeshift shelters from reeds and willow branches. As the decades passed, they were able to build a flourishing village now called Vilne.

When at the beginning of the 21st century ethnographers recorded songs and prayers in Vilne, they reported that all of them were in Ukrainian and the local dialect and phonetics were, despite more than a century of separation, still similar to those in Chernihiv. In the 19th and 20th centuries, an additional influx of people from various parts of Ukraine and the entire Russian empire (later the USSR), resettled in the Donetsk region, in addition to older Cossack settlements, to work in particular in the developing mining industry. The region was mostly populated by Ukrainians, who according to the 2001 census made up 57% of the population. Still, it was much more diverse in comparison with other Ukrainian regions. Heavily industrialized under Soviet rule, the region was also significantly influenced by Soviet propaganda concerning the alleged "friendship of peoples," albeit based on the dominance of Russian language and culture.

\*\*\*

Sisters Svitlana Fomenko and Olena Koniushok dedicated their lives to working with local youth and developing the cultural life of their home village Vilne. Before the Russian invasion in 2022, Svitlana worked as Director of the Vilne Community Cultural Center and Olena headed the Department of Culture in the Khlibodarivska municipality (composed of 26 villages including Vilne). "Someone may not know what their mission is, but I know mine for sure—it's to work with youth," says Svitlana.

Someone once told Svitlana, "You know your work bears fruit, because parents support the 'Russian world,' while their children say they're crazy." Svitlana tells us, "We didn't turn children against their parents, but we managed to foster an awareness of Russian propaganda."

Svitlana and Olena won the regional competition for the right to build a modern, spacious youth center funded with $21 million from the regional budget. They called it "The Free" ("Vilni") which derives from the village's name of Vilne. Since 2021, the village of just 800 people has boasted a large public hall available for films, music, public speaking, and an arena for sports. In addition, various workshops were held there, and the center was used as a study space for languages and the arts.

Initiatives by young people have infused the village with vibrant energy. In the summer of 2021, they organized a charity fair and raised $1,000 for each disabled child in the village. Olena says, "It was very lively. One girl did makeup for visitors. The boys brought a TV and a game console, and there was a raffle and treats. People had fun and they all chipped in."

In early February 2022, Vilne's young people were focused on repairing one of the center rooms for future projects. "There was no sense of a pending full-scale war," says Olena. The team was busy ordering new shelves and a pool table, and promoting a documentary about the history of their village. They had completed it just two months earlier.

However, a young man who had participated in the 2014 Revolution of Dignity in Kyiv, raised concerns about possible Russian aggression when, on 21 February 2022, Putin ordered the deployment of additional troops to the parts of the Luhansk and Donetsk regions that had been occupied since 2014. This was just 30 kilometers from Vilne.

"You know, Putin will try to capture the entire Donetsk region or will launch a full-scale attack against Ukraine," he said to Olena at the time.

"What are you talking about?" she asked. "Putin won't be allowed to do it."

Olena explains to us later, "I didn't even want to hear it. I didn't want to believe that such a war could happen in the 21st century."

On 23 February, the day before the full-scale invasion, Svitlana and Olena organized the Marathon of Unity. Across all 26 villages of their municipality, young people held a public event to thank those who were defending Ukraine's territorial integrity. The very next day, the villagers awoke to Russian bombardment that sounded throughout the whole of Ukraine.

The young man who had warned Olena of the invasion immediately left Vilne, and for good reason. Soon, once Russians occupied the village, they started detaining many Ukrainians: those who participated in the 2014 Revolution of Dignity, those who were serving in the Ukrainian army before 2022, and those who simply wore Ukrainian symbols or had patriotic tattoos.

\*\*\*

Initially, Svitlana and Olena had no intention of leaving their homes, even after the Russian military occupied Vilne in the first weeks of the war as part of its efforts to encircle the port city of Mariupol and take control over Ukraine's south. However, after witnessing their colleagues detained and beaten by the Russians, in mid-March, the two sisters set off together with their husbands and children on a dangerous route via Russian checkpoints to relocate to the Ukrainian city of Poltava, 400 kilometers to the north.

Like most Ukrainians who fled their homes because of the occupation or the approaching front line, they settled in neighboring regions, in the hope of returning soon. Just days after fleeing, Svitlana and Olena learned that the occupiers were searching for them.

The bitter truth was that some of their fellow villagers had assisted Russian occupiers by compiling lists of individuals with an active Ukrainian stance. Based on these lists, the Russians detained people, holding them for several days and subjecting them to beatings and torture. "At first, I was disgusted that people I knew, like teachers, chose to cooperate," says Svitlana. "I wondered how I could ever face them again. But now, I feel differently — let it be disgusting for them. They don't realize that Ukraine will win and we will all return."

In the following weeks, some locals in Vilne and surrounding villages prepared food or did laundry for the Russian soldiers. "These people believed they had no choice. We called them 'conformists,'" says Svitlana. She adds that there were many Russian supporters among pensioners, who referred to the Russians as "our boys." Born in the USSR and brought up on Soviet myths about the 'Great Patriotic War' (WWII) and 'brotherly peoples,' they still considered Ukraine closely dependent on Russia, even after 31 years of independence. "Some villagers were attracted by the low petrol prices in Russia or were brainwashed by Russian TV propagandists like Olga Skabeyeva and Vladimir Solovyov," says Olena. "While others thought that their youth, spent during Soviet times, was returning."

Some initial Russian supporters changed their minds after witnessing or experiencing war crimes in the village. Once, a Russian soldier broke into a house where the mother and her children were alone. He demanded that she prepare a bath and food for him. After that incident, the trauma induced the youngest child to start stuttering. The next time the soldier came, the father was home and confronted the intruder. In response, the soldier fired several shots beneath the man's feet.

*"Mom, don't cry. Everything will be fine," 11-year-old Nastia kept repeating to her mother in the hospital in Dnipro. Her head was tightly bandaged. Now she has a scar.*

*In one moment, the Russian missile took the lives of dozens. The central part of the Building №118 in Dnipro had completely collapsed. In place of the nine floors, there was only a void. On both sides, the surviving sections of the building were still upright: their outer walls had fallen away but the furniture inside the remaining apartments was still in place.*

*Half a year after the injury, Dmytro (right) takes his first walk around the training room. Instead of his right leg, a metal prosthesis is attached to his pelvis. Also in this picture – prosthetists Yuriy Yaskiv (left) and Denys Nahornyi (center).*

*The war caught 63-year-old Kateryna in Hostomel, where fierce fighting had started on the very first day of the invasion. She, her daughter, son-in-law, and grandchildren hid in their basement. "I saw my grandchildren with frightened eyes – I felt helpless," she says.*

*Nearly 75,000 people escaped from Chernihiv via the hidden routes, mainly by volunteers' cars. Those evacuated by Roman Movhans's group were taken to a village kindergarten. Concealed among forests, it had been converted into a layover base.*

*The amalgamated Sloviansk and Kramatorsk are the last two train stops for the Kyiv-Kramatorsk train, also known as the Kyiv-War Train.*

On 10 March, when the Russian military first entered Vilne, a father of the sisters' close friend was in his yard. While he was trying to escape to the basement, a Russian soldier shot and killed him. The soldier then said to the man's relatives, mockingly, "What can I do? I'm a sharpshooter."

Svitlana says, "As time passes, the number of people who understand what Russians really are, grows. But at what price?"

***

Olena and Svitlana's parents and grandparents were among those who remained under Russian occupation in Vilne. At first, the Russians did not touch them. However, in June, the occupiers forcibly transported 41 Vilne residents with patriotic views, to the detention center in Starobiesheve, near the city of Donetsk, along with dozens of people from neighboring villages. This was the largest detention of Vilne residents. In previous weeks, up to ten people had been detained at any one time, held for a couple of days, then mostly released, but this time the repressions targeted not only activists but their relatives as well. In particular, relatives of five of Vilne's youth workers were detained, as were Svitlana and Olena's parents. Those who fled earlier, and were far away in territories controlled by Ukraine, could do nothing but hope and pray.

Russians detained entire families with children. They confiscated people's documents and mobile phones and herded them all into a detention center. The detainees were fed a small portion of soup just once a day.

"Russians have absolutely no pity," Svitlana says. Their father, after three major surgeries, had two-thirds of his stomach removed. He could only eat mashed food; instead, he was given just the same soup, once a day.

At the time, many Russian soldiers had moved into the homes of these villagers and stolen their cars, money and valuables. After three weeks of detention and threats, Russians released the villagers and offered them transport to Russia, but most of them returned to Vilne. Exhausted, the sisters' father was emaciated and could barely walk. With a height of 1.87 meters, his weight had dropped to 65 kilograms.

The mass arrests of patriotic citizens mirror the genocidal policies of the Soviet Union in the 20th century, when thousands of members of the Ukrainian cultural and political elites were executed or deported to Siberia. The extermination of these elites was meant to serve as a warning to others, while structural measures such as the elimination of the Ukrainian language from public use, censorship and propaganda aimed to "reeducate the population" and, over a generation or two, transform them into Soviet people. This strategy was aimed at ruination of national and local communities while simultaneously allowing exploitation of the local population as powerless individuals for the Soviet state's objectives.

Since the occupation began in 2014, and even more intensively after 2022, Russia has employed similar tactics. Ukrainian orphaned children were deported to Russia for reeducation, and the use of the Ukrainian language in schools was severely restricted, with Ukrainian history, literature and language being eliminated from the curriculum. Street signs and city names were changed to Russian in the early days of the occupation, demonstrating Russia's intent to mark the territory as its own and erase any symbols of Ukraine. For example, as early as 5 May 2022, while the Battle of Mariupol was still ongoing, the Russians had already changed signs with the city name to Russian instead of Ukrainian.[29]

The remaining population in the occupied territories was then forced to take Russian citizenship, which subjected them to Russian mobilization; without citizenship, people were unable to register property or vehicles. A local collaborator and governor of the occupied Kherson region, Vladimir Saldo, explicitly indicated the policy of forced citizenship change on 24 May 2024, stating, "There remains a small percentage who have not received Russian

---

[29] This case was described by numerous media, including the Hromadske on 5 May 2022 (https://hromadske.radio/news/2022/05/05/u-mariupoli-okupanty-zminiuiut-tablychky-na-rosiys-ki-v-toy-chas-iak-liudiam-nemaie-shcho-isty-andriushchenko).

documents. The further, the closer this percentage will be to zero."[30] Meanwhile, those who fled occupied territories had their property confiscated by Russia as "abandoned," including land plots and apartments. This property was subsequently resold to settlers from Russia at low prices, facilitating the ethnic transformation of the local population.

Escaping Russian-occupied territories to those controlled by Ukraine became extremely difficult in the summer of 2022 due to severe movement restrictions imposed by Russian troops and disruption of humanitarian corridors. After they had been released from a three-week detention, it took Svitlana and Olena's parents six long days to drive 230 kilometers to Zaporizhzhia, passing Russian checkpoints and filtration camps all the way. They joined their daughters and grandchildren in the Poltava region—a 14-person extended family was together again, although without a home.

***

Despite horrifying news about their parents' arrest, in June the sisters started working on their first project since relocating—to aid those like themselves. They named it Municipality Online (Hromada Online) and created a series of online activities for displaced persons from their native Khlibodarivska municipality so that "after victory, we can all return together," says Olena about their motivation. "We set up this initiative so that we could be small anchors for each other. So that there is someone to return with, and to rebuild and restore order in our municipality."

The online activities for people who hailed from the 26 villages were meant to heal the pain and shared trauma after the harrowing loss of home. "It was easy for us to understand what others needed, because we're not just part of an NGO for displaced people—we're displaced persons ourselves and now we're working for our fellow villagers," says Svitlana.

---

30   Quoted by the RFE/RL (https://www.radiosvoboda.org/a/novyny-pryazov ya-prymusova-pasportyzatsiya-zlochyn-pokarannya-rosiyi/32970887.html)

One activity was the Piece of Home initiative which the sisters arranged through UNICEF. All participants were given a small sum of money (800 hryvnias, 22 euros) to purchase their own "little piece of home." "We know that people put themselves 'on pause' for a very long time," Svitlana says. "We did too—from March to June. It was a lost period for us. We know that displaced persons are reluctant to spend money on things for their well-being, but as part of our project, they had to."

Personal items like headphones, clothes, dishes, books, tonometers, chairs, cosmetics and pillows are some of the simple comforts they lost during forced evacuation and have purchased as part of the initiative. "We didn't want to restrict people and, indeed, there were so many different things people bought," Olena says. "For instance, I wanted a large frying pan like the one I left at home because for me it's not only a household item but a symbol of our family—to make food for everyone."

However, not all things can be bought and simply replaced.

The question asked by Svitlana and Olena echoed one of their Zoom calls, "If you could go home one more time, what would you take away?"

The most popular response was photo albums, especially the ones with old, faded images they never digitized. Now they wonder if they will ever gaze upon their childhood photos or be able to show their children what their ancestors looked like.

Along with these desires people mentioned a rocking chair, grandmother's earrings, a cat, a dog, an unread book, a coffee machine, a large pot, perfume, a camera, and more.

"And I would take my vyshyvankas (embroidery)," says Olena, remembering her beautiful embroidered blouses and her traditional outfits.

Some could not mention anything specific, saying they would like to take no less than "their apartment with everything in it" or their "mother or grandparents" they had left behind.

Only 10% of the residents who left Khlibodarivska municipality moved abroad in the first year of the war. The rest, 90%, resettled in other parts of Ukraine. "People often express their gratitude to those Ukrainians who sheltered them," says Olena. "Now, during meetings we discuss what people like in their current living circumstances, so that they can find something beautiful even in such difficult times." Getting together online from various places across Ukraine and abroad, they discussed which of the local customs they would like to bring back to Vilne after its liberation by the Ukrainian armed forces.

"People have a place to return to," says Olena. "Vilne did not suffer too much from the shelling." She hopes that one day she too will return home, together with other displaced persons from their municipality.

During one of their Zoom conversations, Svitlana asked to finish the sentence, "On the first day following the victory, I will ..."

"... cry tears of joy and mentally and physically prepare to return home."

"... gather all of our local club's artists and publish a collection of poems."

"... buy a ticket home."

"... open my favorite Nova Poshta."[31]

"... there will be joy through tears! We'll pack our belongings and go to our ancestral home. And in my soul there will be the thought, 'Ours did it!'"

"... walk like a zombie and not believe that this horror is really over."

"... there will be multiple victories. For starters, a blue and yellow flag will be raised over our native village. I will take a fast route home and make plans for the future. And there will be joy. I will pray (although I'm not very religious) and thank the Lord. On this day, I will want to hug my family. And I also want to call all those people who helped my relatives and me during a difficult time. And listen to them. To learn that they, too, have the opportunity to hug their closest relatives. And that there will be peace."

---

31  Nova Poshta is the largest and fastest Ukrainian postal service. It became a symbol of the rapidly growing entrepreneurial culture in Ukraine, not only because of its overall success, but also due to a franchising model of operations. Thousands of Ukrainians were opening their own Nova Poshta offices, even in small villages and towns in the 2010s. During the war, Nova Poshta became a symbol of connection between the front line and the rest of Ukraine, delivering parcels to soldiers as close as five kilometers from the front, as well as immediately reopening offices in settlements liberated by the Armed Forces of Ukraine.

# Jungle

Granted the magic to weave love and chords,
Wishing I could be building life, I dive into this surreal subsistence.
For if not us, then we will all be killed by these faces of horde.
Our world is broken again, we are the new engineers of existence.

Beyond the slag heaps, the sun rises on,
The world lets the determined take their own.

— Yarmak,[32] "Babylon," the song was released in 2024

"If you fight continuously for three years, you're almost certain to ruin your health because of difficult conditions and nothing but dry rations," says Volodymyr Hrynchyshyn, a soldier with the Ukrainian armed forces. It is September 2023, and we are driving to the front line with Volodymyr to deliver a donated car to the military. "There were situations where soldiers had to sit in trenches for up to a month without rotation," he says. We are on a new highway through Kharkiv and Izium towards Sloviansk. Paradoxically, the closer to the front, the better and newer the road. The highway had been completely renovated because of President Zelenskyy's pre-war initiative to repair and widen roads throughout the country. Some had complained about poor policy in preparing for the war, when the focus was on renovation instead of additional procurements for the army. Others said good roads made executing military logistics for the front line faster and more reliable.

---

32 Ukrainian rapper Yarmak gained popularity with his Russian-language songs, although he maintained a pro-Ukrainian political stance and participated in the 2014 Revolution of Dignity. In the years leading up to the full-scale invasion in February 2022, he started releasing more songs in Ukrainian and eventually wrote songs exclusively in Ukrainian. After the Russians invaded, he joined the Armed Forces of Ukraine and, as of summer 2024, continued to fight against Russian military aggression. Yarmak says that during the war, he strives to write songs that resonate with soldiers, unlike the pop songs topping the charts. However, his songs have become extremely popular among all Ukrainians. The music video of his song Babylon—excerpt from the translated lyrics above—shows the ruins of Maryinka in the Donetsk region, a town where Yarmak fought. Maryinka was completely destroyed by Russian shelling.

147

The closer to the front, the fewer civilian cars. The last 100 kilometers of the highway were under Russian occupation a year earlier, but liberated during the Ukrainian Kharkiv offensive at the end of 2022. The fields here were unsown and unharvested. In early September, the landscape brims with the crimson-scarlet hues of goldenrods, their stems already dry. Autumn wildflowers bloom among neglected, self-seeded wheat ears, adorned by the rays of the setting sun. Lines of trees and groves of forests stand half-dry and half-burnt in the aftermath of flames from artillery shelling. To the south of Izium, destroyed villages reveal the areas where Russian troops tried to break through the front at the beginning of the war. The most massive shelling leveled entire rows of houses. Now, these villages are razed to the ground, and only half of a wall remains standing from a house here and there — burnt remains without a hint of a roof. Not a single person could be seen on the streets in local villages like Kamianka. This is one of the last villages that the Russians managed to capture. This is the area where they were stopped and later driven out.

On every hill along the highway, blue and yellow national flags, and red and black combat flags flutter — a reminder that each of these hills had to be recaptured by Ukrainian forces at the cost of human lives. Volodymyr says that just a few kilometers away, near the front line, is where the "jungle" begins — wild thickets where no civilization and no rules exist. There soldiers dug burrows in the ground to hold the front, surviving like wild animals to preserve humanity further to the west. Wildlife has bred amply in these deserted lands during the war — hares graze in clusters in abandoned fields. Evidence of abundant foxes is clear from the number of roadkill. At least a dozen red foxes lie dead by the roadside as we drive just 50 kilometers.

"You sit in the trench and look through the thermal imager at night — hares are grazing, foxes are chasing after mice in the field. It means everything is fine, you can be calm. But if there are no animals, it means you have to be attentive," says Volodymyr. He goes on to speak of the time at the beginning of his service in 2020. "That was a calmer period. You could bathe and do laundry, but when the full-scale war began, it was the end of rest and there was no hope of saving strength or health."

The empty roads, now liberated from Russian occupation, run almost parallel to the current front line, only a distance of 30–40 kilometers away. To the east of the road, dense forests stand on the picturesque banks of the Siverskyi Donets River for tens of kilometers — the stretch where Ukrainian forces held the front. Two-thirds of the cars driving here are military. They fly through the "jungle" on the clear, one-lane highway at 160 and even 200 km/h: no speed limits here and no police; just their own rules apply. Occasionally, small potholes from shrapnel and larger ones from projectiles appear on the otherwise smooth road. The presence of death is palpable here through the lingering smell of fires and rusty, mutilated equipment standing abandoned off to the side.

\*\*\*

Sloviansk was only eight kilometers from the front in 2022, but it was not devastated completely because it did not experience occupation or street fighting. In 2023, the front runs 25 kilometers to the east, yet this town is a lively island within the "jungle," even though every second person on the streets is military. The soldiers are mostly more muscular than average civilians, and although their gaze is tired, at the same time it is clear and focused. In Sloviansk, they can be somewhat more relaxed than further along the front line, some servicewomen even wearing clean, laundered uniforms, with their hair loose, not pulled up into a helmet as usual. Only the weathered skin on their faces betrays that they may have been pulling the wounded from trenches or adjusting artillery just yesterday. In general, there are many more men here than women. The town is a border but at the same time it is a bridge between civilization and the front. Here, a soldier can drink coffee, shower, and sleep in a bed, but it is impossible to forget about the war. The town is full of military vehicles. At times the siren of a medivac screams through the street at high speed to rush the wounded to medical care. Sloviansk is sad and tense, but at the same time it is composed and calm, despite the explosions in the distance.

In a rare free hour, military service members come to the town. During a rotation, some personnel can stay here overnight, while others may be stationed in Sloviansk to conduct logistical work and repairs or perform other support tasks for the front. Many apartments in the town are empty — the owners have fled and now lease their flats to the military, with the help of neighbors or acquaintances. Sometimes a soldier's beloved — and more rarely even a whole family — may come here, but only for a brief visit. Such meetings are bittersweet because the inevitable pain of the separation always looms over them. Flat owners who had fled the area often hide the keys to their apartments in nearby locations, like in the mailbox, and provide the flat number and key location to the guests as soon as the payment is confirmed. Most of these apartments still contain personal items, like clothing, photos, books, and other possessions that had to be quickly abandoned. The night silence is filled by crickets and distant explosions.

In Sloviansk it is evident what the struggle is for — life itself — with people surviving despite the attempts of the enemy to destroy them. Everyone in Sloviansk, civilians and military, knows that this town will be next on the Russian path if the front falls. Here, every shop, café, and every surviving building seems much more precious than elsewhere, despite their modest architectural significance. Some of the buildings date back to the time when German and English business magnates participated in the establishment of mines here in the 19th century. Most of the buildings, however, are Soviet-built — featureless five-story blocks with tiny flats.

***

Some local residents who left at the beginning of the war during the uncertainties of the time have returned to Sloviansk. Tetiana is among them. In the morning, she leaves for her sales job in a bold pink blouse, her blonde hair slightly curled, looking forward to her day. Her whole ambience is up-beat, denying war and death.

"I left when the war started, but then came back. Many of my neighbors and acquaintances have also returned. My relatives are at the front, we don't see them." She says she is accustomed to air sirens, the sounds of artillery, and the presence of the military on the streets. She lives her life as normally as she can.

Utility workers nearby mow lawns with the buzz of string trimmers, despite the fact that the majority of the buildings on the street were destroyed or damaged by shelling. A few streets away, where all the buildings have survived intact, someone has hung colorful flower pots on the balcony, radiating yellow, red and orange. They are a bright spot among the drab building facades.

A young woman, Olha, sits on a park bench, focused on her mobile. She works remotely as a consultant at Monobank, an innovative and youth-oriented bank which has an online helpdesk available 24/7. She was born in Sloviansk and has returned here from Kyiv where she spent several months at the start of the full-scale war. She has relatives in the military and worries about them. Once a rocket dropped in her neighborhood but luckily no one was killed.

Another local, Yuriy, used to edit the local newspaper Business Sloviansk. The newspaper stopped publishing at the beginning of the full-scale war. "Everyone scattered, some to the front, some to other places or jobs," he says, hurrying through the town, past the debris of a damaged wall to the town center.

A local pensioner says that in Sloviansk she takes care of her elderly parents. "Have I managed to adapt? How can I put it? Definitely frightening. Air alerts all the time. But both in Kyiv and in Dnipro there are the same air alerts and explosions."

Tamara stands on the street behind a table with 19-liter bottles of milk. She pours it directly into people's containers who stand in line to buy dairy products. She and her husband are from Sloviansk, but in 2014 they bought land east of the town in the Lyman district and started a farm, which grew to 80 cows. In 2022, the Russians occupied the village and she had to leave, but her husband stayed. During fighting the farm burned down, and only 50 cows survived. But after the Ukrainian army liberated the village, Tamara and her husband decided to remain in the countryside and continue farming.

"We work. My pension is small, and my husband's is the same. People come, buy products." Three days a week they sell milk in Sloviansk, and then three days in Lyman, a small town just 12 kilometers from the front. They sell it for only 20 hryvnias ($0.55) per liter, saying their work is partly social assistance for locals.

Soldiers, two men and a woman—Mirazh, Kostia, and Lastivka—are talking in a curb cafe in the town center, using their rotation time to rest. Nearby cafes are crowded with people in camouflage, some just grabbing a coffee and a lunch and rushing back to their military duties.

Lastivka is a communications technician, while Mirazh and Kostia are artillery gunners. They have been fighting continuously since February 2022, and during this time each of them has been able to visit home only once during brief leave. "There are no options other than to continue the fight," Mirazh says. "Everyone has gotten used to it over these one-and-a-half years."

"By everyone, you mean both military and civilians?"

"Well, as for civilians, I would call it a bit differently," says Mirazh, meaning that some civilians in cities far from the front forget about the war. Smiling ruefully, he tugs at his short beard. He has a large black dragon tattoo on his right hand.

\*\*\*

The amalgamated Sloviansk and Kramatorsk are the last two train stops for the Kyiv-Kramatorsk train, also known as the Kyiv-War Train. The new Intercity train, constructed only a few years before the war, arrives at the station, and for a moment, it does not seem like wartime. But on the platform, two or three hundred people have gathered, and most of them are in uniform. A few of them even have prostheses instead of a limb but do not abandon their service.

However, about a third of the people are civilians, mostly women who have come to spend a few moments with their husbands or boyfriends. A few have come with their children. But the visit has ended, and it is time for the soldiers to return to their duties. On the platform, couples are embracing and saying good-bye, knowing that, at best, it will be months before they see each other again. Sometimes it seems that nowhere else is there more love in one place than on this narrow platform.

A young woman and a serviceman hold hands as he caresses her long brown hair tousled by the wind. She boards the train and takes her seat but cannot hold back her tears. She calls him by video link once the train starts moving to say a few more warm words of farewell. During the journey to Poltava, tears trickle down from her eyes more than once. She gazes at the photo on her cell phone dozens of times. In the picture, she and her beloved are standing on the platform — someone photographed them there. Finally, after a few hours of the trip, she sends him a text message, "I blame my-self for falling asleep at 8 o'clock. I should have spent more time with you." Over and over, she checks her phone during the entire trip to see if there is a response.

# Children in the Yard

Just after 3 pm on 14 January 2023 — almost a full year since the beginning of the full-scale war — Maksym and Iryna Shevchuk were dressing their children, nine-year-old Tymur and 12-year-old Karolina, to go to a birthday party. The children went to play outside in the yard of Building №118 on Victory Avenue in the southeastern city of Dnipro, waiting for their parents to come down.

A friend, six-year-old Zhenia, was playing with them because there was no electricity and internet at home due to a scheduled power outage.[33] Parents of children living in the building were not afraid to leave them alone in the yard, Zhenia's mother Anastasiya Khudiakova tells us. Their neighborhood was friendly and safe, where everyone knew everyone else. Besides, she could see her son through her window. BOOM!

Anastasiya found herself on the floor under the shattered window frame. At first, she did not understand what had happened. She looked up. The window was no longer there. "I had only one thought — that my child was outside."

In her robe and slippers, she rushed out. The apartment door was jammed. "I knocked it out somehow, I don't remember how. And I was just running, headlong."

While charging down the stairs, Anastasiya started yelling her son's name once she reached the third floor. When she came outside, the yard was engulfed in smoke and filled with screams. Among them, she heard two children yelling, "Mom!" Her son Zhenia and his friend Tymur ran to her. They were unrecognizable — both boys were wearing hoodies and covered in soot. She hugged them both. At first, she could not believe that her son was alive. "You understand what happened," she says. "Automatically your mind sets you up for the worst, for something bad. And when

---

33  The power outage was due to Russian missile attacks on Ukraine's energy infrastructure in the winter of 2022–2023, which caused significant damage. Consequently, power was supplied to Ukrainian households on a schedule, typically with 4-hour intervals. In the spring of 2024, Russia resumed its strikes against energy infrastructure, causing even more significant damage.

you go out and see that everything is really all right ... you can't believe it."

Anastasiya looked at the boys' ears, checking for blood which would be a sign of sudden deafening. Her son was not wounded, but Tymur had an arm injury. Tymur did not yet know that his parents were no longer alive.

\*\*\*

That fatal afternoon, the tranquil yard of Building №118, 100 kilometers from the front line, became a place of despair. The central part of the building had completely collapsed. In place of the nine floors of apartments, now there was only a void — all the floors had turned into a heap of concrete mixed with remnants of belongings from the apartments. On both sides, the surviving sections of the long building were still upright: their outer walls had fallen away but the furniture inside the remaining apartments was still in place. In one of the flats, in cabinets hanging by nails on what remained as walls, a few cans of food could be seen — although the kitchen no longer existed. Fourteen residential buildings nearby were also damaged because of the explosion's blast wave — most of their windows were blown out. In one moment, the Russian missile took the lives of dozens. The injured could still be saved, but the clock was ticking loudly and terrifyingly.

Just minutes before the explosion, Serhiy Khlibtsevych and his 16-year-old son Volodymyr had decided to visit friends nearby.

"Are you coming?" Serhiy asked his wife Hanna.

"No, I'm not feeling well."

The father and son were only a few dozen meters from the building when the shell exploded behind them. "It's like the ground was bouncing around under our feet, like on a trampoline." The yard was filled with smoke, wreckage flying everywhere.

At the moment of the explosion, Hanna was standing near the window watching the two leave. The blast wave flung her and the window frame four meters back. She lost consciousness.

Serhiy rushed his son to a shelter, then ran back to the apartment, phoning his wife the entire time. The desperate wait to hear her voice felt like an eternity. Meanwhile, his wife was digging through the debris for the phone. She did not yet realize that blood was streaming from her temporal artery. Stumbling through the darkness and toxic smoke, Serhiy found her and raced out of the apartment. Just as they reached the ground floor, the remains of several neighboring flats collapsed with a deafening roar.

A stranger on the street tried to bandage Anastasiya's injury, but her blood was still spurting out. Several ambulances had arrived, but long queues waited by each. Serhiy spotted an ambulance racing toward the site. He waved his arms frantically, and it stopped. The medics jumped out and instantly placed Hanna on the stretcher.

Serhiy waited in the hospital corridor for three hours while Anastasiya was in the ICU. Finally the doctor came out and told Serhiy that on that day they had lost several people with similar wounds,"You were lucky to be close to her and to stop that ambulance. She's going to live."

\*\*\*

It was a true terror to be near Building №118 on the evening after the attack. People who were buried in the rubble were shouting for help. The death toll was rising, as some of the rescues became retrievals of the dead.

Hundreds of people from the neighborhood came to help. Some worked to remove rubble. Others passed out tea and sandwiches to help people keep up their strength and comfort the worried. Rescuers, volunteers, trucks and cars filled the area, blocking access to the street. Many of those who came to help stayed near the building for several nights. Serhiy was there too around the clock and hardly slept. While his wife lay for days in the hospital, he and his son continued searching for survivors. "It was impossible to fall asleep at all for the first two days. And when we did, it was only sporadically, maybe two or three hours."

Clearing rescue efforts started from the top floors and moved down. "On the fifth day, hopes of finding anyone on the lower levels were fading away."

In the yard, Serhiy learned the painful news about his neighbors. When he tells us of 15-year-old Maria, a close friend of the family, he cries. At the moment of the explosion, Maria was standing under an archway on her way out of the building when the shockwave hurled her into the air and killed her outright. Just a year earlier, Maria and her family had moved into the building, escaping the war raging near their home in Nikopol, 120 kilometers to the south. "I constantly think about the people I've lost," says Serhiy. "Such moments in life leave an indelible mark, and I'm not sure how it will affect me in the future. And children ... children are most important ... how will it affect them?"

*** 

"Mom, don't cry. Everything will be fine," 11-year-old Nastia kept repeating to her mother in the hospital. The girl's head was tightly bandaged.

A day before, Nastia's mother, Vlada Samarina, returned from the hospital where she had assisted injured soldiers as a volunteer. She was having lunch in the kitchen at the back of the flat when she heard a boom. "It wasn't very loud. At least, that's how it seemed to me." Her husband and daughter were in the room facing the Dnipro River, while she was on the other side. The glass from the balcony windows flew over her husband's head, but caught Nastia, splitting open her forehead. She felt a sharp pain and covered her head with her hands.

"I'm bleeding," she said.

Her father immediately lifted her in his arms and ran down the stairs to the car, then drove at lightning speed to the hospital. "We didn't even realize it was our building that was hit," Vlada says. "It was only when we were leaving the driveway that I saw out of the corner of my eye that it was our place." As they sped down the street, cars moved to the side to let them through. Nastia's head was so tightly bandaged that she could not see where they were going, but she kept consoling her parents. "We were far more stressed than Nastia was … Nastia is a fighter."

In the hospital, the family met their nine-year-old goddaughter who lived in the same building. "We realized how lucky Nastia was." Their goddaughter's leg had been crushed by a concrete block. For months she wore a special orthopedic Ilizarov apparatus.

On the night after the explosion, Vlada thought, "All the horrors that could happen to us, have happened. We've been living in the war for a year—this is our life now, and we have no other choice but to keep living. The soldiers on the front have it much harder."

"Yesterday, I showed my daughter a video of soldiers driving back from the front line in a car. They were completely covered in dirt and mud. It's terrifying. I've been with them for a year now, volunteering in a hospital. These are young guys who have their whole lives ahead of them and haven't done anything yet. They want to do something good—and now they're sacrificing themselves so we can sleep in our beds."

After a section of the Building №118 collapsed, Dnipro residents gave Vlada's family an apartment to live in. Two months later the smell of smoke in the remaining part of the Building №118 had almost dispersed. Their flat had not suffered much, and they could have returned home once the structural inspection was done. "But I don't have the strength for that yet," Vlada says. "Hopefully, when it gets warmer, we'll be able to move to our small country house outside the city. For now, we don't have the courage to live in this apartment building, knowing what happened."

***

Tetiana remembers the Building №118 when it was newly built. In her childhood, she lived there with her parents and brother. Tears come to her eyes as she talks about her previous home, of which nothing is left. "This is just palpable grief, because so many people's family members died, and they cannot be brought back," Tetiana says, hardly able to speak through her tears.

The flat was given to Tetiana's brother, Serhiy, who went to serve in Ukraine's armed forces. It stayed empty while Serhiy was fighting the Russians at the front, so luckily no one suffered. But it was still hard for Tetiana to call her brother at the front and tell him he no longer had a home to return to.

\*\*\*

For hundreds of families from Building №118, the tragedy was not over after the attack. Little six-year-old Zhenia, who was playing in the yard with his friend Tymur, developed a nervous tic. Months after the tragedy, the little boy is still being treated by a psychologist and a neurologist. His grandfather, who was in the flat at the time of the explosion, suffered a concussion and a minor stroke. He partially lost his speech and the ability to work. "He's still recovering. He doesn't speak well," Anastasiya tells us. "He can no longer work. Well, he will be home with Zhenia, and will help him with homework."

Anastasiya herself sought help from a psychiatrist. "I'm strong. But I understood that I needed help, and now I'm on anti-depressants. But we all believe in the Ukrainian armed forces. We hope the war will end soon."

Zhenia's friend Tymur was much less fortunate. His parents, Iryna and Maksym, were among 46 people killed by the attack. Since then, Tymur and his sister Karolina stay with their uncle's family.

Tymur's football coach, Illia, was home at the time of the strike, just three streets away from Building №118, watching TV with his girlfriend. When they heard the explosion, they did not think it was in their neighborhood, assuming that it hit the power station located nearby. However, just three minutes later, social media exploded with posts about the tragedy. Since the parents of Illia's trainees lived in the affected area, he immediately posted in the parents' group chat. There was no response from the family in

Building №118. When Illia arrived at the site of the disaster, he discovered the parents of his trainee Tymur had been killed.

Illia decided to help Tymur and Karolina by collecting donations from the football club's community. The local football federation and teams of all ages participated, donating to Tymur's guardians. Illia's former teammate—today the world-famous Ukrainian footballer Olexander Zinchenko—recorded a video in support of Tymur. Tymur's fellow teammates visited to support him, and he was able to return to football several weeks after the tragedy.

***

Dnipro, Ukraine's fourth-largest city, was just 100 kilometers from the southern front line and 200 kilometers from the eastern. It became Ukraine's key logistical and medical center closest to the front. Wounded soldiers are brought to Dnipro's hospitals, where the most urgent operations are performed. Many Ukrainians who lived in territories that are now occupied by Russia, or in areas that are close to the front line, have chosen to live in Dnipro until the end of the war.

In March 2023, Dnipro was vibrant and alive, with many children from relocated areas playing in the streets. Here, sirens may wail less severely than in many cities further from the front, but they do wail more often—every few hours, sometimes several times in an hour. Most city residents use chatbots to know if the threat is tangible or not because often the sirens are set off because of Russian training flights close to Ukraine's border. When a siren blares in the park on a Saturday morning, people mostly continue strolling, not rushing to shelters. It may seem that they have gotten accustomed to war and are less fearful. In reality, it is simply impossible to live in a constant state of tension and fear for a long time. Their lives are a testament to the resilience of life, fighting its own battle against war and destruction. People, playing with their kids in the park or chatting leisurely over a cup of coffee, often bear the scars of war that do not fade.

"People have become kinder, more merciful, and more understanding," Serhiy Khlibtsevych says. For him, as for many Ukrainians, the Building №118 explosion is not the only scar of war. Serhiy's mother has been living in a town under Russian occupation for a year. When there was still a chance for evacuation, she lay in hospital with heart disease. Her husband, Serhiy's father, died under occupation in August 2022. At that time it was still possible to bring a deceased person to Dnipro for burial. "Now evacuation is incredibly difficult. We're waiting and hoping for victory and an opportunity to reunite. People who are in occupied regions also lose hope after living under occupation for so long, downtrodden by harsh Russian directives and violence."

A lot of Serhiy's acquaintances and friends were fighting. Some had been in France, serving in the French Foreign Legion, and came here to fight when the full-scale war started. "They serve in Ukraine's special forces. Many have had injuries, have been in the hospital for three months, and then gone back to the front. Of course, our soldiers — many who are my age or younger, even children of my friends — are brave and courageous. I would like to believe that the war will end. I think that if we were given more weapons by our partners, we would have ended the war a long time ago. Because donating 'four tanks a year,' I think, is only enough to keep us afloat. People are dying and people are breaking down psychologically, because how much longer will it last? It's already been a year and what if it's another year and then another? We are adults and can cope somehow ... but what about children?"

# Wings

When in 2015 Maria Berlinska, who volunteered to serve in Ukraine's armed forces, returned to Kyiv, she was bitterly upset that Russian pop singers and stand-up acts still toured Ukraine's capital concert halls and the Russian language was heard at every street corner. Nine years later, when we meet her in the Kyiv-based Dignitas fund office, she says she is not surprised that people refuse to admit danger, even when it breathes down their necks. In parliaments and governments in Western countries, which she frequently visits, she says, "I am not surprised that you do not believe that the war will affect you. My own society was at war for eight years, and many people did not believe the 2022 full-scale attack would happen until the first light of dawn on 24 February."

Maria continues to repeat that the Third World War has already begun, with the axis of democratic and the axis of authoritarian regimes already formed. Even if thus far the war is visible only on the Russia-Ukraine front line, where aerial bombardments and combat operations are daily events. Yet war is ongoing in Western countries as well invisibly — through economic, informational and cyber warfare.

"Ukrainian soldiers are buying time, not only for their families, at the cost of their lives and health, they are buying time for the entire Western civilized world."

***

"The small Soviet-style army won't win over the big Soviet-style army," Maria concluded after fighting Russians in the east of the country since 2014. Having extensively studied Russian history, Maria learned that Russia is ready to use the "meat waves tactic," sacrificing the numerous lives of its people for military victories and expansionism. She realized that the only way for Ukraine to win over Russia is through technological superiority.

"Technological militarization of society is the only way to save people and statehood," Maria continuously repeats, stressing that drones can execute a lot of tasks in place of soldiers, saving their lives. "Our most important strength is not HIMARS or F-16, but people." In 2015, she founded the Aerial Reconnaissance Support Center (Tsentr Pidtrymky Aerorozvidky) and later initiated the Victory Drones project, which is part of Dignitas, a charity fund established in 2013 during the Maidan Revolution. As of 2023, 65,000 service members had undergone a Victory Drones training program.

"If a Russian tank emerges and causes damage to infrastructure and human lives, the restoration of the destroyed areas, prosthetics for wounded soldiers, and compensation for their families will be very costly. We need to address the causes, not the consequences. We need to destroy that tank before it can inflict harm," Maria asserts, adding that it is necessary to destroy military targets on Russian soil as much as possible, before they even reach Ukraine.

While meeting with world leaders, she advocates more critical weapons delivery to Ukraine: to sacrifice drones and weapons, not human lives. "Steel is the cheapest price the Western world can pay," she says, warning that Western countries may eventually face Russian troops on their own soil. "The Western leaders were late with weapons deliveries and because of this, we lost tens of thousands of people, both dead and wounded, who could have been saved."

\*\*\*

On social media, especially at the beginning of the full-scale war, Ukrainians often raised money for Mavics for their relatives and friends fighting on the front line. These inexpensive Chinese drones, typically used for photo and video shooting, have become essential tools for reconnaissance at the Ukrainian front, serving as the army's eyes. While reconnaissance is the primary aerial drone function, many strike drones are also capable of directly attacking enemy positions and equipment. They proved to be a game-changer in the Russia-Ukraine war.

Many models of strike drones were developed by Ukrainian grassroots teams and companies and then immediately tested on the battlefield. One of the most cost-effective and devastating weapons that has inflicted enormous damage on Russian military equipment is the R18 drone, developed in 2016 by the Ukrainian Air Reconnaissance (Aerorozvidka) non-governmental organization together with the Ukrainian military. The R18 gained a good reputation in 2018 when it was in active use by Ukraine's armed forces in the east of the country. Aerorozvidka, which has hundreds of active members, was founded around the same period as Maria Berlinska's Aerial Reconnaissance Support Center, in 2014. The organization states, "Our goal is for robots to fight, instead of people, because the lives of our defenders are priceless!"

Using the R18 octocopter, which can fly into dangerous areas such as minefields, ambushes, and behind enemy lines, allows soldiers to complete missions while remaining at a safe distance. This drone, equipped with a thermal imager, can fly up to 13 kilometers, and carry and drop explosives on military equipment or other targets. Aerorozvidka assesses that for every $1 spent on these drones, the Russian army incurs $670 in losses.

"This is a fully Ukrainian-developed drone, which is impressive in comparison to other drone bombers made from repurposed agricultural drones. Of course, some parts come from China, however, the overall design is our own—making it highly convenient, especially because of the dynamic nature of the current war and the opportunities for constant improvements," Aerorozvidka instructor Serhiy Ristenko tells us at the training field where each R18 drone is subjected to thorough testing before being deployed to the front lines.

The February 2022 Russian invasion caught Serhiy in the part of Chernihiv region, which was quickly occupied by Russian troops. A renowned photographer, famous for his photos of Kyiv taken by drones, had been learning to operate military drones since 2017. Serhiy decided to join Aerorozvidka once his family had left the occupied territory for safety. With non-military drone flights strictly prohibited in wartime Ukraine, many photographers like

Serhiy, who previously flew drones, decided to use their skills to contribute to Ukraine's fight against the Russian aggression.

In 2022, on the approaches to Kyiv, the Russian forces moved in long, multi-kilometer columns, creating many opportunities for R18s to strike. Several crews operated simultaneously, working tirelessly in a continuous cycle, targeting any enemy movement they spotted. Their R18 drones destroyed targets along the strategic Zhytomyr highway west of Kyiv, including tanks, infantry fighting vehicles, armored personnel carriers, and other military vehicles like the Urals.

R18 drones are designed for night-strike operations featuring a thermal-imaging camera. Typical tactics involve preliminary use of electronic warfare systems for reconnaissance and intelligence gathering, before deploying the R18 for a direct attack. The complex includes two drones, so that if one is destroyed, the other can be used to complete the mission.

On one occasion, an R18 was hit and badly damaged. One of its batteries malfunctioned and fell off, while two of its propellers were destroyed by Russian troops. Despite this, the drone managed to fly back home. Many drones such as the Mavic typically have only four propellers with power distributed evenly among them, each blade with 25% of the total power. However, the R18 has eight blades, each with about 12% of the total power. Thus, even if one or two blades are damaged, the drone can still return safely.

"Our task is to minimize the risks to personnel and cause as much damage as possible. Thus, our perfect offensive is carried out almost without any personnel," says Serhiy. Although striking enemy positions is the most needed and widespread use for the R18, it also functioned as a transport drone—for instance, it has carried ammunition and medicine to enemy-surrounded units.

Comparing this war to other drone wars in places like Afghanistan, Serhiy points out that US Navy SEALs encountered much less electronic warfare. The absence of these countermeasures made it easier for them to carry out their missions. In contrast, in Russia's war against Ukraine, the widespread use of electronic countermeasures makes it difficult to operate drones and necessitates frequent changes in technology and tactics to adapt to ever-evolving conditions. Serhiy says the Russians should not be underestimated, since they learn quickly and adapt quickly. For example, the tactics used in the summer of 2022 were no longer effective in March 2023 because the Russians had developed new countermeasures. In this war, both sides are constantly learning from each other and the primary goal is to stay one or two steps ahead.

"One of the major advantages of having this drone developed in Ukraine is that we have a department of engineers here working on improvements," says Serhiy. Aerorozvidka's engineers analyze almost every case where their drones are lost or destroyed. They identify how the Russians destroyed a drone and use the information to develop new countermeasures. "However, we understand that we have a limited amount of time because sooner or later, the enemy will find a countermeasure to this too. I know engineers who are already thinking about how Russians will counteract the drones that are flying now, and how to bypass the future countermeasures that the Russians are only just developing." The engineers expect that the Russians will develop and use new countermeasures within about four months. "By the time they do so, we must be able to bypass it."

Competition for better drone development has been proceeding non-stop in Ukraine "between garage cooperatives and aviation modeling clubs," as well as defense technology companies. "It's very good when there's such a push," says Serhiy. "In 2022, few people thought there would be so many drones. But it's been a year, and now there are a lot of Ukrainian strike kamikaze drones."

Aerorozvidka exchanged know-how with other grassroots teams developing drones, and at the beginning of 2023, Serhiy tried operating kamikaze drones developed by the Magyar's Birds (Ptakhy Madiara) combat drone unit. "Operating them is even more difficult than R18 because they are unstable. Ukraine's kamikaze drones also have a bright future," he said then, guessing right.

\*\*\*

In the winter of 2023–2024 the various types of drones, including drone bombers like R18, but especially numerous small FPV kamikaze drones, saved thousands of Ukrainian soldiers. They critically slowed down the Russian offensive amid a deficit of artillery shells caused by the delay in American military aid. Meanwhile, Russians have started copying Ukrainian tactics of drone use, also developing their own strike FPV teams to target Ukrainian positions. The density of various drone use made the front line transparent for both sides, complicating any concealed movements.

In 2024, Ukrainian engineers started testing and using the first drones with artificial intelligence. They are capable of detecting the target with a machine's eye and subsequently striking it without human intervention. The calculation behind this new technology is to make drones less dependent on constant operator control and radio signals, rendering Russian electronic warfare unable to stop them.

In addition to strike drones, Ukrainian enterprises have developed a number of long-range reconnaissance drones, such as the Leleka-100, Valkyrja, and Shark. They also continued the development of more long-range drones capable of striking not only within Ukrainian territory, but also targeting locations deep inside Russia, such as during the 2024 campaign to strike Russian oil refineries and military airfields almost 2,000 kilometers away. Beyond aerial drones, Ukrainian forces also effectively utilized domestic-made marine drones, such as the Magura-5, which was the nautical weapon used in sinking a large part of the Russian Black Sea fleet, forcing it to retreat from the open sea and unblocking Ukrainian Odesa ports for trade, even though Ukraine does not have a strong navy. As well, since 2023, some units of the Ukrainian forces have been actively using ground drones to conduct tactical missions, including mining and demining, delivering ammunition to military positions, evacuating the wounded, and even conducting assault operations.

Company commander Oleksandr Yabchanka of the Da Vinci Wolves battalion told us that his battalion was one of the first to use newly-designed Saber automatic turrets in 2023. They were capable of firing machine guns with the operator sitting 100 meters from the drone position in a dugout and operating the turret via cable. "The enemy shells the position of the turret intensely, thinking you are there—and you are just drinking a coffee 100 meters away, underground, and monitoring the surroundings by camera," he says, enthusiastic about these drones. "Of course, it doesn't eliminate the danger completely, but in order to win, we should make Russian losses disproportionately larger than ours."

Other types of turrets were installed on unmanned, wheeled drones, also operated from a distance. They were modified to fire from grenade launchers. In the battles for Bakhmut, in the spring of 2023, Commander Yabchanka's unit, along with others, successfully protected the key road to the town for weeks, repelling wave after wave of Russian attacks. They maintained their positions until the last Ukrainian troops withdrew from Bakhmut. Yabchanka was wounded three times but returned to service each time after treatment.

Small aerial drones, like FPV (first-person view) drones, can be created by any citizen after little training. In 2024, Maria and the Dignitas Fund launched the People's FPV (Narodnyi FPV) project as part of the wider Victory Drones initiative. Any citizen could pass a free course learning how to create an FPV drone from scratch. These drones are further tested by specialists and sent to the front line.

One day, upon entering the apartment of our acquaintance in Kyiv, 27-year-old software engineer Mykhailo Karpyshyn, we noticed several FPV drone frames on his wall. It turned out that he had already built 20 such drones and delivered them to the Ukrainian armed forces. He bought the parts for the drones with his own money, which was significantly less costly than purchasing ready-made drones.

On his desk, two 3D printers work almost around the clock. He uses them to print plastic weapon parts, in particular for drones and drone munitions. The digital models for these parts come from the Printing Army (Druk Armiya) NGO initiative. It unites a group of online coordinators and volunteers who determine what soldiers need. The volunteers then develop 3D models and distribute these digital models on a specialized online platform, indicating how many parts are needed. From there, all who have 3D printers can download the models, print the necessary amount, and then send ready parts for testing to coordinators, after which they are dispatched to the front lines for military use.

While small, cheap drones were initially promoted for military use by Ukrainian grassroots initiatives, months into the full-scale war, the Ukrainian government started considering the new weapons seriously and launched the Army of Drones project. In 2023, the state provided over 300,000 drones for the Ukrainian army through this project, according to Ukraine's Minister of Digital Transformations, Mykhailo Fedorov, aiming for one million in 2024. A total of 90% of the drones were made in Ukraine by domestic companies, while more than 200 Ukrainian companies were engaged in the production of UAVs, striving as far as possible to localize the production of parts in Ukraine. Adapting to the new tactics of drone warfare, the Ukrainian military has become the first in the world to introduce special strike drone companies in each brigade and other big units—a total of 67 such companies by the beginning of 2024. On 6 February 2024, President Volodymyr Zelenskyy signed a decree creating Unmanned Systems Forces as a special branch of the Armed Forces of Ukraine.

*** 

As Serhiy finishes another test of the R18, he steps out from the dirt road to the field. His friend, the drone operator, guides the R18 in for a landing, bringing it steadily lower just above Serhiy, who raises his arms, preparing to catch the large, over one-meter-wide drone from the air. The freezing wind cuts to the bone, and Serhiy, in a dark-green raincoat and hood, resembles a sorcerer practicing levitation.

"I understand that after the war, we will be one of the most powerful drone nations in the world. Because even some grandpas in villages know how to operate drones. It's nationwide. It's as if a child who has just learned to eat with a spoon is immediately taught to operate a drone," says Serhiy, smiling.

*** 

"The unified axis of evil—Russia, China, Iran, North Korea, Belarus—poses a significant threat," Maria says. "There are unstable processes that could devastate Europe very quickly. The closer to Ukraine geographically, the more countries realize this. In the Baltic countries, it is not a question—their territory is the size of one or two Ukrainian regions. The farther away from Ukraine, the more it seems distant. They believe that as NATO countries, they have the NATO umbrella. But then they start to sober up—what does it really protect against? Let's model a situation—several thousand attack drones fly into Brussels. What happens next? Is it followed by a nuclear strike on Russia? Seriously?"

By raising these complex and uncomfortable questions, Maria simultaneously offered a part of the solution on how to counter the significantly larger armies of authoritarian regimes—through technological superiority and the necessary technological militarization of society. Ukrainian society proved ready and effective for asymmetric warfare against the Russian forces. What it needs are more resources, says Maria in 2024.

"Ukraine is currently investing tens of thousands of lives in global security. All the West needs to do is provide weapons. In fact, this should have been done a long time ago. It's a very cheap price to pay."

# How Is It Going?

Two neighbors occasionally meet on the village sidewalk.

"So, how's it going, Yuriy? Is it going to take much longer?"

"What do you mean?" says Yuriy Kovaliv.

"The war. Is it going to take much more time?"

"How can I know?"

His neighbor says something about being happy to see Yuriy after two years and each go their separate ways.

This is the second time Yuriy has been asked this type of question today. "They ask, when will it end? But how do they contribute to ending the war sooner?" Yuriy tells us in November 2023. He has given up responding sincerely to the question "How are you?"—since it would take a long and heavy monologue.

"Anyway, my leave was coming to an end in five days, and I'd have to go back to the front," Yuriy says. Caring for his family and keeping his business above water was about all Yuriy could manage while at home in his village of Murovane, 1,000 kilometers from the front. He processes and markets different kinds of meats, including beef, poultry, pork, sausage, and others. He only had a few days left to arrange for all the operational tasks to keep the business functioning during his absence.

The proceeds are not just for himself and his family; the army needs funds too. Yuriy has already spent thousands of dollars to buy a new car he needs for his work at the front, not to mention the cost of all the maintenance. Oil and filters have to be changed every two weeks, while tires need to be balanced. He has been putting at least 700–800 kilometers on the engine every day for almost two years.

\*\*\*

Yuriy received a call from a military enlistment office on the second day of the full-scale war. He then contacted his employees: 45 workers, two senior managers and an accountant, saying, "That's it, I'm gone. You manage here. Everyone work together."

He served in the special forces of the Airborne Forces in 1994–1996 — almost 30 years ago. Now, entering the military enlistment office, he did not know which position he would be assigned.

Dozens of conscripts were already inside and an officer asked who had B or C category driving licenses. Those who did stepped forward.

"Who is not afraid to do the work that not everyone can do?"

No one knew what kind of work he was talking about and stood still.

"Is it very necessary, and are some people already doing it?" one of the conscripts piped up.

"Yep," the officer said, nodding.

Some five more men stepped forward.

The officer's final question was, "Who has a big vehicle, preferably with a refrigeration unit?" Yuriy was the only one: he used it to deliver meat products to customers. Thus, he discovered that his assigned task was to drive to locations where fatalities had occurred and evacuate soldiers killed in action (KIA).

Yuriy started serving on the Kyiv front line on 26 February, responsible for a wide swathe of territory from the Belarusian border with the region of Zhytomyr to Kyiv itself. In those first days of the war, there was a shortage of vehicles and drivers for evacuation, and Yuriy had to do transport after transport. One time, a couple of French journalists rushed up to him.

"Tell us what you're doing here, how are you taking bodies out?"

"Go away. There's no time."

Yuriy tells us, "The father of a dead soldier was sitting on the curb crying, because he had not been able to retrieve his son from the morgue for three days. There was no one to help, and the journalists were just running around looking for hot news."

After the Battle of Kyiv was won in April 2022, Yuriy took up his duties on the southern front line near the cities of Mykolayiv, Ochakiv and Kherson. Three months later, he was relocated to the eastern front line in the Donetsk region. There, he covered nearly 80 kilometers, from Velyka Novosilka to Avdiyivka, transporting the bodies of fallen soldiers to Dnipro, where other crews would take them on to their homes, all over Ukraine.

\*\*\*

Every day at 6 am, Yuriy leaves Dnipro and drives 200 kilometers to Velyka Novosilka, continuing along the front line according to the coordinates sent to his phone. In every spot, he picks up bodies. One, two, three, four … in late afternoon he drives back to the Dnipro morgue. He prefers to complete the transport before nightfall—near the front, drivers have to turn off their headlights while on risky field roads. Better to do it early, "because time can get away from you, and you can end up in great jeopardy."

"I would like to put, let's say, three body bags in the car and not crowd them," says Yuriy. "But this rarely happens, mostly there are more. Of course, I would like to carry one, maximum two or three. Then again, I would like to sit at the base and drink tea and coffee, and not do that work at all. But it's necessary."

\*\*\*

Sometimes, while driving to the front, Yuriy turns on the radio. Initially, it works just fine, but as he gets closer to the front line, the signal of Ukrainian stations is interrupted from time to time, and instead, Russian stations play. "You can listen to them out of curiosity—get a better understanding of what's in the mind of the enemy, but it can be harmful for people who don't think," Yuriy says.

In the spots where he retrieves dead soldiers, he puts them in body bags and loads them into the car. Sometimes he speaks briefly with local troops.

"How are you? Ok?"

"The usual," says a soldier. "Shelling was heavy today, and projectiles hit us. We're completely fed up with them. Bastards."

Yuriy is not much of a talker, and in the first days of his service he chose the call sign of "Tykhyi," meaning "Quiet Guy."

He fills out and signs the document with details of the deceased — name, date, manner of death, description. A local commander co-signs. Yuriy starts filling out the form for the next KIA when his daughter calls from home. It's Sunday afternoon.

"Dad, how are you?" she asks.

The Russian artillery and mortar shells start hitting the Ukrainian positions nearby. It is still not close enough to take shelter, but the explosions are getting louder.

"What's that noise?" she asks.

"They're picking up the garbage and it bangs around."

"Ok," is all she says. Maybe she believes his answer or maybe not, but they don't say anything else about these sounds. He always leaves out the details so as not to worry his daughter. She recently had a baby girl and Yuriy became a grandfather. He wants to keep them safe and as far from the horrors of war as possible.

Yuriy loads the KIA body bags into the evacuation van, takes the signed documents, and drives off, heading for the next spot, wasting no time. As evening approaches, he stops near the last checkpoint, and asks what the situation is further down and whether he can drive on. The soldier snaps,

"Go, go."

"Is it okay … quiet?" Yuriy asks.

"Yeah. Okay. Go, go!"

They don't ask for any particulars about his trip or documents. This is not unusual for Yuriy. "It's not because they don't care," he says. "They can see it's urgent. They want me to get to the pick-up spot, do my work and get back as soon as possible out of respect for the fallen soldiers."

When there is an ambulance on the road, Yuriy pulls over to let it pass. An ambulance has priority, because it transports the wounded. "The ambulance goes first, I go second. We all understand that we need to do this as quickly as possible — to deliver the deceased to their parents and loved ones, to return the body to the earth, to bury."

Some say they would prefer to fight in the trenches than evacuate bodies. "After all this, I must be crazy," Yuriy says, admitting the psychological toll of his job. The only way to handle it is to joke.

"Did you tie the bag well so he doesn't trundle too much," the driver may ask another one. "You can skip a meal," Yuriy says, "but you have to joke and laugh to keep going."

"I no longer know whether we laugh more or cry," he adds. Being in an actual situation, or recalling it, can strike so hard that even well-weathered souls can crumble. "When I'm home, during my time off, I watch the news, and tears well up in my eyes. I go to church, I'm standing there, and I weep. Why? Who knows. Maybe I let go and soften for a moment. During the day, you're alone in the car, and you can cry two or three times while driving. You're alone, and the whole thing just overwhelms you. Like when I see a boy, only 19 years old. I need to find out who he is, where he's from, what happened. Or when I take a KIA's ID and notice he has a letter with him. His daughter has written to her father, 'Dearest Dad, please come back soon.' And you cry.'"

***

The evacuation unit that Yuriy joined rapidly expanded after 2022. It was placed under the command of the General Staff of Ukraine's armed forces, and received its special insignia with the inscription, "On the Shield" and an emblem of two Knights shaking hands to highlight the spirit of solidarity. The phrase "On the Shield" is derived from an ancient tradition symbolizing the honorable return of warriors who have fallen in battle.

Every section of the front line is covered by two soldiers, each driving a car. This allows them to take turns to drive and "have the occasional day off—at least to wash some clothes and have some sleep."

The first car Yuriy used on the front line started breaking down too often. He then bought another vehicle with his own money—a big white van on which he stuck a huge emblem with the inscription "On the Shield."

One time, in the first months of the war, Yuriy ran out of fuel near Pereyaslav in central Ukraine. Most gas stations were closed because of Russian missile strikes on fuel depots and the resulting disruptions. Yuriy tried asking at the military checkpoint but soldiers couldn't spare even 10 liters of fuel, and the curfew was about to start. He decided to sleep right there on the roadside, and since it was cold he had to sleep in the van. "There were seven soldiers in my van, but I had no choice. I just plonked down and conked out," he says. The next morning a driver passing by towed Yuriy's car to a gas station that still had fuel, and he kept on driving.

A few months later the fuel situation got better, and the army started providing it. Still, Yuriy had to pay for the car maintenance, at less than full price because many car shops gave a discount to the military. "We're still in a relatively safe position," he says about his group of drivers evacuating KIA. "We still have a place to sleep in a bed, since we are based in Dnipro, and usually return there every night. We have tap water, electricity and heating. We can cook for ourselves and don't have to live on the front line."

"The guys on the front are always wet and cold, and it's much more difficult for them," says Yuriy. His brother-in-law is fighting near Kupyansk and another relative is guarding the border in the Sumy region. "When it rains, and you've only been in the trench for five minutes, you're completely wet. And you can't do anything about it, because you have to stay in your position. Consider if you live in a trench for two weeks: what do you do about underwear and socks? Do you take them off and go wash them in a puddle? Of course not. It's good if you have taken enough new ones to change. Toilet tissue and wet wipes are needed, but will you substitute them for more cartridges and ammunition? It's hard everywhere, but for the guys in the trenches, it's wet, dirty, with mice running around and over you all the time. It is hardest for them."

\*\*\*

Yuriy's duties include identifying the KIA, a task that is not always easy. He shows us pictures of bodies on his phone. These are part of the documenting process. "Three handfuls of ash — three bodies." It is his most extreme case yet. Literally three small heaps of ash are carefully collected in plastic bags, with a number next to each. Yuriy found the remains in a military vehicle which took a direct hit by a projectile and incinerated completely. He tried to identify where each individual body was, according to metal objects nearby, such as belt buckles or ID tags. Having done his best, he placed the packages in his van. Another photo shows half of a soldier's body. His head and chest are intact, but the entire lower part of his body has been pulverized into a mush of entrails and blood. There are many more horrible photos of mutilated bodies. Some are completely impossible to identify.

When identification is complicated, Yuriy tries to collect as much information as possible on the spot. Some of the soldiers nearby may have witnessed how a soldier died and who he was. However, if not properly recorded, all details that might aid for identification will be lost. At the very least, Yuriy tries to record the unit name of the soldier, narrowing down to the smallest detail. If he finds a phone, a ring, or any personal item, he collects them and always records such information in the documentation for a KIA soldier, which he will later submit officially.

Once, a deceased soldier was hard to identify, but he had a notebook with phone numbers. Yuriy dialed one of the numbers. The person on the other end answered, not understanding who she was talking to. Yuriy heard a woman's voice. Wife? Mother? Sister? With a heavy heart, he asked about the features of the soldier who had fought near Avdiivka. In response, he heard sobbing. A sorrowful task, to inform the death of a loved one but it is better for the family to know than hope in vain.

Yuriy is not obliged to inform relatives of their loss. But when there is no other way to identify the body, he still tries all possibilities. Otherwise, the soldier will be added to the list of missing personnel. The body will be placed in the morgue, and documented as "Unknown." The unknown body will lie for months, or even years, and relatives will not know whether the soldier is alive, or in captivity, or dead. The best information that can be provided to the family in this case is MIA (Missing in Action).

A DNA test is the final option for identification but is possible only when relatives already suspect that a particular body might belong to their loved one but are not 100% sure. "DNA is used when a potential relative has arrived to confirm the remains but cannot recognize the body or does not want to look," Yuriy says.

Sometimes soldiers' relatives find Yuriy's phone number, call him and say, "My husband died, could you help find the body?" One example of this is Yuriy's village neighbor who had been fighting since 2014, and was killed during the fighting in Bakhmut. The neighbor's family asked Yuriy to go to the area to find him, but Yuriy was unable to even start a search in the town amid constant fighting. Months later, he was likely still lying somewhere under the rubble in the now-occupied town.

\*\*\*

During his four-week leave, Yuriy saw his newborn granddaughter for the first time. They scheduled her baptism specifically during his time off but planned the celebration to be modest, at home with only close friends and family.

"Even when our defenders are risking their lives every day, people should have some pleasure, not only walk gloomily and sad in black scarves. But one should also know the limits," Yuriy says. "Especially when people on the front are already very tired and need to have some change. It's very sad that a part of society doesn't contribute to the war effort at all, while others sacrifice not only money but their health and life."

Very liberal mobilization laws adopted before the war meant that mainly those coming forward voluntarily joined the military. The wide range of exemptions from mobilization allowed many to stay home and failed to create a sense of urgency for all. Yet in 2024, these laws began to change, allowing inspectors to check military documents on the streets, lowering the age requirements for the draft, and increasing fines. These changes have helped to start mobilizing more people, at a time when the front line was experiencing an acute shortage of reserves.

When Yuriy first came home on leave, for three days he just walked around the house, slept and ate, gradually returning to his normal self. "First, you feel as if you're recovering from a knockout. Later you start to see the world around you with criticism for some features of peaceful life. Then you start to give up on criticizing, but instead you start thinking about what things to take back to the front. You're not here at home, the front is constantly with you. You stay active in all the chats, still connected with commanders and comrades."

Ukrainian service people have the right for 30 days of leave per year to meet with their family and rest. However, instead of resting, many use this time to visit doctors, repair equipment, or organize new supplies from volunteers to help fellow soldiers when returning to the front. This is exactly how Yuriy used his time off, not to mention spending another UAH 40,000 ($1,100) to make long overdue repairs to his car. Yuriy's municipality added more to this sum—one of many ways the municipality helps its own people serving in the military. However, at the same time, many who serve in the military criticize the officials who devote revenue to repair sidewalks or renovate public spaces. Even though all national taxes (81% of the total collected) go to defense, the remaining local taxes (19%) are distributed by municipalities, as they wish. "We have martial law," Yuriy says. "And what would the police do if I violated a curfew? The maximum penalty would be to take me to their office and then release me. Why adopt curfews or any other rules if there is no penalty?"

One acquaintance recently told Yuriy, "I want to give 20,000 euros to the army. Let's buy a new van for you." "No," Yuriy replied, "I can manage with this one. I'll fix what's most necessary and keep driving. Better to find the guys who need to buy drones."

"20,000 euros seems like a large amount, but there are people who give this kind of money and that's normal," Yuriy says. "I believe that if we walk on good sidewalks, relax and celebrate in nice parks, replace cobblestones and everything else, then we probably don't give enough to the army. And it's wrong to say that I won't personally donate unless an MP or someone else does. Our guys are already there, fighting, but the victory won't come by itself. There will always be a part of society that is indifferent to anything but their own personal comfort. But that isn't an excuse for anyone else to do less or fight less relentlessly."

In the past, before the full-scale war, Yuriy often confronted the passive attitude of some people when he took part in local political activism. In one case, the municipality paved new roads, but Yuriy protested, saying the funds were used ineffectively and more could be done. He would bring up this subject with his fellow residents, but some replied, "Well, it's fine. At least the municipality did something. Before, it didn't even do that."

"That's the logic of many people," Yuriy says. "But I don't want to be a fool, to attend the unveiling of a monument or the opening of a new roadway, knowing that they have deluded me as a taxpayer and a resident."

***

Yuriy was retrieving the remains of Ostap Onistrat, the 21-year-old son of the prominent Kyiv banker Andriy Onistrat. Ostap was the first in his family to volunteer to take up arms, but soon thereafter his father followed suit. Ostap's life was cut short near the village of Pavlivka in the Donetsk region, when he was struck squarely by a shell. He was maneuvering a drone at the time. "It seemed to be a relatively safe task, simply launching and piloting the drone," Yuriy says. "But when I collected him, the body before me was beyond recognition."

"He went to war and I could do nothing but go too," Andriy says during an interview, crying.[34] Andriy had become a millionaire, having established his own bank. He was able to avoid going to war and his son Ostap was not even eligible for mobilization at 21. Now, when asked if he would dissuade his son from serving after everything that happened, he says no, even though he is crying.

"Logic urges me to say that I would not have allowed him to go. But he changed during his service. He became a different person. Now the question is, could everything that happened to him have been erased ... could things have been different? He would

---

34   Andriy Onistrat's interview was shared on his YouTube channel on 2 December 2023 (https://youtu.be/LsvRoqWp97E).

not have gained such respect from people had he not joined the army. People around him started to see him in a completely new light. This affected all of us — his mother, his grandparents. Everything around him seemed to sing ... He opened up."

Andriy was Ostap's commander. The day his son died seemed to stretch into eternity. He knew his son was on a mission. Andriy stopped by a well to scoop up some water to drink, his glasses fell into the well, and an unexplained sense of anxiety overtook him. A few minutes later he pulled a phone from his pocket and saw a stream of calls. The commander of the second battalion, Khazik, had left him an audio message, "I know there is a problem. I can send my evacuation team."

"Something stirred inside me. I started calling Ostap, but he didn't answer. Then I called Khazik, and he told me my son was gone. Then it was an hour's drive to get there. I arrived at the site, and they had already loaded him into a personnel vehicle. I wanted to see him. They wouldn't let me. I followed the vehicle that was transporting him for a long 30 minutes. I couldn't believe it. They didn't show him to me, and later I understood why. Because there was nothing left of him. They gave me the phone number for the morgue. I didn't talk to anyone. I just went to the morgue and saw everything for myself."

\*\*\*

Sometimes, when returning to Dnipro after a hard day, as he lies down and drifts off to sleep, Yuriy has nightmares. He tells us of one where bones and skulls are swirling above his head. "I'm aware that I'm sleeping, that it's just a dream. Then an old, shriveled hand, as if the hand of death itself, offers me a drink from a scoop filled with blood. The hand scoops out some blood and gives me a drink. I woke up and went for a smoke."

Yuriy says he is relieved that he does not dream of the boys telling him he did something wrong. If they do appear in his dreams, they tell him everything is alright. There are many more horrible situations that Yuriy has experienced.

Once he was on his way to pick up a fallen young soldier. The soldier's father had also fought, but in a different unit, and he drove with Yuriy to the site to retrieve the son.

On the way back, Yuriy was driving fast, as he always did, but the father said, "Wait, don't hurry."

"Why?" Yuriy asked.

"Just let me spend a little more time with my son. Don't rush, let me stay with the boy a bit longer ..."

# What Can I Do?

With a population of just over 50,000, the small town of Novovolynsk, built in the 1950s, is one of the few mining towns in the west of Ukraine. After mines became obsolete, the town launched a new approach to its development, building a huge industrial park for a growing number of enterprises. The effort was led by a new mayor elected in 2020, Borys Karpus, but the war changed the ambitious plans for Novovolynsk.

In the fall of 2022, we met with Mayor Karpus at the town council, renovated just before the war. A wooden map of Novovolynsk and the surrounding villages hangs on the wall in his cabinet—Novovolynsk is located just five kilometers from the border with Poland, in the Volyn region. "'Contra spem spero,' we believed that the invasion would not happen," the mayor says, quoting the Latin phrase, "Against all odds, I hope" that was popularized by the renowned Ukrainian poet Lesia Ukrayinka from this region. "Yet many cities prepared, and we did too. Apart from military and medical training for our residents, we thoroughly checked basements, although we couldn't fully imagine what their purpose would be."

When Russia attacked, long lines of vehicles set out from Kyiv and other cities to safer areas in the west or abroad. However, seeing the extremely long queues at border crossings, many left them and stayed in Novovolynsk—the last town on the main highway from Kyiv to Poland. To encourage people to stay in Novovolynsk, town authorities set up an information booth at the town's outskirts. The mayor himself stood at the booth, encouraging would-be evacuees to stay, while local volunteers offered to host them. The town's population rapidly grew by 10,000.

The first IDPs (Internally Displaced People) who arrived in the town on 25 February were from Kyiv. Yuliya Lefter, the Novovolynsk deputy mayor, says that many of them came to the town council saying: "I am an IT specialist. I am an accountant. I have a car. I can do this and that. Tell me how to help."

***

Just three days before the full-scale war began, 32-year-old Katia Nakonechna was planning to move into her new apartment in Kyiv. At the same time, she prepared an "emergency suitcase" containing all the essential items she would need in case of evacuation if war broke out. International travel is essential to her work as a senior telecommunications director for Europe and Israel. Nevertheless, Katia and her husband had decided, "We would not go abroad if something happened." Instead they went to Novovolynsk, Katia's hometown.

"How can I be useful?" she wondered, and her aunt advised her to go to the town council. Learning about Katia's professional logistics experience, the mayor told her that many organizations from abroad were transporting humanitarian aid to Novovolynsk. "We'll be a transit hub, so we'll need to organize logistics. Try to organize the process."

The town council gave up some of its free offices to volunteers like Katia. Along with her, marketing and IT directors, several senior managers, businesspeople, and lawyers—mainly from Kyiv and Kharkiv—began working together from the second day of the Russian invasion without pay. "Ten strangers who had never seen each other before had to create new procedures from scratch," says Katia. They organized the delivery of tons of humanitarian aid, calling their logistics center UHelp.

The UHelp logistical center ensured that a transparent process was in place, so that assistance could flow directly from donors to drivers, and then to defenders on the front and people affected by the war. "We could not allow any truck to be lost," Katia says. "And there are a million ways it could get lost. There have been cases—not with us—but in general, where trucks were lost. We organized work so that each truck had a specific team leader. It was a supertask to develop such a system from nothing, in mere days."

In the first two months alone, the UHelp team organized and managed the delivery of 200 trucks of aid for the military and civilians. The aid came from various countries, but mostly from

Germany, Poland, the Netherlands, Italy, and the Baltic states. There was no boss in the logistical center, and no one gave orders. "Everyone understood that if there was a task to be done, it should be taken on and resolved. Some drivers took time off from their regular jobs to volunteer with us."

In the first few weeks, border crossing was extremely slow, with queues stretching out for seven days. One driver proposed to install flashing headlights and large signs that read "Humanitarian Aid" in English and Polish on their cars. As a result, everyone pulled over to allow them to pass the queue. Now volunteer drivers were able to leave Novovolynsk and return with aid the same day.

Often foreign volunteer drivers refused to cross the border into Ukraine, and just left aid sitting out in the open at the crossing. To make it faster for drivers from Novovolynsk to make pick-ups, Katia's team sought out a local man with a warehouse in Poland near the border. He generously lent it to them for aid transfer. "Everything was based on trust," Katia says. "Of course, we tried to control the process, but we didn't have cameras everywhere. It was clear that if a driver didn't transfer the complete cargo, we wouldn't assign them any more jobs."

After two months of full-time volunteering, Katia resumed her regular job, part-time. She worked in the morning, "Because as soon as you arrive at the volunteer center, there is such a conveyor belt of tasks that you really can't leave until evening." As time passed, volunteers used donations to purchase items for the military, including thermal imagers, drones, helmets, and later Starlinks.

"There was a moment when we were overwhelmed, and everyone started taking 20 tasks at a time," Katia says. "It was the worst, because in this manner you won't finish any. I then said that if you each take one task and complete it today, it's much better than if you take ten and don't finish a single one. There are 45 million of us: that is, if every Ukrainian were to complete a task a day, there would be 45 million completed tasks. It's effective."

\*\*\*

The war caught 63-year-old Kateryna in Hostomel near Kyiv, where fierce fighting had started on the very first day of the invasion at the local airfield. She, her daughter, son-in-law, and grandchildren hid in their basement from the Russian shelling. "I saw my children and grandchildren with frightened eyes—I felt helpless," she says. They fled from the town and later found out that on that same day the Russians advanced to their house.

Kateryna's family was getting ready to go to the US and pleaded with Kateryna to go with them, but she decided to return to her hometown of Novovolynsk instead. "Grandma, will the Russians come to America?" her seven-year-old granddaughter asked at the border crossing, before saying goodbye. The little girl forgot her phone in Hostomel and later sent a voice message for the invaders to find, "Russians, you are the worst people on Earth. You will listen to my message, but know that you will die a second after you listen!"

"I have a very strong desire to wait for victory here in Ukraine, so that my children can return," Kateryna says. On 26 February, she arrived in Novovolynsk and immediately contacted the mayor. "On the 26th, everything in Novovolynsk worked like a Swiss watch. The matter of displaced persons was already organized, and the matter of humanitarian aid was well in play. Now it was necessary to account for all the aid and to find warehouses to sort everything and send it on. Our task was to organize everything quickly."

Very soon, the aid arriving in Novovolynsk was sorted and packed in 14 warehouses across the town, managed by ordinary people who wanted to help. "There are no cities in Ukraine where volunteers did not come to Novovolynsk. Bucha, Irpin, Borodianka, Kherson, Mykolayiv, Kharkiv," Kateryna says. And since the volunteers maintained connections in their hometowns, the hub was able to organize local deliveries directly to the points where help was needed most. For example, when the Irpin hospital relocated to Lutsk, displaced persons reported that wounded soldiers had to sleep on the ground. "Meanwhile, proper beds arrived from The Netherlands. We packed them up and delivered them to the hospital."

Kateryna manages one of these warehouses, where both locals and displaced people have been volunteering. 20-year-old Danylo from Bakhmut in Ukraine's east came to Novovolynsk in August 2022 and decided to volunteer in the warehouse. He had been hit by shrapnel in his leg when a Russian mortar shell fell several dozen meters away. Svitlana from Novovolynsk previously owned a pharmacy but sold it before the war. Now she and her husband were helping the medical department of the warehouse to acquire medications. They sew and assemble first-aid kits themselves and provide them to the military.

In addition to supplying the military, the warehouse also helped displaced people. A young woman, 24-year-old Aliona, had moved to Novovolynsk from Shchastia in the Luhansk region. Once a month she comes to the warehouse with her friend to obtain hygiene products for their babies. "Novovolynsk is great. Kind people, good infrastructure and many cafes and playgrounds. I can't say yet whether we'll stay here. I want to go home, but no one knows what'll happen next. However, with the latest counteroffensive, the news is good now," Aliona says, reflecting on the latest events in November 2022.[35]

Everyone who receives aid is registered on a database so that the aid is distributed fairly, Kateryna tells us. The database includes information on all forms of assistance and all donors across Novovolynsk. "When we open the database, we can see what kind of help a person has already received to avoid waste or worse—double dipping—with someone reselling the aid."

There were 23 spots across Novovolynsk where volunteering for the army and war-affected civilians was ongoing. For instance,

---

35 The Ukrainian 2022 autumn counteroffensive in the Kharkiv and Kherson regions proved highly successful, with Ukrainian forces advancing nearly 60 kilometers toward Kherson and 100 kilometers in the Kharkiv region. However, in the following months, the front remained relatively stable, aside from localized Russian advances in the Avdiivka and Bakhmut sectors and Ukrainian in the Tokmak sector.

in just a few months the clothing bank sorted and distributed 20 tons of donated clothes. On the premises of the Inter-school Resource Center, 1,500 locals received training in first aid and basic rifle-shooting — 40% were women.

Before the war, the Novovolynsk public canteen provided free food for about 70 people with disabilities and for the elderly. Afterward, they fed 500 people a day, most of whom were displaced individuals who had lost everything. The canteen worked ceaselessly, including at weekends. They also collected money by baking and selling pastries and bought a car for the armed forces with the proceeds. The canteen provided buns and biscuits for Novovolynsk volunteer drivers who were on the road for hours.

"In the first days of the war, you felt as if you were on some kind of drugs, you just worked and worked," says volunteer from Kyiv Serhiy Kornyliuk, Novovolynsk native, who works as a city development consultant. "I sincerely believed that this Novovolynsk volunteer drive could turn into a national level of warehouse storage. And then, after the Russians were ousted from Kyiv, and many volunteers returned to the capital, the gigantism decreased, but the initiative remained. This is still an imperfect model, but I believe it could work even in peacetime after the war. Dozens of grassroots initiatives and a mayor willing to support coordination — it's a model for the future and for the reconstruction of Ukrainian regions."

\*\*\*

"Life Goes on Without Proofreading" (Zhyttia ide i vse bez korektur) — this poem by modern writer Lina Kostenko inspired Serhiy Kryzhanovskyi "to enroll in medical school and to change something, to leave something behind." In 2008, while working in the pharmaceutical industry, Serhiy learned of the Mayo Clinic in Rochester, US — one of the world's leading research hospitals. Nobel Prize winner Sir Alexander Fleming, credited with the discovery of penicillin in 1928, was closely associated with the Mayo Clinic. Serhiy was especially struck by the fact that a world-renowned hospital was established in a modest US town, "It was neither in New York, nor in Los Angeles, but in the small town of Rochester with a population of 3,900. This encouraged me that I don't have to go to some kind of Kyiv or Lviv. I can be in cool Novovolynsk and set up a clinic here, attracting clients from Kyiv and Lviv. This was my goal and we are making steady progress toward it," he tells us in the cabinet of his Bodro clinic.

Along with polyclinic, surgery, and rehabilitation, Serhiy's clinic specializes in leading-edge pain diagnosis and control. The clinic is powered by solar roof panels, and offers hotel accommodation for visitors, as well as innovative Tours for Health programs that combine preventive health checkups with local tourism. "Of course, like everyone else, I have some commercial interests," says Serhiy. "But my main goal is a successful project. Because an unhealthy obsession with money actually keeps one from working. It's uncommon for a bad person to be a good doctor."

On 23 February 2022, the Bodro clinic was undergoing the final phase of its X-ray licensing, a process that had taken Serhiy two years to complete. Next day at 5 am, he went to the window and saw a column of refueling tanks and armored personnel carriers. On those first two days of the war, the clinic was still taking patients. Some of those who arrived in the initial hours of the attack had no idea the war had begun.

"We decided to work and see. If we earn money, there will be salaries. If we don't, there won't be any." Bodro announced online that it would definitely continue working. Fortunately, only one doctor left the clinic to go abroad.

"From a logical standpoint, I did not understand at all how one can attack a country whose army is prepared for a full-scale attack. I told everyone that it was simply unbelievable and a form of stupidity. However, this stupidity happened," Serhiy says. In the initial days of the war, he contacted a Malaysian friend telling him that tourniquets for the military were desperately needed. Together, they started a project to collect 100,000 tourniquets and very quickly got the first 400. Later, the rate of delivery slowed. "Malaysia is far away—they don't understand our war very well. Now, eight months into the war, money is collected much more slowly."

At the same time, Serhiy contacted his French acquaintances and, within a week, humanitarian aid with highly specialized medical supplies arrived, as well as two field hospitals packed into two military containers. Moreover, doctor and professor Philippe Juvin came from France to help. He was serving as a member of the European Parliament for two terms, practicing as a surgeon in the Afghanistan war, and later treating patients in the aftermath of the 2015 Paris terrorist attacks. He became an active supporter of Ukraine.

Initially, having arrived in Ukraine Juvin intended to work as an anesthesiologist. However, Serhiy offered him a different role.

"Philippe, it doesn't make much sense for you to work as a hospital anesthesiologist here, even if you'll be close to the front line," Serhiy told him. "However, your experience of working with military operations — since you went through Afghanistan and coordinated the emergency service actions — is important to us. It is also important that you can help not only in Ukraine but also when you return to France." Serhiy says he spoke openly, "Because there is nothing to hide here. We want France to assist Ukraine."

As a result of his visit to Ukraine, Juvin presented recommendations for military personnel on how to aid the wounded on the battlefield, as well as recommendations for hospitals on how to organize assistance in emergency circumstances, such as mass destruction. His lectures on all of the topics have been recorded and distributed. "When Juvin returned to France, he wrote a great article about Ukraine in Le Figaro called 'What I Saw in Ukraine.' He also communicated with French President Macron on our behalf."

At first, the number of patients in the Bodro clinic dropped sharply, but when refugees from Kyiv and Kharkiv settled in Novovolynsk, the numbers rose again. Wounded soldiers started to appear among Bodro's patients. The hospital's team decided to accept two new soldier patients every month at no cost. "We can donate some of our resources. But it still won't be sufficient to assist everyone."

One of the clinic's patients was a Georgian soldier in the Ukrainian army who suffered from a sciatic nerve injury. Before arriving in Bodro, he had already been hospitalized for 40 days and was switched to narcotic analgesics to alleviate the pain. "He was prone to a medical addiction. And we alleviated his pain in a different way, so that he will definitely not be on narcotic painkillers. It was a cluster injury, very difficult, and there is still much work to be done, but he is already smiling. It's encouraging."

Bodro employed seven doctors who fled the east of Ukraine — from Mariupol, Kharkiv, Kramatorsk, Zaporizhzhia, and Kherson. "We took them in with their families, helped them find housing, integrate, and did everything possible to make them feel at home here. This is one of the missions, because we don't make any profit from them yet," says Serhiy.

"I feel a sense of my mission in this, because I am not fighting. And hence, I feel a certain amount of guilt, especially when you see that your friends are either fighting somewhere or doing something more vigorously than you. I think that everyone often feels this way. And then you wonder, what can I do? Maybe I can at least help the resettled doctors."

Novovolynsk businesses collaborate on a common chat platform to raise funds for the military. In the early days, Serhiy's friend's foundry made anti-tank hedgehogs from its metal. A local car service repairs military vehicles at no cost, doing so for vehicles procured by volunteers. Another of his acquaintances, in the real estate business, routinely brings material from abroad and sends it to the front. Serhiy says, "Volunteering is good, but it's equally important to keep working."

\*\*\*

Nearly 30 businesses throughout Ukraine relocated to Novovolynsk just half-a-year into the full-scale war. Vladyslav Budayev was forced to move his company Amrok which produces military combat-unloading systems and other army materiel from Kharkiv to Novovolynsk. The town council granted him the use of educational institutions' premises where tailoring courses were held.

By chance, Nina, a women's clothing designer from Kyiv, and Olena, a children's garment technologist from Russia-bombed Mykolayiv in Ukraine's south, have also moved to Novovolynsk because of the war. "I am actually a women's and children's clothing technologist. But life led me to these strict boundaries," Olena says, showing us their products: a first aid kit, grenade pouches, dual and single magazine pouches, and a military combat unloading system. The company works directly with Ukrainian soldiers, constantly receives feedback and improves products to make them more advantageous in combat. "And I have to admit that our military cares about their appearance, in terms of the color and design. As one soldier said, 'It will be elegant for me.' Even on the front lines, they strive for elegance."

Halyna from Avdiivka in the Donetsk region has been working here since March 2022. "We want the war to end and to return home," she says. But, unfortunately, there is no place now, because everything in Donbas is either occupied or bombed. We realize that this will last for some time." Halyna says a mining town like Novovolynsk is similar to her hometown. "Everything is the same here, except for the fact that the Ukrainian language is spoken everywhere. But for me, Ukrainian is my mother tongue."

*** 

The blue design of the Sleep Sugar Coffee Point, near Novovolynsk park brings to mind a coastal city cafe. This is no coincidence, because before the full-scale war the owner worked in Odesa, on the Black Sea. "Many displaced people from Kherson and Mykolayiv visit us. When we talk to them, they all want to go home. Even though Novovolynsk is a pleasant place to live."

*"I constantly return to the thought that I have nothing," Tamara tells us, her gaze sad and introspective.*

*The smell of burned-out military vehicles, recently shelled civilian cars, remnants of projectiles are commonplace – they all speak of fierce fighting in the Chernihiv region not long ago. The photo was taken near the village of Lukashivka.*

*The freezing wind cuts to the bone, and Serhiy Ristenko, in a dark-green raincoat and hood, resembles a sorcerer practicing levitation.*

*In 1989, Oleksandr had moved to Bucha, built a new house here and planted cherry and apple trees in the yard. For years, the family lived in tranquility.*

*"Here, there was a hit at 4:45 am," Taras Hrynchyshyn says, showing us a photo of himself near a huge, three-story facility, reduced to a heap of white bricks and remnants of walls. "And just 15 minutes earlier my group had left there for a mission."*

*"There are 45 million of us: that is, if every Ukrainian were to complete a task a day, there would be 45 million completed tasks. It's effective," says Katia Nakonechna in Mika cafe in Novovolynsk opened by displaced persons from Kyiv in the spring of 2022.*

*"Eros and Thanatos — Love and Fear — battle within everyone. Everybody feels fear sometimes, but what wins in this internal fight finally defines everything," Taras says, reflecting on the start of the war and referencing one of his songs.*

Another café, Teddy Coffee, was opened in Novovolynsk by Vitaliy and Valeriya, who fled the embattled town of Irpin with their 10-month-old baby. Their original Teddy Coffee, which they had managed for 10 years in Irpin, remained abandoned until the town was liberated.

Spouses Yuliya and Ihor had been working in the music industry in Kyiv. Yuliya was a concert director and Ihor a sound producer for popular Ukrainian singers. While in Novovolynsk, they opened Mika café, emulating their favorite spots in Kyiv. Near the café, they would host concerts with top Ukrainian artists to raise funds for the military.

Local cafes supported the military too. For instance, Felicita Novovolynsk redirected 100% of the proceeds from several menu items for the Ukrainian army.

\*\*\*

In one of the corners of the Novovolynsk History Museum hangs an embroidered portrait of Taras Shevchenko, the most-honored poet of Ukraine. Although it does not seem particularly unusual, it was created under extreme circumstances. Kateryna Kochmar, who was deported by USSR from the west of Ukraine to a Siberian labor camp after WWII, embroidered this portrait on her bedding by memory alone — without any image of the poet — using twisted fishbone as a needle. She pulled the threads from the stockings of young women imprisoned with her. Upon returning to Novovolynsk after her term ended, she donated the portrait to the local museum.

Another woman from Novovolynsk, Hanna Ditchuk, was imprisoned in a Gulag labor camp at the age of 17 for reading the works of Ukrainian historian Mykhaylo Hrushevskyi who provided a detailed and scholarly account of Ukrainian history from the ancient times to the 17th century. In the train, Russian authorities purposefully gave the prisoners salted fish and forbade them to drink water — they sucked on icicles for mere drops a day. In Siberia, she and other young Ukrainians were forced to clear forests and build railroads. They were only permitted one piece of bread and a liter of water per day.

Iryna Kostiuk tells us these stories in detail, despite our arrival 10 minutes before the museum closes. She has been working for seven years — since the age of 24 — as the museum's director. Such stories have been compiled in official records, along with stories of Ukrainians deported from the nearby Khelm region of present-day Poland.

After their Siberian exile, many Ukrainians settled in Novovolynsk, because under Soviet law they were prohibited from returning to their homes for 10 years. Besides, Novovolynsk had jobs while the mines were being built. Authorities settled in the town too — mostly Russian-speaking managers to whom former prisoners were subordinated. "It was a town of contrasts: on the one hand, the Soviet Russian-speaking population; and on the other hand people returning from Siberia, originally exiled for speaking Ukrainian and singing Ukrainian songs," Iryna says. Despite such contrasts, the town ultimately became Ukrainian-speaking. There was no church in Novovolynsk when it was being built under Soviet rule because of their policy of atheism. Since Ukraine's independence in 1991, more than 20 churches of different denominations have emerged here.

For two years, Iryna made regular business trips to Kyiv trying to get on the list for restoring 17th-century cultural artifacts. Her challenge was that each year the government only funded restoration projects for two museums and the competition was extremely high. Paradoxically, the war conditions made her dream come true. In spring 2022, restorer and artist Artem Pohribnyi from Kharkiv asked Iryna whether there was anything to be restored in the Novovolynsk museum. To receive his salary from the Kharkiv Restoration Center, he needed to report his activities.

"A respectable person, with an international restoration license, with several exhibitions, suddenly asked us if he could restore something for free," says Iryna in astonishment. "The concentration of qualified people from big cities was so high in small Novovolynsk." Artem restored a 17th-century shroud and an ornamental gate from the beautiful five-domed church built by

Adam Kysil not far from Novovolynsk. In a dozen of his own paintings, now displayed in the museum, Artem tried to convey how much he missed his city. One of his paintings features a close-up of a girl's eyes, with Novovolynsk depicted in one eye and Kharkiv in the other. These are the eyes of his daughter. In another painting, a wooden trunk contains memories of his home. After a few weeks in Novovolynsk, Artem returned to Kharkiv.

Iryna says that one day she hopes to return to her ambitious pre-war plans, one of which is the interactive Museum of Mines. First, she wanted to create the museum in the mine and went down to the mine together with colleagues. "That plan failed, because it's very expensive. Now, I want to establish a virtual 3D museum. I would like there to be sound, water, and smells to give the impression that one is walking on coal. I visited the very beautiful Museum of Ukrainian History in Kyiv — one installation portrays Volodymyr the Great sailing on the Dnipro, and a viewer can almost smell the grass on the hills and hear the splashing of waves against the ship."

\*\*\*

In 2021, 18-year-old Mykhailo enrolled in the Ukrainian Leadership Academy, a year-long residency program for personal and social development for high school graduates. Anticipating the war, the academy transferred this group from Kyiv to the western city of Ternopil in the winter of 2022. When the war ignited, students opened 44 volunteering centers, packing tons of humanitarian supplies for Kharkiv.

One evening, Mykhailo and his friends called officers of the local territorial defense, "We want to join." Asking their age, the enlistment officer laughed and said, "Go to sleep."

When the academy's program ended and Mykhailo returned to his hometown of Novovolynsk, he got involved in the New Wings (Novi Kryla) youth center that had just opened on 5 May 2022. Some of the young people joined in to renovate the center from an old Soviet-style library to a modern youth center. "At first, I thought everyone would leave Novovolynsk. But it turned out to be the opposite." Each month, the center organized more than 15 events, including recent acoustic evenings, painting tote bag master classes, and anti-bullying lectures, while also raising funds for the army.

Their mural project, Walls Are Not Silent, has focused primarily on Ukrainian cultural and political themes. "We gathered all the youth who used to draw random graffiti to give it more artistic meaning." For instance, one mural depicts Ukrainian Soviet-time dissident Levko Lukyanenko and includes his citation, "Anyone who says that independence fell from the sky doesn't know that we endured 10 years of prison and exile."

Once, when they were creating a mural, a pensioner passed by, looked at it and said, "God, that's beautiful. It was a gray town, but now it's so bright." Mykhailo says, recalling this story, "I never expected any praise about our business from seniors. That's understandable, given our target audience. Often, older people do not understand what we do, especially with the posters that we hang sometimes."

\*\*\*

There has been no Russian shelling in Novovolynsk, so most of the locals who went abroad at the beginning of the war have since returned. The town council estimates that their town that once only had 50,000 residents has grown by 10,000 because of IDPs[36] — a rare occurrence in a country where the population is decreasing significantly due to war and, consequently, migration.

In the first days of the war the mayor learned that the modular towns for relocated people are a failure story, because they become

---

36   The town tries to attract international organizations helping refugees to work in Novovolynsk as these organizations usually do not have specific lists of places to help. In total, 13 organizations helped local IDPs, including UN Acted, Triangle, and UNICEF: some people received one-time help of up to $550, and others had an additional $55 monthly. The town council attracts partner towns from Poland, Germany, Lithuania, and Chezhia. During the war, Novovolynsk schools developed summer projects with partner cities in Germany and Poland, and approximately 300 children went to Poland, Germany, and Lithuania for summer camps.

ghettos. People who have higher levels of education and income look for better living conditions, while the less fortunate move in. "That's why we didn't do it," the mayor says. "Displaced people moved into dormitories or into the homes of their friends and relatives. This is better, even though domestic conflicts may arise, especially when three generations live in the same house."

In Ukraine, the children of IDPs could continue studying online at their former schools or study in schools where they relocated because of the war. Half of the Novovolynsk IDP-student population chose local schools. However, for Ukrainian refugees abroad it was not easy to study in their former Ukrainian school online—according to EU legislation, they must attend school in the country where they are based. On 24 March 2022, 37% of Novovolynsk children who attended preschools had left the country. In September 2022 the figure was at 14%, according to Serhiy Moroz, Head of the Education Department of Novovolynsk. He hopes to return one day to his previous projects like the partnership he developed with a Mariupol lyceum: in 2018, children from Mariupol and Novovolynsk took part in an exchange program.

Many European countries have created favorable conditions for Ukrainian refugees, but a significant proportion of these countries are addressing their own demographic and labor challenges, which are much more severe in Ukraine. Since Ukrainian men of conscription age are mostly prohibited from crossing the border, the majority of refugees are unmarried women and women with children. Besides, many of these refugees have higher education and professional skills. People remain the primary asset capable of driving local development, but in times of war their presence is also crucial for the country's normal functioning and survival.

# Second Life

"The company commander was killed, and my leg was torn off," Dmytro, a Ukrainian soldier says, recalling that fatal day in June 2022. A nearby explosion of a Russian 120-millimeter mortar shell knocked him to the ground, severing his leg up to the knee. He managed to apply a tourniquet to stop the bleeding. Initially he could not feel the pain due to shock. But when he did, it was excruciating.

At that time, he was defending the hottest spot on the front line—Sievierodonetsk—a small industrial town in Ukraine's east, on the bank of the Siverskyi Donets River. Encircled on three sides and constrained by the river, Ukrainian troops had been defending the perimeter of the town for several weeks. Under Russian artillery shelling, the evacuation of the wounded was complicated, and Dmytro was transported to the hospital too late. Doctors told him they needed to amputate his entire leg to save his life.

Born in the Cherkasy region in the very center of Ukraine, Dmytro lived not far from the picturesque banks of the Dnipro River, Ukraine's longest river, where the hills to the west of the river stood high above the water. He was 26 when he fought the Russians in 2014 in the east of Ukraine. Having lived through the difficult battles during the first months of the war, he resigned from the army and returned home in 2015. Dmytro married and had two children, but in 2022 their peaceful life was shattered by a new wave of Russian invasion. Dmytro anticipated these events and knew he would have to take up arms once again.

"My backpack was always prepared," he says.

After the injury and initial operation, he was transported to Lviv in the west of Ukraine—the city that soon became a major medical and rehabilitation hub. "When I arrived here, I weighed 57 kilograms. Before the injury, I weighed 90. I lost a lot of blood, and over the next two months survived only thanks to painkillers," he says.

Like all soldiers with amputations, before any recovery treatment can begin, he had to wait for all his wounds to heal and for the pain to become tolerable. This phase often takes months and may involve several additional operations. The next phase is to make and install a prosthesis, which is a relatively fast process, taking only two to four weeks. Afterward, the rehabilitation and ongoing adjustment of the prosthesis begin. While most soldiers can take cautious steps within a few days, strengthening muscles to support the prosthesis and learning how to walk again can take several months of hard work.

***

Half a year after the injury, Dmytro takes his first walk around the training room. Instead of his right leg, a metal prosthesis is attached to his pelvis. By slightly bending his spine, he thrusts the prosthesis forward. The knee of the prosthesis is locked to simplify the task. Later, once his back muscles strengthen and he is able to move better, the knee mechanism will be released to more closely mimic normal movement.

"Is it better now when I turn it up?" asks prosthetist Yuriy Yaskiv, adjusting the height of the prosthetic leg by rotating screws with a screwdriver.

"Yes, but when I take a step, the prosthesis touches the ground," says Dmytro.

"Because you need to increase the length of your step. Muscles of your back have not yet developed. Try."

"Will I run?" Dmytro asks.

"Realistically?"

"Yes, realistically."

"Realistically, no," says the prosthetist. "I have never seen someone with a full leg amputated who could run. When there's still a hip—it's possible. But with a complete removal—no."

Yuriy has worked as a prosthetist since 2008. He, like other Ukrainian prosthetists, has worked with soldiers who have required amputations since 2014. However, with the onset of the full-scale war, not only did amputations increase dramatically, they also became much more traumatic—mainly due to the increase in Russian artillery, including cluster munition.

"We work 24/7 when needed. We work on Saturdays, until eight o'clock … until nine o'clock. My family has to take a back seat because these men," Yuriy gestures towards the soldiers who are learning to walk again, "are of primary importance." Tears well up in his eyes, and he returns to his work.

\*\*\*

The small clinic of the Ukrainian prosthetics company Without Limits (Bez Obmezhen) in Lviv, where Yuriy works, provided more than 70 prostheses for soldiers in the first half of 2022. Overall, Without Limits had clinics in ten Ukrainian cities, but in the first year of the war, half of them could not function at full capacity because of constant shelling, missile threats, and evacuation of employees to safer Ukrainian cities. The situation was the same in nearly half of the 80 other Ukrainian prosthetics centers.

In the first three days of the war, prosthetist Denys Nahornyi witnessed the Russian bombing of his workplace, Kharkiv Research Institute of Prosthetics (Ukrayinskyi Naukovo-Doslidnyi Instytut Protezuvannia) which develops and produces electric chips and sensors for myoelectric prostheses that read impulses from human muscles. Denys had to relocate to the city of Dnipro and then to the west of Ukraine, but he continued working with myoelectric prostheses at the Without Limits clinic.

"All my hand prostheses work from just two sensors that are attached to the muscles and act as antagonists—flexor and extensor. According to different combinations of signals, the electric hand is quite flexible and can perform various gestures. This hand can hold up to 20 kilograms and helps with complex tasks," he says, showing us a black hand with a wrist and forearm up to the elbow.

A myoelectric prosthesis has several joints, and can only be controlled sequentially, by tensing muscles. A mechanical hand may not match normal contours and have unsightly attachments, such as hooks, but in some cases it holds an object better.

Myoelectric prostheses look like ordinary hands, and many people think that if a prosthesis looks like a real hand, it will replace a real hand. "In fact, no prosthesis can replace a lost limb. Depending on whether a person types on a computer, wants to lift something heavy, or rides a bicycle, a myoelectric prosthesis is programmed differently," says Victoria Olih, a director of the Without Limits clinic.

Since 2022, the clinic has mostly served the military, working with complex, traumatic residual limbs. "The traumas are extreme—a residual limb will alter its positioning a lot throughout the day. The weather, medication, and workload—everything has an effect. But we have learned to manage it, and both the quality of the equipment we can purchase and the available specialization are very high. The speed and success of rehabilitation largely depend on the will and effort of the soldier."

Besides quality prostheses, injured soldiers receive higher salaries and compensation. "These payments from the state sustain many people psychologically, they feel self-sufficient," Victoria says. After rehabilitation, most of the injured soldiers return to their homes all over Ukraine. "They are not afraid of war. Many of them say, 'Give me a prosthesis, and I will go to the front.'"

\*\*\*

"I started to think that guys who had fought in 2014–2015 gave me the opportunity to study at school and get an education. And now it's my turn to give someone such an opportunity," says Maksym, who turned 25 in 2022. He enlisted in the military in his native Kropyvnytskyi region in central Ukraine, on the fourth day of the invasion.

For a month, he fought in an artillery unit but was wounded on 24 March 2022. An explosion tore his leg up to the knee. "We were among the first wounded who needed prostheses. Almost immediately, the specialists from Without Limits arrived at our rehabilitation center and exhibited available prostheses. I decided to go with one of theirs, to be able to walk as soon as possible."

At first, Maksym received a temporary prosthesis and gradually learned to walk. After a second surgery and full rehabilitation, he was fitted with his permanent prosthetic leg. "When wearing trousers, sometimes I forget I don't have a leg. I was amputated below the knee, so I even went to my sister's wedding and danced there. I can run with this prosthetic leg and play football. We have the best doctors. They quickly put me back on my feet and motivated me. You need the will, the time, and the patience—these are the three factors, and everything will be fine. I don't even think of it as some kind of amputation. Sometimes, our guys joke that if a leg is amputated below the knee, it doesn't count."

He decided to continue his military service despite the injury. His dream is to join Ukraine's Paralympic Team after the war. "Now I have a reassessment, one could say, a life from a new page. I started trying everything because life is short."

Volodymyr, another soldier with a prosthetic leg, is returning to his home in Mykolayiv at the end of 2022 after several months of rehabilitation. He just turned 49.

"Of course I'm returning. My family is there … my job. Mykolayiv is already liberated." He wanted to continue working, repairing equipment at the armored vehicle plant in his city, less than 100 kilometers from the front. Volodymyr first fought in the military in 2015 and 2016 in the east of Ukraine, then returned to service when the full-scale war began in 2022. It took him three months to learn to walk again.

\*\*\*

Although the complete official data is unavailable, multiple sources indicate that by 2024, the total number of Ukrainian soldiers who had undergone amputations and were receiving prosthetic limbs had reached tens of thousands.

In 2014, when the war had just begun and the first amputees arrived at Ukrainian clinics, it became evident that the healthcare system had neither the facilities nor expertise to provide help for all of them. Doctors were used to dealing with only a small number of amputations caused by illness or traffic accidents. To expand and modernize the Ukrainian prosthetics industry, a team of volunteers created the Center for Prosthetics Support in 2014, which later became Protez Hub. This nationwide NGO consults, trains, and provides support and materials for Ukrainian private and public companies producing prostheses. They have pulled together dozens of Ukrainian companies and have involved both national and world-class professionals for training.

In 2017, it became clear that ordinary prostheses were not enough for military veterans, who often also require special prostheses such as for sports or heavy physical activity. "We provided training, and all this was also developed. As of now, 99% of the Ukrainian guys who have participated in the Invictus Games and the Warrior Games[37] received prostheses in Ukraine made by Ukrainian specialists," says Olena Tsymbaliuk, director of logistics and operations at the Protez Hub.

If a person has lost a limb, they will need to wear a prosthesis and have it serviced throughout their entire life. It is important to find a prosthetist near their location, which is why it is crucial to make all necessary prostheses available in Ukraine, rather than sending soldiers for treatment abroad. "A prosthesis is a mechanism that needs constant maintenance, just like a car. You don't go to a service station or a tire repair shop in another country."

Each prosthetic limb consists of two parts. The first part includes the main components for feet, hands, elbows, and knees. It is mostly generic and purchased from the best international manufacturers. Only two companies produce these components in Ukraine but cannot meet the full demand.

The second part includes the custom-made socket of the prosthesis into which the recipient's partial limb is inserted. The function of the prosthesis depends primarily on how well this second part is made. It cannot be factory-made, and the entire process requires the prosthetist's personal attendance.

Despite the 2022 Russian invasion, the Center for Prosthetics Support continued training professionals to cover the growing

---

37   The Invictus Games, inaugurated in 2014, is an international multi-sport event for wounded service members and veterans, founded by the UK Prince Harry in collaboration with the British Ministry of Defence. The Warrior Games, organized annually since 2010 by the US Department of Defense, serves a similar purpose for American service personnel and veterans with injuries, illnesses, or wounds.

demand. "For example, in June 2022 we took prosthetists to the Netherlands and Sweden. We are promoting direct socket technology, whereby the socket is not made from a plaster cast but is produced directly on the person. It anatomically corresponds to the limb much better, and the process is faster," says Olena.

The war has made Ukrainian prosthetists highly experienced. "Some are even more qualified than their colleagues abroad," Olena says. "Our prosthetists handle traumatic amputations from explosions, dealing with irregular shapes and hastily stitched-up wounds from stabilization hospitals near the front line."

\*\*\*

The policy of the Ukrainian government has been to fully pay the costs of prosthetic limbs for soldiers, regardless of whether they are for a private or public company. The state allocated up to $50,000 for one prosthetic limb, depending on its complexity. When prosthetists make artificial limbs, they consider the person's future plans — physical work, driving, mobility needs, or only basic functions, such as walking.

At the same time, state funding did not cover training for prosthetists, innovation, or the construction of new facilities to serve the increased number of amputees. Donor efforts helped build and open a new Superhumans Center in Lviv in 2023. That year, the center treated its first 290 patients, fitting 413 prostheses (some had double and triple amputations). Yet, its total capacity is expected to reach 3,000 amputees per year. Another similar rehabilitation center, Unbroken, was created in Lviv in 2023. Funded by external donations and the city council, it had by June 2024 treated close to 15,000 patients wounded by the war, both military and civilians, including 350 children.

Olha Rudnieva, the head and co-founder of the Superhumans Center, says that some of the people they have worked with were not expected to survive. These fighters were occasionally saved after evacuations that took five or six hours due to difficult battlefield conditions, far longer than the standard one-hour operation. One soldier they worked with was saved from the battlefield after his rescue lasted 21 hours through a minefield. "You see them coming in a wheelchair, and within a week, they're walking and hugging you."

"Had you ever run a marathon before your trauma?" Olha asked one of the patients.

"No."

"Have you ever been to the mountains?"

"No."

"Have you ever played golf?"

"Never"

"So why are you doing all of that now?"

"Because I could be dead. I realized that I could have died without having accomplished so many important things. Now, my second life starts."

Once, the Superhumans Center sent one of their amputees to Antarctica because he wanted to see the penguins. Olha's friend, coincidentally, was on the same trip, and told her, "Never, ever, again, will I go on a trip with a superhuman. Because he wants to do everything. He wants to climb the mountain, he wants to jump in the cold water because he's so restless and so impatient to live his life. Because he was so close to death."

***

"Dad, is your leg made yet?" Dmytro's five-year-old twin daughters once asked him over the phone.

"Yes. Soon I will be home."

"I would like to return to my unit, but I can't be a burden on the boys either," Dmytro tells us, continuing his first training on a full-leg prosthesis.

While undergoing rehabilitation, Dmytro visited his home in Cherkasy twice, where his wife and children awaited his return. "There was an opportunity to bring my family here, but I didn't want the kids to see all this rehabilitation. It was already a trauma for them when I arrived home. They were scared. They didn't understand at first, but now they call me to ask whether my leg is already made. Of course, I will return to Cherkasy where I was born."

Dmytro longs for the days when he will once again sail on the Dnipro. "Although I was on business trips all my life, I never considered living anywhere else. I can't stay somewhere without the Dnipro," he says, taking one more cautious step.

# War Generation

At 8 am on Monday, 10 October 2022, Ukrainian Member of Parliament and former Deputy Minister of Education, Inna Sovsun, prepared herself for another busy workday, as she had become accustomed to during the war. Her husband, a surgeon, had been serving in the military since the early days of the full-scale invasion, while Inna focused on the crucial task of updating legislation to meet the challenges facing the country. She also traveled abroad, speaking to parliaments and governments of other nations.

"During our first year of foreign visits, it was most interesting to explain that we had a functioning parliament, that we convened and voted," she recalls. "Western politicians were largely unaware of this, as the media primarily showed the president and the front lines. Regarding lawmaking, first and foremost, we were passing laws related to the war. Next came everything pertaining to integration with the European Union, followed by everything else. At some point, I started to get irritated by the phrase 'We will support Ukraine as long as it takes,' because it became an excuse to prolong the support indefinitely. I don't want it to take long. Give us everything now so we can win faster. Because while we keep playing 'as long as it takes,' my life passes by."

High-ranking officials such as the President or Prime Minister had state bodyguards, but MPs did not, even at the start of the war. Unlike many MPs, Inna commuted to work by metro and continued doing so during the war. For the first six months, her 11-year-old son Martyn stayed with his grandmother in the west of Ukraine, where there was less shelling, but then Inna decided to bring him back to Kyiv. "In our district we rarely get shelled; there's no critical infrastructure or military targets nearby, so it's relatively calm."

However, on 10 October 2022, Inna heard loud explosions nearby. Initially, she decided to wait out the situation with Martyn in the bathroom of their apartment in a highrise, behind two walls from the street, which would protect them from shrapnel or blast waves. But when the next explosions sounded closer, she decided to run to the metro, which also served as a shelter. They grabbed sleeping mats, water, and some food.

"Mom, am I going to die?" Martyn asked while running.

"I will never forgive those responsible for putting my child in a situation where he had to ask that question," Inna recalls. "Then I told him, no, it's okay, we're just having an adventure."

As they neared the metro, Martyn suddenly stopped and asked, "Mom, is this a regular bomb or a nuclear one?"

"Don't worry, it's a regular bomb ..." Inna replied, uttering the strangest sentence of her life.

Martyn looked slightly disappointed, saying, "Well, if it's a nuclear bomb, we learned at school what to do."

"It was just a child's disappointment, wanting to impress his mom with something he learned at school," Inna says about the situation. "These things are of course very frightening. Talking about reality without scaring a child is a delicate balance. On the one hand, he should have a childhood: on the other, he needs to understand the situation. He is, after all, already 11 years old."

During the full-scale war, Inna took Martyn abroad for a vacation only once. "I didn't have the internal strength to do it, but I thought my child wouldn't have another childhood. I must do this for him, because who else will?" Martyn's father, Inna's ex-husband, and her current husband are both serving in the army. She also took Martyn twice on her three-day working trips abroad. The rest of the time, since the summer of 2022, he has spent in Kyiv.

"I think he's luckier than many other children," Inna says. "He lives with both parents, two weeks with me, two weeks with his dad because he serves in Kyiv. This is a much better experience than many other children who live with one parent. His school has a shelter. He can attend school, unlike 60,000 children in Kharkiv who haven't been to school for five years due to the war and previously the coronavirus lockdown."

Many schools didn't have shelters that could accommodate all children. Therefore, children took turns attending school one week and learning online the next. "The fact that my child comes home and says, 'Oh, there were no air raid alarms today, it was a good day', or 'Today there was only one alarm, it's okay.' This is unacceptable; childhood should not be like this."

In January 2024, Inna gathered a team to completely rewrite the outdated "Defense of Ukraine" curriculum for high school, using her previous experience in the Ministry of Education. In less than six months, the parliament adopted the updated law, despite Inna being from an opposition party. The old curriculum had been divided by gender and included many unnecessary topics, such as studying military charters. Now, it is a uniform, more practical curriculum for all students.

"We tried to balance two perspectives. There was a demand, especially from some military personnel, for it to be almost a basic military training course. On the other hand, others said it should just be a course discussing values. We aimed to find a balance where we don't militarize children like in Russia. On the other hand, we are a country at war, and people need a general understanding of what war is, the various situations that may arise, how they can help, and how to respond to different challenges."

By May 2024, the team at the ministry had launched training for teachers. They also began creating regional centers at high schools for the renewed Defense of Ukraine subject. The government allocated funds to improve the quality of defense teaching and, most significantly, purchased various equipment for this purpose, such as tourniquets, mannequins, and weapons.

This is just one example of the laws initiated by Inna during the war. The other included simplifying the import of volunteer aid for the military and updating the tourniquet certification system. In 2023, volunteer organizations raised concerns about the quality of tourniquets. With advice from her military surgeon husband, Inna found a solution to recognize only tourniquets approved by the US Army. This was successfully passed into law.

One law, which still lacked a majority in Parliament as of 2024, but which Inna continued to push for, was regulating service terms for soldiers, so far set indefinitely "until the end of martial law." This law, which set limits on the length of service, could be harder to pass because not all MPs have close relatives on the front lines and were also not very eager to widen mobilization for training reserves.

"I don't hide my personal bias in this situation. I've spent two summers without my beloved husband because he's been on the front line. We saw each other a little bit only in wintertime. Now I think, will there be a third summer, and then a fourth where we won't be together? We can't even plan going to the Carpathians for five days. We just don't have that luxury, while 90% of the country does. It's psychologically hard, feeling this injustice. And it's physically hard for service members—their health deteriorates with each day of war, making them less effective as soldiers."

Despite dissatisfaction that not all important decisions can be made during wartime in the current parliament, Inna adds that this is how the democratic process works worldwide. The majority party passes laws in parliament, while the minority tries to exert some influence "through political discourse and shape policy somewhat. The fact that our parliament sometimes passes laws from opposition parties is rather an exception from the norm for European democracy."

"Democracy is less effective at war. But we have to persevere, and I think we need to work on explaining and educating people that we will only win together or lose together. We will win when everyone does at least 15% more than usual. Not just energy workers, not just emergency services and firefighters. The military is doing 300% more. And every time someone tells me that MPs' children should go to war, I say: first, my son is 11, and second, there isn't a single MP you didn't vote for."

***

Two days before our conversation with Inna, on 29 May 2024, journalist and paramedic Iryna Tsybukh was killed at the Kharkiv front. Almost three weeks before, Russians had started their new incursion across Ukraine's border towards the city of Kharkiv, which was quickly stopped by Ukrainian forces amid heavy fighting. Iryna took part in the defense operation there as a member of Hospitallers Medical Battalion and was killed just two days before her 26th birthday.

On the eve of Russia's full-scale war against Ukraine, on 22 and 23 February, she presented her documentary film 'Distance,' which focuses on children from remote villages in the Donetsk and Luhansk regions. The presentations took place in the towns of Pokrovsk and Kramatorsk in the Donetsk region. A few days later, she volunteered to fight, interrupting her Master's program in Public Governance.

"I want children, I want a house, I want to plant tomatoes ... But ending the war is the most important thing," Iryna said in one of her interviews.[38]

Inna speaks about her former student and good acquaintance with great sorrow. "If we had everything we have now two years earlier—back in April-May 2022—the level of losses would certainly have been significantly lower, and perhaps we would have already won. Maybe Iryna Tsybukh would have survived. I read last night that Biden allowed strikes on Russia. If that decision had been made two days earlier, maybe Ira would have lived. It is a huge loss for the country. Ira was one of those who would help to build a new Ukraine. But she did not survive because consultations were needed to decide whether it was permissible to defend the Kharkiv region by striking Russian territory."

***

On 5 March 2022, 52-year-old Iryna Filkina was biking back to her home in Bucha. As during the previous few days, she had been preparing food for the Ukrainian soldiers in the town engaged in fierce fighting with the invading Russian forces. Before leaving, she spoke with her 26-year-old daughter Olha, who had moved to Poland and now tried to dissuade her mother from cycling alone. "Olha, don't you know your mother? I can move mountains!" That was their last conversation.

---

38    The interview was shared by SvoiCity YouTube channel (https://www.youtu be.com/shorts/9xCOPyWFkzc).

An aerial video published by the New York Times[39] shows a person on a bicycle making a left turn on a street in Bucha, who was then immediately shot by a Russian tank. It is presumed the person was Iryna Filkina.

The woman's body remained at the site of the murder for nearly a month. Journalists, among the first to enter Bucha after its liberation by Ukrainian forces, found her near her bicycle in early April. During the month-long occupation, Russian forces killed and tortured hundreds in Bucha. Many of the 501 victims, who were mentioned on the monument to the Bucha massacre, were buried in mass graves, while other victims could not be removed from the streets because of the occupation, and lay there for weeks. Dozens of dead civilians were found with their hands tied behind their backs, tortured, with some being found in the cellars.

The photo of the hand of the murdered Iryna Filkina, with its bright-red manicure, became widely circulated in the West. One day in April 2022, Iryna's manicurist, Anastasiya Subacheva, who was in Lithuania at the time, saw the photo on social media — four red nails and one with a purple-silver heart. When Anastasiya recognized her work, she started crying. "I cried on my mother's shoulder, I felt very empty and hurt."

The terrible news was hardest on Iryna's closest ones.

"Mom, I cried and no one came, and I cried and screamed even more bitterly … I thought you would hear that and come by," wrote Iryna's daughter Olha Shchyruk on 7 April. "Today, I woke up for the first time without tears, because in my dream, I heard a small girl crying somewhere. A kid smaller than me and in more pain. The girl cried because she didn't know where her mother was, and would she ever come back and kiss and hug her again." These were the words of the first post on the Mama Ira Foundation's Instagram page, which Olha founded in memory of her mother to help Ukrainian children who lost their parents in Russia's war against Ukraine.

---

39  The New York Times published the video on 5 April 2022 (https://www.nyt imes.com/2022/04/05/world/europe/bucha-shooting-video.html).

"This experience is dreadfully stressful. If at the age of 26 I'm under such big stress, then I understand how hard it must be for the kids," Olha tells us.

According to Vasyl Lutsyk, Ukraine's head of social services, 1,759 children had become orphans due to Russia's military aggression after two years of the full-scale war.[40] However, since there was no access to the Russian-occupied parts of the country, this number was likely higher. Thousands of Ukrainian children deprived of parental care were also deported to Russia from Russian-occupied Ukrainian territories and subsequently re-educated to internalize Russian identity.

Before 2022, Olha worked as a psychologist helping children with disabilities and internally displaced persons from Donetsk and Luhansk regions who were forced to leave their homes after the start of Russian aggression in 2014. In her Mama Ira Foundation, she wanted to use her psychological expertise to help those whose pain she understood too well. "This is not just some new project idea. It should be a soul that cares for the future of children, just as much as their mothers might have cared for them."

Having contacted other foundations that also work with children who lost their parents at war, Olha found that approximately 80% of the children are reluctant to communicate with psychologists directly. Mostly, relatives call on the children's behalf.

"Too often, children just don't speak at all. They lock themselves in a room and refuse to communicate with their relatives. They also stop communicating with each other," Olha tells us, adding that some children become completely numb. "You understand how stressful it is if a child at the age of 13–14 just stops talking at all and does not say a word." The psychologists who Olha was in touch with agree that the level of trauma is usually so dire that it would take much more time than one year to help these children cope.

---

40  Vasyl Lutsyk spoke about this number in his interview for The Radio Svoboda / Radio Free Europe on 4 March 2024 (https://www.radiosvoboda.org/a/sy roty-bizhentsi-vidibrani-dity-italia-usynovlennia/32844308.html).

"Children are afraid: some strangers came into their country, killed their parents, and went away. No one was able to protect their parents, or them. Their parents, who they had considered to be the strongest people in life, were shot and killed by these people. There is no one in the whole world left to protect them ... Children have been taught from birth that human life is sacred, that they are safe from harm, and that they need to love all others. Now, the cognitive dissonance created in their minds, which are not fully shaped, can have grave negative implications for the future."

Some children pretend that the tragedy has never happened to them. Other victims think that he or she deserves what has happened. "They mistakenly think that something was wrong with them. This might result in serious mental issues. Girls who have been abused will avoid discussing these topics but there will be triggers." Olha says that in order to heal it is important to express your feelings and later accept the situation and move on with your life.

Olha says that the volunteer psychologists working with this problem display a lot of kindness and loyalty. "They communicate with children as friends. They are from Ukraine themselves and tell children stories about their sufferings." The problem is, however, that the available textbooks offer little help in dealing with these problems, and psychologists have to develop real-time treatment plans. Olha and her partners decided not to publicize the children's stories because this could potentially harm their fragile psyche. Another challenge they face is explaining to people, "who never lost their relatives, how to talk to those who did. People often demand that they talk about the details that victims are not yet ready to talk about."

Apart from psychological support, the Mama Ira Foundation covers the basic needs of children who have lost parents at war, including assistance with transportation to relatives or other safe places, food and clothing. "Also, the important issue is burial arrangements for their parents. The costs of proper burial start at 25,000 hryvnias ($800). If a child loses both parents, these expenses have to be covered."

Olha says that before the adoption, children should have enough time to process the traumatic events from their past. "A child is not a toy to be passed around. Children need to know where they are going and how they are getting there, and that nothing will ever be the same. It is necessary to prepare the children for this."

\*\*\*

"On 25 February 2022, I changed my perspective on when I wanted to have children. I had always told my husband that I didn't want children before I turned 35, as I was working and was thinking about my career. But on 25 February, I realized that I want to have children now."

Sofia-Julia Sydorenko met her husband Oleksandr in Lviv in 2019 when she was 28. Sofia-Julia, the head of the nationwide Zero Waste Alliance Ukraine, works on waste-management issues. She also owns a shop selling eco-friendly zero waste products, 90% of which are made in Ukraine. Oleksandr, a user-experience designer from Dnipro, joined a volunteer battalion at the beginning of the war in 2014 and served until 2015. After that, Sofia-Julia tells us, he went through a crisis. With his acquaintances unable to understand why he had gone "there," to the front, and why he had completely switched from Russian to Ukrainian, he decided to move to Lviv.

A few days before the escalation of the war in 2022, Oleksandr received a call from the military telling him not to go anywhere. The couple had tickets to fly to Cyprus for the weekend on 26 February, but "of course, we were not in the mood for vacation anymore."

When the war began, at 8:30 am on 24 February, Oleksandr received another call telling him to report to his military unit in Dnipro as soon as possible. "My 24 February was all about packing," Sofia-Julia recalls. "We washed everything that needed washing, bought everything that was needed." Oleksandr's train was scheduled to depart late in the evening, just before midnight.

"I don't want to go to war," Oleksandr told his wife that day — which Sofia-Julia didn't fully understand at the time.

Oleksandr explained, "Look, I know what war is like. It's not a place you want to return to."

In the third year of the full-scale war, with Oleksandr still serving, Sofia-Julia tells us, "Only now do I understand how much sense that makes because, fundamentally, a sane person cannot want to be at war."

That day, 24 February 2022, the entire train station in Lviv, where Sofia-Julia saw Oleksandr off, was filled with military personnel. "And all trains departing in the following hours were heading east. I was amazed at how many people had come to defend the country."

All day, Sofia-Julia had tried not to show her husband her sadness, but as soon as she said goodbye and walked away from the station, she began to cry. "I cried until about three in the morning. And in the morning, with a friend, I immediately started volunteering."

Sofia-Julia repurposed one room of her zero-waste shop into a shelter where she housed three people from Kharkiv, and in another, they organized a storage area for aid to be sent to the east. Many of these items were donated by friends from abroad, and the people from Kharkiv helped manage the logistics. "Volunteering really saved me. You just work and don't think about anything else."

Oleksandr was involved in aerial reconnaissance and initially fought in the Zaporizhzhia sector. Sometimes he was given a few days to go to Dnipro to repair drones. During these days, Sofia-Julia would come to "help" him. "You come, you see your person, the city is completely filled with military. You drive to change tires at a service station, and that's our date ... Despite this, I've come to love this city so much, it has come to hold a very special meaning for me."

She became pregnant in August 2022 and no longer visited Dnipro. The couple agreed that Oleksandr wouldn't come for the actual birth, as it would be impossible to travel almost 1,000 kilometers in time, but he would use his leave to come to take them home from the maternity hospital. "Honestly, I don't know how they let me go," Oleksandr said then. He had come from the Avdiivka front, where very active fighting was taking place and it was nearly impossible to take leave.

"It was like a fog," Sofia-Julia recalls. "I was postpartum, he arrived after a long sleepless journey. Despite this, I'm very happy he got to see Matviy." However, after a day and a half Oleksandr had to return to the front.

"I joke that during Covid we were together 24/7, both working from home, and now it's 0/7," says Sofia-Julia.

Her mother moved in from Vinnytsia to help her with household chores, as well as with their cat and dog. Sofia-Julia continued working. "I was sending my coworkers their salaries while still in the maternity hospital. What else could I do? The baby was sleeping." She told her colleagues that during the first month of the baby's life, she would try to understand how actively she could be involved. "Matviy slept next to me, and I could work. I just didn't see the need not to work if it was possible."

Sofia-Julia would clean while her son played in the morning and work while he slept. "When your child sleeps, you get work done. I really got into this rhythm. When I have slots, I work; when I feed him, I think about what I need to do. And my mother's help is very important ... Unfortunately, all this is happening without my husband."

In addition to the Zaporizhzhia front, during the two-and-a-half years of full-scale war Oleksandr fought in Chernihiv, Kherson, and Donetsk regions. "We joke that he's traveled a lot during this time. I've barely traveled at all."

Very rarely, about once every six months, Oleksandr manages to come home for a few days to see his wife and son. "It's a certain challenge and fear that we're living in very different contexts. I live in the context of a child, my husband lives in the context of war, and despite the fact that we talk a lot on the phone, I understand that when he returns, we'll have a lot of adapting to do. I see that even when he comes back on leave, it's as if he's returning to our world before we had a child." Sofia-Julia believes that this gap will affect many families with children. "But I decided that I would just take a long time to explain. What I'd like him to understand in half a word, he simply can't understand in half a word, because he hasn't had that experience. There will be difficulties after his return, but nothing we can't work through."

In 2024, Sofia-Julia campaigns for Ukraine to reduce its reliance on single-use plastics. Among other numerous benefits for the society and the environment, this will help to decrease financial support for Russia, a major supplier of the oil and gas used in plastic production. "I wouldn't want us to enable our enemy in this way. Because this is one of the biggest resources which Russia receives income from: 9% of the total final gas consumption and 8% of the final oil consumption in EU countries is used precisely for plastic production, with 40% of this production being packaging.[41] Governments often tell citizens to save gas, but they don't tell manufacturers not to produce plastic. And that's not right."

In 2024, data regarding the demographic situation in Ukraine projected a nearly 30% population decline over the next few decades in the already underpopulated country, primarily related to the fact that many women with children have gone abroad — an indirect consequence of the war. Still, in 2024, one could see many people with babies on the streets of Ukrainian cities. "I can't generalize, but in my circle, there are parents who have realized that it's not something unrealistic, that a child gives a lot of hope, gives understanding and vision for the future. You understand that you have this little person, who will live in a prosperous country." "It's not unbearably difficult," Sofia-Julia said during conversations with two couples who did not want to have children. However, one couple later had a baby, and the other is now pregnant.

Twice a week, Sofia-Julia and Oleksandr video call each other. Oleksandr makes funny faces for his one-year-old son as little Matviy smiles happily. "Of course, this doesn't replace having a dad," says Sofia-Julia.

---

41   This data was publishes in the report "Winter Is Coming: Plastic Has To Go: A Case for Decreasing Plastic Production to Reduce the European Union's Dependence on Fossil Fuels and Russia" in September 2022 (https://www.ciel. org/reports/winter-is-coming-plastic-has-to-go/).

When Oleksandr came home after months of not seeing his son, who was almost a year old, Sofia-Julia was afraid that Matviy would be scared, but upon seeing his dad, the baby immediately broke into a smile and started playing.

Learning in the spring of 2024 that the demobilization of current military personnel was being postponed again and it was again unclear how long Oleksandr would have to fight, the couple was saddened. However, Sofia-Julia says they realize there is no choice but to defend Ukraine from Russian military aggression. "We both understand why he's there. We both don't want this war to be left for our son, for it to drag on into the coming years. We both want to live in a country where there isn't this constant background of war-war-war. We want to live in a boring country that we are developing, where we need to deal with children's playgrounds, deal with things that don't relate to existential problems."

# The Commander

"Life in the army is living one day at a time. You live one day, and if you succeed, perform your task, and keep people alive—it's a good day," says Taras Hrynchyshyn, a 32-year-old Ukrainian commander who has dedicated six years of his life to fighting Russian invaders. Having spent his childhood near the town of Horodok in the west of Ukraine and graduated from a program in banking, he never envisaged pursuing a military career. However, after Russia occupied Crimea and launched its attack on the Donetsk and Luhansk regions in 2014, he volunteered to fight. Taking several breaks during the relatively stable phase of the war between 2016 and 2021, he never completely left military service. Entering service in 2014 as an ordinary infantry soldier, by 2022 Taras was already a platoon commander and has since moved up in rank. He has engaged in combat across almost every sector of the front.

\*\*\*

While the battles were ongoing in the north, east, and southeast of Ukraine at the beginning of Russia's 2022 invasion, people were wary of a larger Russian attack from Belarus to the northwest. Belarus had become a de facto Russian ally in the invasion, allowing its territory and airspace to be used by Russia's military.

---

42  Rome is a Luxembourgish neofolk music band centered around Jerome Reuter. In 2023, Rome unveiled an album titled "Gates of Europe," entirely dedicated to Ukraine's fight. "Gates of Europe" encompasses songs dedicated to specific events and places—such as "Olenivka Rain," "The Ballad of Mariupol," and "Going Back to Kyiv"—as well as those capturing the spirit of Ukrainian resistance against Russian aggression, including "Yellow and Blue," "The Black Axis," "How Beauty Emerged Against This Darkness," and "Eagles of the Trident."

Taras's anti-tank platoon formed part of the Ukrainian forces in the Rivne region, and was tasked with guarding the border with Belarus. Russian troops were located just behind the border and could cross into Ukraine at any moment.

His platoon initially had only 12 people, mostly experienced reservists who had also fought after 2014, while the mobilization of new recruits was still ongoing. Expecting to be the first to meet a possible Russian attack from Belarus, the platoon had been equipped with NLAW and Panzerfaust man-portable anti-tank systems.

Positions had not been prepared in advance, as nobody before the full-scale war had been expecting an attack from Belarus. At first, soldiers lived in a ditch among fields and pine forests in the frosty air, waiting, and gradually preparing trenches and dugouts. "You sleep in three pairs of pants, a jacket and a sleeping bag, but you still feel the early spring wind chilling you to the bone," says Taras. After several days, local townspeople organized themselves and brought some hot meals and tea to soldiers. Finishing the dugouts, the soldiers made rough heaters that could warm them a little.

One day, intelligence notified them that a Russian convoy from Belarus was heading in their direction. "Stop the column, bomb it to bits!" was the order. Taras grimaces, recalling this first chaotic month of the war. "I counted all my rockets. Even if we fired all of them precisely, to put it bluntly, we wouldn't do anything to the column."

Still, he deployed his 12 men at the crossroad in several ambushes which they had prepared in advance not far from the border to create crossfire, hoping to hit at least the first vehicles, slow down the column, and then adjust artillery fire.

As luck would have it, the column did not dare cross the border—perhaps the Russians had either realized that ambushes might be awaiting them, or they had already changed their plans, given that the offensive near Kyiv was failing to achieve its objectives and reinforcements were needed there. The first months of full-scale war ended relatively calmly for Taras's unit. Until he was redeployed to Ukraine's south, where "the real hell started."

\*\*\*

The town of Snihurivka, located between the southern cities of Kherson and Mykolayiv, was occupied in the first days of the war. It was the Russians' most forward stronghold, preventing Ukrainian troops from advancing towards Kherson. Taras's unit was redeployed near the town. In the summer of 2022, fighting positional warfare, they were mostly using old SPG-9 anti-tank guns which, with a range of up to five kilometers, could reach various Russian positions, albeit with low accuracy at such a distance. His platoon also helped adjust artillery fire, conducted reconnaissance and repelled Russian assaults.

A lot of digging was necessary to hide from the dense artillery barrages. While in the forward positions, they lived in dugouts covered with pine logs topped with ground. When on rotation in the second line, they could spend a night in abandoned public buildings. However, nowhere was safe for them near the front. Russians constantly "covered" Taras's positions and nearby settlements, not only with artillery but also air-dropped bombs and missiles.

"Here, there was a hit at 4:45 am," Taras says, showing us a photo of a huge, three-story facility, reduced to a heap of white bricks and remnants of walls. "And just 15 minutes earlier my group had left there for a mission."

Taras's 30-person platoon was part of Ukraine's efforts to expel the Russian army from Kherson. As of September 2022, Ukrainian military units started pushing the Russian forces from the north, out of the Kherson region. Step by step, Ukrainian forces liberated village after village, with the Russians ultimately forced to surrender the entire west bank of the Dnipro River, including the city of Kherson. Thus, the only regional center that the Russians had managed to occupy since the beginning of the 2022 invasion was liberated.

In the final stage of the Kherson operation, Taras's unit cleared Snihurivka and villages near Kherson of the remaining enemy forces. The locals greeted the soldiers with tears in their eyes.

However, although the battle ended with victory for Ukraine and was joyfully celebrated by media and public alike, Taras says that for him "there were only sad battles during this period." He lost comrades not only in active combat but also due to mines. The Russians had laid extensive minefields during their retreat. Several of Taras's comrades accidentally detonated a mine after the western Dnipro bank had already been fully liberated. Three of them were injured, one severely, and saved only because of timely evacuation to the hospital, while another soldier, 27-year-old Andriy Khalak, was killed. He was a friend of Taras who lived in a neighboring village and a commander of one of the squads directly subordinate to Taras. "Offensive military operations, especially those like the operation near Kherson, are incredibly difficult. And the price is very high."

***

Just weeks after the liberation of Kherson, when Ukrainian troops reached the Dnipro and were no longer needed in large numbers there, Taras's unit was redeployed to the vicinity of Bakhmut. This town in the Donetsk region, with a pre-war population of 70,000, became the epicenter of that winter's battles.

There, at the beginning of December, Taras would witness for the first time the large-scale Russian military tactic, known as "meat assaults." Near Bakhmut, the Russians tried to outsmart Ukrainian forces by the sheer quantity of manpower. These were mainly made up of so-called Wagner mercenaries, consisting primarily of prisoners. "Wagner mercenaries are like meat. Nobody values them at all. But it doesn't mean it's easy for us during these attacks," Taras says.

During the nine-month Battle of Bakhmut—from September 2022 to May 2023—Russian troops managed to advance by 15 kilometers on a 25-kilometer-wide section of the front line and were ultimately able to occupy the town. However, this turned out to be a Pyrrhic victory, given that they lost between 60,000 and 100,000 soldiers killed and wounded in the Bakhmut operation alone, according to US, UK and Ukrainian estimates. The number of killed was abnormally high among Russian Bakhmut casualties, because of a lack of medical evacuation. In May 2023, Yevgeny Prigozhyn, commander of the Russian Wagner PMC, said that Wagner saw 20,000 mercenaries killed and another 20,000 wounded in Bakhmut, not counting other units. Even with the most moderate estimates, Russia was losing about one soldier killed for every 50 centimeters of advance in the Bakhmut section of the front.

In many places, the dead Russian soldiers were literally scattered on the fields, one on top of the other. When the pressure exerted by the Russian forces became too heavy, Ukrainian troops would retreat to the next positions behind. The lack of ammunition and heavy infantry weapons, along with exhaustion, were the main challenges for Ukrainians in the Battle of Bakhmut, as various soldiers who participated in the fighting told us.

"I don't understand how it's possible for Russians to crawl among corpses like that and just keep on crawling. They are under the influence of some drugs, definitely," Ukrainian machine gunner Artem tells us of his experience in Bakhmut. He was wounded on 28 February 2023 by Russian mortar fire, sustaining shrapnel wounds to the cheek.

Artem joined the army on 25 March 2022, saying he did not want to see Russians and their atrocities in his home city of Dnipro. After almost a year of fighting elsewhere, he was deployed to Bakhmut, where street fighting had already commenced. Attacking day and night, Russians were pouring into the town in huge numbers, crawling towards the windows of the building where Artem's positions were located. "They liked, most of all, to crawl towards us at night with grenades."

"Meat assaults" should not be perceived as the only Russian tactic. They would use poorly trained soldiers in these early attacks, as well as drop air bombs and fire from artillery a lot to exhaust Ukrainians and disclose and destroy their positions. Afterward, Russians would send in more skilled troops. "I was lucky to survive in Bakhmut for 16 days," Artem says. "The Russians fired mortars constantly, from morning to night. We couldn't do that." Even during intensive Russian attacks, when his unit especially needed more ammunition, it was not always available and they were told that "everything is limited."

Ammunition scarcity was on everyone's lips during this period. Operating a machine grenade launcher in Bakhmut, Yuriy Syrotiuk, a member of the Ukrainian parliament between 2012 and 2014, says that "ammunition is the only thing missing here."[43] Petro Kuzyk, a former member of the Kyiv city council and commander of the volunteer Svoboda battalion, also fought with his soldiers in Bakhmut. He says that the tactic Russians used in Bakhmut was the same as in the earlier battles for Rubizhne and Sievierodonetsk, albeit different in scale. Russia's goal was to look for weak sections in the Ukrainian defense lines and exhaust the Ukrainian defenders with constant attacks and shelling. Forcing Ukrainians to retreat at a particular point, they would send troops in to cement their gains and repeat the process all over again.[44]

Infantry soldier Liubomyr, who was also wounded in Bakhmut, tells us that it was most difficult at night and especially in winter — the mud prevented most of the available trucks from reaching the battle lines, and soldiers had to carry supplies on foot. Such conditions were very dangerous for the wounded, who also had to be evacuated on foot — sometimes carried for several kilometers — with every minute critical.

At the same time, Russians used a slightly different tactic near Vuhledar town — 100 kilometers south of Bakhmut — in a supportive effort to exhaust Ukrainian troops. They were marching towards the town in huge mechanized assaults, but were hit by Ukrainian artillery, blown-up by mines, and ultimately stopped by infantry anti-tank weapons. Stanislav, who operated the American MK-19 automatic grenade launcher in that sector, witnessed how his comrades destroyed four tanks, and how the rest of the column retreated after that. He was wounded by Russian shelling, saying the artillery and mortars "covered constantly" before tank assaults.

---

43   Yuriy Syrotiuk's story was recorded by a Ukrainian journalist Yanina Sokolova in an online interview in March 2023 (https://www.youtube.com/watch?v=Zo4WN_8Yb2w).

44   Petro Kuzyk's story was recorded by a Ukrainian Youtube project ISLND in March 2023 (https://www.youtube.com/watch?v=F_9OCyvBIes).

"Everyone in any country would do the same and go to protect their nation," he says evenly about his decision to fight. During those intense winter hostilities, Ukrainians managed to hold Vuhledar, unlike the fate of Bakhmut.

While the Ukrainian army was suffering far fewer casualties than the Russians, at the forefront were Ukraine's best troops, a large number of whom had volunteered to fight in the initial days of the invasion. In contrast, Russia pressed into service prisoners and compulsorily mobilized soldiers from geographically remote regions who were used for "meat assaults."

One of the Ukrainian elite groups defending Bakhmut was the Da Vinci Wolves battalion, which brought together many first-rate fighters who expressly wanted to be in this particular unit. They were protecting the key supply road to Bakhmut, which lay under constant Russian bombardment, enabling the continuation of defensive operations in the town. On 7 March 2023, the first commander and founder of Da Vinci Wolves, Dmytro Kotsiubailo, fell in the Battle of Bakhmut. His grandfather had fought with the UPA (Ukrainian Insurgent Army) during the Second World War, and Dmytro joined the 2014 fight against the Russians at the age of 18. He became one of the most effective and famed representatives of the new generation of Ukrainian commanders. On that March day, having visited frontline positions on the supply road together with his deputy, they were returning to the town of Chasiv Yar when they came under enemy artillery fire. Dmytro was at a doorway when the explosion occurred. He turned, gasping with his last breaths that he was wounded, then lost consciousness. Despite swift medical evacuation efforts, Dmytro's injury to his neck proved fatal.

\*\*\*

"When you are in a war zone for a very long time, the sense of danger dulls a bit," Taras says about his feelings during the fighting in Bakhmut.

One day, at the beginning of the siege, they were returning to Bakhmut after driving a soldier and supplies to the front line east of the town. Their Volkswagen T4 had been purchased for $1,700, supplied by volunteers, and "was already crumbling, falling apart from the fighting." They were returning by the Bakhmutka River dam, close to the Russian positions. Here they saw a Ural truck, totally destroyed because its ammunition cargo had exploded, and assumed it was hit by a Russian Kornet anti-tank guided missile with a range of 4.5 kilometers. There was a hill nearby occupied by Russians within range from where they had a view over this part of the town.

Taras immediately recalled that earlier the same day, a Ukrainian Kozak armored vehicle was also struck nearby and its crew was killed. He regretted taking this route but there was already no other choice than to press down on the gas pedal and drive as fast as their old T4 could manage.

Several mortar shells hit nearby. "We realized that we were just like a sausage on a plate, waiting for a rocket to drop on us," he recalls. Nonetheless, they still managed to pass quickly into the safer town center, hiding among taller buildings.

Later, Taras's battalion commander also perished at the very same dam. Unfortunately, this time, a Russian ATGM managed to hit, and he died of his serious injuries. "That day a total of four vehicles were destroyed. We also drove through there the same day but were lucky. The Russians may have decided not to waste a rocket on an old, dilapidated T4."

On another day near Bakhmut, Taras and his unit were standing in a muddy trench, having grenades prepared in the event of a Russian infantry attack and breakthrough. Meanwhile, they were firing mortars towards Russians who were trying to approach Ukrainian positions.

His platoon prepared five firing positions in the area. They would choose one at a time to fire a few shells, then immediately take shelter or relocate before a Russian drone would detect them and pass coordinates on to mortar or artillery crews. On this occasion, Taras's fighters waited in dugouts and then relocated and worked again from another position. But this time the Russians randomly aimed their mortars at one of the five positions in the hope that soldiers would appear exactly there. They guessed right.

After Taras's unit fired, it usually had at least a minute to hide — Russians would need time to aim their mortars in response, load them and several more seconds were needed for the shell to "arrive." But this time the Russian response "arrived" seconds after Taras's unit fired. A powerful explosion of a 120-millimeter mortar projectile ripped through the air just 15 meters away from Taras. It was very close and normally would kill because the spread of debris from that kind of shell can reach up to 250 meters. But a small elevation near the trench saved them. Since the shell hit the elevation, its fragments flew right over the soldiers' heads. Nobody was even injured that day. Instead, the trunk of a heavy chestnut tree was sheared off, just a stone's throw away.

"We all inhaled, then exhaled, and ran to the shelter."

***

Having survived the deadly roulette of Bakhmut unscathed, Taras was transferred slightly northward to the Lyman sector and promoted. He now assumed the role of commander for an extended fire-support company. Instead of 30 people, he was now responsible for 130.

After Bakhmut, he still had to spend some days in the hospital to "restore himself." Many soldiers, after 20 months on the front line, eating mostly canned food, sleeping in trenches or underground cellars, and taking on heavy workloads every day, needed to undergo some form of treatment, even if not wounded. Afterwards, his new work started which would turn out to be no less difficult than Bakhmut.

The new company was reinforced by drone detachments, but he had yet to organize and coordinate the new team's work. During our conversation, he answers more than ten phone calls and voice messages. These are all coming from officers and sergeants in his company who are readying people, equipment, and ammunition for battle. He barely has time to breathe: here he needs to arrange the repair of cars; there he needs to submit someone's furlough report; and then suddenly, his priority is to appoint recently mobilized service members. Since February 2022, Taras has used only ten days of his annual 30-day furlough. "There are many wounded, there are many tasks — it's war."

The new company is composed of people from all over Ukraine and — unlike his previous battle-hardened platoon — the new soldiers arrive with varying levels of skill and motivation. Some have come from a reorganized detachment that lost combat capabilities, a so-called "battalion of deserters." These, to his surprise, became good fighters. Their battalion had been dissolved early in the war after their commander ordered attacks without proper reconnaissance. That commander was removed and soldiers appended to other units. Others in Taras's new company were stress-resistant, professional military.

Others still were newly mobilized recruits. "I have a medic, for example," he smiles. "I turn, he's already sitting. I turn again, he's already lying down. You tell him to stand, he stands. You tell him to bring something, and he brings what you asked for, but nothing more, and sits down again."

On the other hand, there are fighters who take the initiative themselves — rather than wait for orders — and they commit 150%. One of these was the deputy commander of Taras's company who works "like an enterprise." While the deputy took on all the paperwork, which is "a freight-load of bureaucracy," Taras could dedicate his time to working with soldiers and executing his main task as commander — to make everyone work together efficiently.

"A soldier at war should be a person with a broad profile," he says, drawing upon his experience as an infantryman. "They must be able to drive a car and start a chainsaw. They need to want to do the work. From typing reports in Word to hammering a post into the ground, cutting a log, digging a dugout, not to mention orientation in the area."

Besides drone operators, a platoon of mortars reinforces Taras's company. They work with American 81-caliber mortars, which are "good," according to Taras, although he wished they had 120-mm calibers, which are "better" due to their longer range and wider radius of explosion. His company also had NLAWs, Javelins and Stingers — soldier-portable, anti-tank and air defense systems — as well as heavy drone bombers capable of lifting 30 kilograms of explosives at a time and dropping them on Russians from above. "This is a remake of an agricultural drone," he says, displaying one. Bombers and inexpensive FPV kamikaze drones became a unique Ukrainian innovation, proving extremely effective against Russian armor. However, the Russians later copied and adopted these tactics as well.

"I have two flags on my body armor—Ukrainian and American," Taras says with gratitude for US military support. The current state of weaponry in his battalion and brigade is a combination of mainly Ukrainian and American weapons, as well as a few German and Italian anti-tank systems. The only issue is the lack of quantity. "And that's why people die. That's why cities are destroyed. Society might have thought that a new century had dawned on normal life, but unfortunately, we still have the killing and atrocities as we do now."

Taras says it is better to pay $3,000 for ten kamikaze drones and destroy a tank than to send an operator with NLAW that will need to trail around seeking a target, with a high risk of detection. "People are the main value. Soldiers win wars while commanders only command. It all starts with people. Only after people should technology be valued. For me, commanding a company means more responsibility. More responsibility, and then again, even more responsibility."

*** 

In September 2023, the Russian brigade that was positioned across from his units in the Lyman sector changed. Fresh Russian 25th Army reserves were deployed to replace previous brigades. "Their effectiveness had increased due to better training, better coordination and motivation," says Taras. "New forces want to prove themselves. Fighters who sit in one place for a long time experience fatigue, burnout and demotivation. When new soldiers arrive, they start thinking, 'Now we'll show them who we are!'"

Taras denies TV reports that portray Russians as an untrained, mobilized mass of so-called mobiks who are an easy target. In reality, the Russian army fights with different levels of professionalism, utilizing both "meat assaults" and trained soldiers. And while, from the Western point of human value, such a tactic may seem barbaric, it is militarily effective and sustainable in the Russian imperial system of values. Moreover, Russians are constantly working on shortcomings and refining their tactics.

The difference between various Russian units can be easily detected on a drone video showing who is moving into which positions. Taras says, "If mobilized infantry troops are approaching, they walk in groups, confused, looking around, hiding behind trees. But when the Russian paratroopers come in, it's 'Go for it!' Carrying heavy backpacks, they walk at a distance of 50 meters from one another. They stretch out. No one would shoot at them from artillery or mortar like that. They are such wolves, you know. You can identify the type of fighter simply by their manner of walking."

In the autumn of 2023, Taras was sure that the Russian potential was not yet exhausted, and a difficult fight was still ahead. At that time, the Ukrainian brigades in his sector, north of the Donetsk region, were mainly on defense, holding off a huge Russian grouping. "We fly with drones, observe, and calculate when they have a replacement at a particular point. We mark it and then strike there intensively. In the evening, our SPGs grenade launchers and mortars are already aimed. And the Russians do the same."

Holding positions in a village is slightly safer than in a field: soldiers can conceal themselves from shelling not only in trenches but in better-secured cellars as well. Still, nothing protects them during rotations when they need to shift to or from ground positions. Units closest to the front line are mostly unable to stay in one place for longer than three days, as fighters become too exhausted if they do not have proper sleep. However, during some hot battles such as Bakhmut, timely rotations were not always possible.

\*\*\*

A Ukrainian counteroffensive in the summer of 2023 achieved only moderate results, with advances in the Melitopol and Berdyansk sectors in southern Ukraine of about 10 kilometers. Russia retained control of the Azov Sea coast, Crimea, and a large part of Donetsk and Luhansk regions in the east, and was clearly mobilizing people and preparing industry for a long war. Although Ukrainian troops succeeded in repelling the first Russian attack and continued holding off the invasion, it became evident that achieving victory would require more from Ukrainians than just heroism. "Victory loves preparation. Victory happens if you teach specialists, prepare equipment, train people," Taras says.

On the bright side, the Ukrainian Army of Drones (Armiya Droniv) state program has been working rigorously providing Taras with the means to fend off Russian attacks. Ammunition has been flowing to the front, including domestically produced since 2023, although it only meets the "basic demand." "Reserve positions are being prepared, drones are being supplied, that's for sure," Taras says, refuting the excessive criticism circulating at the time. "But questions should be asked in a slightly different way. In a psycho-emotional manner, about the unity of people. We need this emphasis — unity between the military and the civilians who are far from the war. Here, we have the impression that a section of society says, 'You fight the war there, and we just do business here.' We all studied history. The economy shifts in wartime. Economic priorities are redirected to the military." At the beginning of 2024, the state finances were unable to cover entirely existing weapons production capacities in the country — only 35% of the necessary sum was available in the budget.

"My mood often depends on who I talk with," says Taras. One day, they are volunteers who have just delivered a car or other aid for his unit, but another day, he sees online that some men from his village have quit jobs to avoid being drafted or reads that someone tried to illegally cross the Tysa River flowing along the border of Ukraine and Romania to avoid mobilization.

"Participation in the war, despite all difficulties, will turn many people into military professionals with a whole new set of skills. And those skills will stay with them — to their benefit. When people are forced to live under constant stress, they begin to realize that there is nothing to be afraid of. This can lead to personal growth precisely because of the harsh demands of war. Their

leadership and management capabilities will have been highly am-
plified." Even if tomorrow the Ukrainian army liberates all the
Ukrainian lands that Russia has occupied and the war ends, another one may lie in the future. Therefore, "the army and its read-
iness will always remain the main security guarantee."

In 2024, in the 10th year of the war he had been fighting since
the beginning, Taras was promoted to Chief of Staff of the fire support battalion. The battles of the Russia-Ukraine war had become
increasingly reliant on drones. The latest tactics involved sending
flying or ground-based drones into Russia's rear and deploying
mines there — an unexpected strategy for the Russians. Shortly before his appointment as Battalion Chief of Staff, Taras went home
for a few days. He spent a week in the hospital recuperating after
his health had deteriorated during the battles. However, he managed to spend a couple of days with his family and by his village's
lake, "where it's very beautiful and peaceful," before returning to
the front. When someone messages him, "How are you?" he usually responds with, "It's tough. We hold the line."

# Cherries by the House

A cherry orchard by the house,
Above, the cherries' beetles hum,
The plowmen plow the fertile ground,
And girls sing songs as they pass by,
It's evening — mother calls them home.

A family sups by the house,
A star shines in the evening chill,
A daughter serves the evening meal,
Time to give lessons — mother tries,
But can't. She blames the nightingale.

It's getting dark, and by the house,
A mother lays her young to sleep,
Beside them she too fell asleep,
All now went still, and just the girls,
And nightingale their vigil keep.

Taras Shevchenko, 1847
Translated by Boris Dralyuk and Roman Koropeckyj

This famous poem by Ukrainian 19th-century writer Taras Shevchenko is often associated with the Ukrainian idyll — a house nestled in a blooming garden, the serenity of a common family supper, and the peacefulness of the surrounding village life. Even in modern, highly urbanized times, many Ukrainians, while living in cities, still have their own cottage with little gardens, or visit parents' and grandparents' homes in villages. Despite food being very inexpensive, many still grow fresh food themselves — even if in only small quantities — as a hobby or custom. If they do not do so themselves, they usually have parents or grandparents who do.

From behind the garden fences of Bucha's quiet streets, away from the local high-rises, peek apple, plum, and cherry trees. Many of them have branches that are broken or cracked due to shelling, but new leaves swiftly conceal the damage. With a pre-war population of 30,000, this quiet, cozy suburb of Kyiv nestled gently among pine and oak forests—until it was invaded by Russians. Bucha became known worldwide as the site of the Bucha massacre—the murder of civilians, widespread torture, and mass graves. Anticipating their possible defeat near Kyiv, Russian soldiers committed hundreds of war crimes, especially in the last two weeks of occupation. Immediately after the town's liberation, over 400 civilian bodies were discovered, many simply lying on the streets, in basements and backyards, shot, with their hands tied behind their backs. Many of them bore signs of torture. Rape took place too. One dead woman was found in the cellar of a house where Russian soldiers had stayed. Her body was found naked, wearing only fur.[45] Another case, reported by the Ukrainian prosecutor general's office, details how a Russian soldier, after breaking into a house near Kyiv, shot the man and then repeatedly raped his wife, while threatening her and their young son with a weapon.[46]

The names of 501 victims of the Bucha massacre have been identified and commemorated on a memorial created in Bucha a year after the tragedy.

Living at the site of atrocities is painful and difficult, yet the majority of residents have returned to their homes after Ukrainian forces expelled Russian invaders.

***

On one of the first days after Russian forces entered Bucha, 61-year-old Nina stood in her yard and counted the tanks passing by in a column. She tallied them as they rolled through, "One, two ... five ... twelve ..." She counted a total of 18 Russian tanks and armored vehicles rumbling down the street past her house. The situation in her hometown was rapidly worsening—fortunately, she

45  This testimony was published by The New York Times on 11 April 2022, along with the description of other Russian atrocities in Bucha (https://www.nytimes.com/interactive/2022/04/11/world/europe/bucha-terror.html).

46  Catherine Philp recorded this testimony for The Times (https://www.thetimes.com/uk/politics/article/one-soldier-raped-me-then-the-other-as-my-son-cried-7xbqwzdqw).

and her family managed to escape amid the fighting before the Russian soldiers cemented their control over the town and forbade departure, making it nearly impossible to get out alive.

They relocated to the west of Ukraine and only there learned about Russian atrocities in Bucha. Nina assumed the Russians were living in their home and looting it. She was hoping they would not steal her cross pendant that had huge symbolic and spiritual meaning for her.

A month after the Russian retreat, Nina's family returned home, not knowing if their house was still standing. Together with them were many other Buchans, even though Ukrainian authorities had warned that the post-occupation areas were still unsafe and were contaminated by mines and explosive devices.

Standing in front of her home, Nina saw that her neighbor's house, just three away from her own, was completely destroyed. They were lucky to find theirs still standing. "We saw blood on the floor and a broken window," says Nina. "The Russians probably tried to climb into the house and gashed their hands on the broken glass. They broke down two doors, including the one to the shed, and took a camera, a speaker, and some minor things. In our house, not very much." "But looting took place all over the town," adds Nina's son, 37-year-old Vitaliy. Some local people told us that they threw away all the furniture that was left to remove traces of the Russians.

Nina's gate and fence were badly damaged. Overall, over 1,000 houses were damaged and more than 200 were destroyed in Bucha. "Where a Russian missile might have missed your house, it hit your neighbor's, reducing it to ruins," Nina's son, 37-year-old Vitaliy says.

\*\*\*

In 1989, 36-year-old Oleksandr, together with wife and two daughters, had to flee the Fergana massacre in Uzbekistan, leaving behind the flat he owned and the job he loved. "Most of all, I was afraid for my daughters who were 12 and four-and-a-half," Oleksandr tells us. He had moved to Bucha, built a new house here and planted cherry and apple trees in the yard. For years, the family lived in tranquility

On 28 February, four days after the invasion, the Russian army pummeled one of the rooms of his house with machine guns — they set the sofa and curtains on fire but the house survived. However, within a matter of days, on 5 March, as the family hid in the basement, a Russian infantry fighting vehicle fired at the house again. Emerging, they tried to extinguish the raging fire but failed. This time the house could not be saved. The only thing left were bare brick walls covered in black soot.

Moving to the garage basement, they started planning an escape, but Oleksandr refused to leave his home although it stood in ruins. The family tried to convince him to go, but he was adamant. A few days later, his wife, disabled daughter and grandson were lucky enough to escape with the last convoy of evacuation buses. The Russians allowed a few such evacuations from Bucha and nearby occupied settlements after arduous negotiations, but not all of the evacuations succeeded — often blocked at the last minute by the occupiers.

Having stayed behind, Oleksandr was not able to venture past his yard because it was becoming more and more dangerous — the Russian military banned any movement, killing anyone spotted on the streets. Just past Oleksandr's fence, a dead man lay — he had been killed by Russian soldiers on 1 March. He lay there throughout the entire occupation.

In the basement, Oleksandr ate garden vegetables stored from the last season and canned food. He was fortunate to be able to cook on an old stove in the garage. Most of all he missed the taste of bread and butter.

On 31 March, the thunder of intense fighting raged around him. Oleksandr lay hidden in the basement, having resigned himself to meeting his end. After a while it was silent, and the next day he learned that Ukrainian forces had pushed back the Russian troops.

Breathing the air of freedom, Oleksandr left the basement and took to repairing the still-standing annex where the storage rooms were located. He was busy turning them into a comfortable space in the hope that his family, staying in the town of Truskavets in western Ukraine, would return home.

\*\*\*

17-year-old Vladyslava lives on Yablunska Street in Bucha — the place of the famous photograph in which dozens of Russian tanks and military vehicles destroyed by Ukrainian forces stand deserted among family homes. This shot was a testimony to the first Ukrainian successes at the beginning of the invasion. Later, however, this street and many more like it were captured by the Russians.

For three weeks, Vladyslava and her family sought refuge in their cellar. In the first days of the invasion, Russian soldiers entered their cellar and confiscated their mobiles, but returned their sim cards, in an attempt to appear "good" while at the same time they were looting Vladyslava's house above. Vladyslava's family managed to leave Bucha before the worst of the atrocities began, during the last two weeks of March.

"We left through the last evacuation corridor and saw a lot of corpses and shot-up cars," Vladyslava says. Her house, already looted by the Russian soldiers, was completely pillaged after they left. Still, in early May when the family was finally able to return to Bucha, Vladyslava was happy to learn that most of her friends had returned as well.

\*\*\*

While walking in Bucha, it is easy to find yourself in Irpin without even realizing it — the two towns blend seamlessly together.

Nataliya, the owner of a small bakery in Irpin, told us that during the occupation of this part of the town, Russian soldiers stole a large bin by the cafe which the owner says was creatively decorated. The Russians did not go inside — Nataliya's acquaintance covered the windows with boards after they were shattered by explosions.

The cafe reopened as quickly as one month after the Russians were forced out. "We'll renew everything step by step," Nataliya says. "Many people I know who had fled the 2014 war in Donbas were forced to flee again … A lot of terrible things happened."

***

The home of 50-year-old Tamara is among more than 100 houses in Irpin that were completely destroyed in the 2022 Russian invasion. During a Russian shelling, Tamara's house took a direct hit while the neighboring houses survived. The ceiling, roof, and furniture were all burned and only remnants of the walls were left standing. "The kitchen was here. And over there the living room," she says, leading us through the rubble that still has a strong acrid smell. She remembers well how her house burnt furiously after it had been hit. She called the emergency services, but they were no longer in Irpin. Neighbors tried to extinguish the fire from the side of the house, but all in vain. "I constantly return to the thought that I have nothing," Tamara says, her gaze sad and introspective.

Together with her son, Tamara takes care of her elderly mother and her husband, who recently had a stroke. A few weeks after the house burned down and the Russian forces retreated, the local authorities offered her family transit to special modular housing for people whose homes had been destroyed by shelling, but she declined. Throughout the spring and summer of 2022, the family lived in their garage which, unlike their house, had survived the Russian bombardment. "The local authorities offered—I'm not saying that they didn't—to put us up in a temporary shelter," she says. "But that doesn't work for us. I have two older people to take care of and there is only one common toilet there. Here, this is our own garage, you know? Our dog Masha is much calmer here. After all, this is our own plot of land—to be in your own place is completely different."

At first, they had to ask for help from neighbors and cooked on an old grill. "But we can't go to our neighbors all the time. We had to get out of this situation," she says. They bought an electric stove and put four old beds in the garage.

"We managed to save our homemade food in jars. Some food I could buy in the store. Some things, like today's lunch, were given by volunteers. They also gave us clothes."

While Tamara is talking to us, a local volunteer Andriy from Irpin Bible Church asks her, "Did you get food kits?"

"No, we only have coupons for lunches."

"Then come to our church. I'll bring you food sets, or you can come and take them yourselves."

"You say this, and I am so ashamed that I can't even express it. You see, I'm not used to it. I'm used to solving problems myself.

# The Song That Will Last

Taras Kompanichenko was born in 1969, spent his childhood in Kyiv and, at the time of massive Russification of language and education in the 1970s, studied at one of the few Ukrainian-language Kyiv schools, School №200.

"Are you in favor of an independent Ukraine?" Taras once asked his father when he was a child.

"Be quiet. We are. But we can't talk about it."

His parents were not the first generation of his family to oppose Russian expansionism, which forbade Ukrainian culture and language, let alone statehood. Russians deported his mother's family from the village of Derkachivka, in present-day Sumy region, to Russia, and only later was she able to return to Ukraine.

In the early 1970s, with the end of the the Khrushchev Thaw, the Soviet Union carried out a severe policy of repression against the "Sixtiers" — Ukrainian intellectuals who opposed Soviet control. Among the most prominent were friends of Taras's parents: writer and essayist Yevhen Sverstiuk, who was imprisoned in a Gulag labor camp; and painter Alla Horska, who was killed. Taras's parents were lucky to be "only" threatened, possibly because they were technical specialists in physics and chemistry, rather than artists. The latter were considered more dangerous by the Soviet authorities, since their work could be symbolic and could reach a wider audience.

His parents made every effort for Taras to grow up in a Ukrainian environment. One of their gifts, a traditional Ukrainian string instrument called the bandura, proved to be pivotal along his life path. He has since developed into a professional musician, embodying a modern interpretation of the ancestral bard role.

*\*\*\**

Only later did Taras fully understand the horror of repression his parents' friends faced at the time of his childhood.

252 DARK DAYS, DETERMINED PEOPLE

He witnessed the collapse of the Soviet Union in 1991 and the subsequent flourishing of the arts, when he was in his twenties. He then began studying, reconstructing and performing (mostly forgotten) Ukrainian music from the late Medieval, Cossack Baroque (also known as the Ukrainian Baroque), and Romantic eras, as well as later compositions from the era of the Ukrainian Republic, during its war with the Russian Imperial and Bolshevik armies (1917–1921).

A significant part of Taras's repertoire hails from the times of the Cossack state. Even though the Russian Empire destroyed it completely in 1768, the musical tradition was largely continued by kobzars — bards who traveled from village to village reciting historical tales and ancient lore, especially those of the glory of the Cossack state. Despite Soviet repression, when the kobzar repertoire was strictly censored, the tradition has survived to this day, both in Ukraine and within the Ukrainian diaspora. In his youth, Taras learned his skills from renowned masters.

"I taught all the kobzars to sing 'Hey Ukrainians, Our Holy Deed Is Still Alive,'" an esteemed kobzar Ihor Rachok once told Taras with pride.

"Who are these 'all?'" Taras had asked.

Ihor replied, "Well, you, Kompanichenko, and Taras Sylenko.[47] Mainly, you two."

***

The advent of freedom of speech after Ukrainian independence in 1991 allowed Taras to study sources that had been banned by Moscow. When he began his research, the songs and names he discovered were mostly unknown, and preserved only in archives. The Russian and Soviet authorities managed to consign a large part of Ukrainian music and literature to oblivion by banning, exiling, or executing artists who were in any way contrary to official ideology. In the opinion of Russian imperial censors and, later, the Communist Party, all artists had to assimilate Ukrainian culture and

---

47   Kyivan bandurist, 1972–2021.

collective memory into a "Greater Russia," and later into an "all-Soviet" narrative.

Taras spent years researching archives and libraries in Ukraine, Poland, the US, Canada, and other countries. Fortunately much music was mainly preserved in various old publications: Ukrainian newspapers, collections of ethnographers, and antiquarian church documents.

He discovered old-world Christmas carols, but the melodies were not always preserved. "That's why I sang them to melodies I had recorded from Ukrainian elders. Sometimes, I composed my own melodies for carol lyrics published in the 19th century by historians and intellectuals, like Volodymyr Antonovych, Mykhailo Drahomanov, and Yakiv Holovatskyi." He then focused on Ukrainian Renaissance and Baroque poetry and recorded audio versions of 16th to 18th-century authors Demyan Nalyvaiko, Danylo Bratkovskyi, Ivan Velychkovskyi, Theofan Prokopovych, Hryhoriy Skovoroda, Tarasiy Zemka, and Herasym Smotrytskyi.[48]

Taras set to music poems by classical Ukrainian writers, such as Panteleymon Kulish, Lesia Ukrayinka, Oleksandr Oles, Vasyl Stus, as well as the lesser-known Yakiv Shchoholiv, Liudmyla Starytska-Cherniahivska, and Vasyl Vyshyvany. Vyshyvany was the Archduke Wilhelm Franz of Austria who decided to fight alongside Ukrainians. He became a colonel of the Ukrainian Sich Riflemen.[49] The riflemen originated from the Ukrainian units of the Austro-Hungarian army and later became part of the Ukrainian regular army during the short period of Ukrainian independence from 1917 to 1919. Taras composed melodies to some Ukrainian language poems by Vyshyvany. "My colleagues have commented

---

48  Some of these songs can be listened in Taras Kompanichenko's YouTube channel (https://www.youtube.com/@choreakozacky) and in the YouTube playlists.

49  The famous song "Oh, the Red Viburnum in the Meadow" ("Oy u luzi chervona kalyna"), written by Stepan Charnetskyi in 1914, was dedicated to the Sich Riflemen. Based on the original version of the 17th-century Cossack melody, it was officially published in 1875, by Ukrainian historians Volodymyr Antonovych and Mykhailo Drahomanov. Since 2022, this song has come to be known internationally, when it was performed by Ukrainian singer Andriy Khlyvniuk, who later became a soldier.

that these verses have become of interest to students at last, because they are no longer just dead poetry."

Taras believes that historical songs and poems should not just atrophy in archival records, but be performed both traditionally and through contemporary interpretations. For that purpose, in 2005 he created his band Khoreya Kozatska, where eight musicians play various ancient Ukrainian instruments, including: basolia, similar to a cello; hurdy-gurdy, fiddle-like and hand-cranked; sopilka, flute-like woodwind; several percussion instruments; and more. The band's repertoire is broad, covering works from Ukrainian medieval poets to Vasyl Stus, who tragically died in 1985 while incarcerated by the Soviets.

To find new cantos for his repertoire, Taras dreamed of getting Bohohlasnyk of the Vasiliyan Fathers, a liturgical anthology containing 248 Ukrainian religious songs with musical notation, published in various editions during the late 18th and 19th centuries. "I could only dream of having this collection. Then one day, a music book was lying in a far corner of the Skovoroda Museum in Pereyaslav, and it was the Bohohlasnyk. The museum director loaned it to me for a year, and my wife wrote her bachelor's thesis on this particular copy."

Several times, people simply gifted old manuscripts to Taras. They would get in contact and ask him if he already had a certain publication.

"No, I don't."

"Well, you do now."

Another family gifted him an Irmologion of the late 17th to the early 18th centuries from their private collection—a valuable liturgical book of religious chants including musical notes. In 2021, Taras visited the frontline town of Shchastia to support the 79th Brigade with his songs, and during this visit, Father Serhiy Tsioma gifted him a collection of church hymns printed in Lviv in 1700. On other occasions he bought valuable antique books in antiquarian shops, or researched musical libraries and archives, like the Koshyts Library in Winnipeg, Canada.

\*\*\*

A few years before the full-scale war, Taras joined a project led by the Ukrainian Institute of National Memory to discover and record lost songs from the Ukrainian Republic of 1917–1921. Starting his work at the Ukrainian National Library of Chicago, he found numerous compositions, primarily military marching songs, by Ukrainian composers such as Yaroslav Yaroslavenko, Kyrylo Stetsenko, Yosyp Kyshakevych and Vasyl Barvinskyi. He thought it was already a great discovery, but when he later researched undigitized materials in the Ukrainian Library of Vernandskyi in Kyiv, he discovered a number of newspapers from the era of the Ukrainian Republic that had printed a huge number of songs previously unknown. "We sat in the library for three months, without interruption, scanning page after page."

It was extremely valuable to find the original publications of these songs because the Soviets later intentionally altered their lyrics. They incorporated Soviet ideology into many Ukrainian songs which had become too popular, and therefore impossible to ban. New versions of these songs were published and distributed, while original versions were forbidden. "When the choir opens notation and begins to sing, it sings the Soviet-approved texts."

One example of such falsification is from the lyrics of Spyrydon Cherkasenko, written towards the end of the Russian Empire and the abdication of Tsar Nicholas II: "Ukraine-mother, the executioner has perished" ("Vkrayino-maty, kat skonav"). Cherkasenko, from the contemporary Mykolayiv region, was one of the leading young poets of 1917–1921.

The Soviets made several changes to this song. For instance:

> Ukraine, Mother, your gem of tears and blood will shine,
> It will glow in the diadem of *universal love*. [Ukrainian original]
> It will glow in the diadem of *the friendship of peoples*. [Soviet altered][50]

---

50  Vkrayino-maty, blysne vin, tviy samotsvit iz sliz i krovy,
    zasiaye vin v vintsi vseliuds'koyi liubovy. [Ukrainian original]
    zasiaye vin v vintsi druzhby narodiv. [Soviet altered]

"These changes are seemingly simple, seemingly minor, but they completely pervert the content and make the song some kind of collective farm anthem," says Taras.

"The Ukrainian movement for universal love and for their own national state was falsified and lied about by Bolsheviks ... When a lie is told—especially when it's a big lie—it becomes hard to turn it around. It is as if a man publicly says, 'your daughter is a whore.' 'I don't have a daughter,' you answer, but this already doesn't matter. A lie has been said, and people have heard it, regardless of what you say or do later."

Taras researched dozens of newspapers extensively because "they showed what people fought for at the time, what were their ideas. And it turns out their ideas, songs, and poems are relevant in 2022 more than ever. As if these people just returned from 100 years ago and continued their fight with the new support and new power Ukraine has today, but didn't have then."[51]

***

Taras highlights the verse "My friend the foe" ("Druzhe miy vorozhe") from Hrytsko Chuprynka, illustrating the Ukrainian poet and military commander's principles for conducting battle honorably.

> My friend the foe, to stand in battle
> We are all compelled by the call of honor.
> Let us honestly and openly
> Carry our flags.
> We shall employ the pure means,
> So that bystanders may respect us.
> Proud and brave,
> in every place, all are immaculate.[52]

---

51   In these newspapers, Taras discovered many missing verses by Ukrainian poets. For example: Hrytsko Chuprynka had many of his works published in the Narodna Volia newspaper; Stepan Ivanchenko, a colonel of the Ukrainian Republic Army, was published in the Respublikanka newspaper; and the first poems of Volodymyr Sosiura, who was then a fighter of the 3rd Haydamatskyi Kurin (battalion), were published in the Ukrainian Kozak newspaper—all their verses were prohibited and forgotten during 70 years of Soviet censorship.

52   Druzhe miy vorozhe, staty do boyiu vsikh nas prymushuyiut' poklyky chesty.

"This is an appeal, if you are already waging a war, then use fair means," says Taras. "We still can understand the soldiers who fight against us. They have their own way of thinking, which does not correspond with ours. We defend our truth, and still use fair means. But they don't use fair means because such a notion never existed in Russian culture. Nobody wrote such a poem, nobody called for such a thing. Moscow culture failed."

Chuprynka was arrested for the first time in Irpin when Bolshevik occupiers conducted repression and numerous executions during their first occupation of Kyiv. Chuprynka managed to escape from guards, led an anti-Bolshevik uprising in occupation and later took part in the liberation of Kyiv in 1920 by the Ukrainian Republic's forces, this time allied with the Poles. However, after the Bolsheviks occupied Kyiv again they arrested and shot Chuprynka in 1921.

At the time of Chuprynka, Ukraine did not have a strong enough army to win, and lacked military support and recognition from other European states. Ukraine lost the 1917–1921 war, but at least, Taras says, Ukrainians remained humane.

***

In 2021, Taras expected a new big war. He discussed its potential with friends and some relatives, but no one believed it could happen. Taras was not in a doomsday mood either, despite many military analysts predicting that the Russians would overrun Ukraine in a week.

During the first night of the invasion, Taras, like most Ukrainians, did not sleep. The outcome of the first battles was not yet clear, but Taras wrote the first verse of "Chivalric brotherhood" ("Brattia lytsarstvo") that later became his first new wartime song.

---

Budemo zh chesno y odverto, my z toboyiu prapory nesty.
Budem vzhyvaty my zasoby chysti, Shchob povazhaly nas liude pobochni.
Hordi y odvazhni, na kozhnomu mistsi vsi neporochni.

"It was time to put all political squabbles aside. 'Get rid of our house quarrel,' Ivan Styshenko, Ukraine's 1918 Minister of Education, who was subsequently killed by Bolsheviks, once said."

Taras was offered refuge in Germany, Poland, or the Ukrainian Carpathian mountains in the west of the country, but deemed it "unethical" to flee after "calling to fight for Ukraine in songs and fighting for Ukraine through culture." During the early days of the war, Taras's friend, a Ukrainian writer and publisher, phoned him:

"Taras, do you realize that if you die, your entire unique world will go with you, and all your knowledge will pass away? There is nobody who can replace you. It would be a catastrophe for Ukrainian culture."

"And for whom will this entire culture be, if we don't save Ukraine?"

"Go to the Carpathians. Anyway, your main weapon is the bandura."

"Excuse me, but no," Taras said. Yet, he questioned his own mind, thinking, "Maybe he's right."

"I'm crying now," his friend confessed. "I feel very uncomfortable and like a coward."

"Stop, nobody is a coward. I'm also afraid," Taras replied.

Taras says that if the war had happened in 2003, when he was younger and his children were still small, he might have hesitated more. But in 2022, his two sons and two daughters were already adults themselves. On the third day of the war, when Kyiv was bombarded by Russian missiles, Taras was with his family, collecting precious artifacts: valuable paintings, sculptures, banduras and other musical instruments, and their entire library to transport to the west of Ukraine. They loaded everything and sat down for a few minutes in their house in a suburb of Kyiv, Boyarka, before departing, when Taras said,

"You know, I'm not going."

"We too. We've had enough of running—our forefathers fled and were killed," one of his sons said. Being 21- and 23-years-old, the young men were not yet formally subject to mobilization.

They exchanged hugs and decided that the father and two sons would stay to defend their country, while his daughters would evacuate the precious collection.

***

Taras called his acquaintance Andriy Kovaliov, a cultural researcher who served as a spokesperson with the Kyiv Territorial Defense Force.

"Your weapon is a bandura," he responded to Taras's request to join the ranks. Other territorial defense friends made another analogy, saying that if Taras were to fight, it would be like "driving nails by iPhone" or "driving nails with a microscope."

"I just didn't want to be shot on my knees," Taras tells us. "I wanted to die with dignity, with a weapon in my hands, protecting my family and our world. Or to survive and win, not allowing our world to be destroyed."

Finally, on 28 February, Andriy agreed to enlist him.

"You have 15 minutes to collect your things," Andriy said.

The same day Taras joined the territorial defense, he gave an impromptu concert for soldiers who were in the city on rotation. "At first, they refused to give me a weapon, insisting that my weapon was a bandura. However, a gun was finally issued a few days later."

During these same early days, his aunt, uncle, and two sisters found themselves under Russian occupation in Kherson, 500 kilometers to the south, close to the Black Sea, watching Russian troops take over the city. Taras had wanted to send them west in the first days of the war, but they refused to leave their home.

Meanwhile, his 80-year-old mother was in Sumy, 250 kilometers to the east, also under constant Russian bombing. She was upset that she could not plant a vegetable garden as she usually did in spring. His brother, a police officer also in Sumy, joined the Territorial Defense Forces and fought in the Battle of Sumy. Initially, they faced a shortage of weapons and body armor, but the territorial defense and the regular army successfully held the city.

"Eros and Thanatos—Love and Fear—battle within everyone. Everybody feels fear sometimes, but what wins in this internal fight finally defines everything," Taras says, reflecting on the start of the war and referencing one of his own songs. "Kyivans were willing to eat anything, sleep anywhere, just to repel the invasion. Everything worked like a hive."

***

Many Kyivans who joined the territorial defense decided to marry during the war. Taras remembers them feeling that "all matters should be resolved now." Some had lived together for years before taking their vows, seeking to "close this gestalt and be in love before God." Others, who only recently met, chose to marry.

"On the one hand, these were risky decisions because you never know what will happen the next day. However, it was a life affirmation that inspired hope and faith, assuring us that there would be a tomorrow, that there would be children. Young, beautiful men and women were getting married, and it was just impossible that this would not go on. Although we are at war here, life wins over death."

Couples wore helmets instead of wedding wreaths during these simplified wedding ceremonies—green veils could be made from military camouflage nets. People would sometimes greet the couples with roses. Taras and guests performed numerous variations of the Ukrainian traditional song of congratulations on these occasions, "Many Years" (Mnohaya Lita), as well as church chants and other songs.

Military oaths were sworn by new recruits right near the front line, mostly in small groups or individually. One day in Novi Petrivtsi, north of Kyiv, the military oath lasted four hours because soldiers were taking them one by one, not altogether as usual. Taras and a few other musicians sang 20th-century and earlier Ukrainian military anthems during these oaths.[53] One day, the

---

53   In particular, they sang the anthems of UPA (Ukrainian Insurgent Army) that fought for Ukraine's independence at the time of WWII: "We Were Born at the

112th Brigade invited Taras to sing at the consecration of an icon of the patron of Kyiv Archangel Michael, commemorating the 1658 battle of Ukrainian Hetman Ivan Vyhovskyi against the Moscovites.

Sometimes, while sitting in underground shelters waiting for an air raid alert to pass, Taras would sing with the soldiers. Along with the familiar songs, soldiers learned many new Ukrainian songs they had not known even existed. Taras also presented his new songs. "It will be forever unforgettable when the counter-subversive brigade joins me in singing 'Azovstal.'" The song was written to support Ukrainian soldiers surrounded at the Azovstal steel plant during the siege of Mariupol. The Russians bombarded and stormed the site from March to May.

The refrain in another of his songs, "The spirit is stronger than cannons" ("Dukh harmat mitsnishyi"), written at the end of February 2022, describes the types of indispensable weapons for the Battle of Kyiv. "I tried my best to add NLAWs and Stingers in the song, as well as Ukrainian Stuhnas and Vilhas. Still, many weapons could not be included in the song," Taras says. "However, its main lyric—'The spirit is stronger than cannons'—was borrowed from an old motto about the 18th-century Cossack state, written by Ivan Kotliarevskyi, a Ukrainian writer who was the first to publish a book in the modern Ukrainian language, *Eneida*, in 1798:

> Where love for the motherland leads heroes,
> There, the enemy's power shall not stand,
> There, the spirit is stronger than cannons.[54]

Since 2014, Taras has composed numerous songs about the modern Ukrainian army, and from 2022 he has written even more.

---

Great Hour" ("Zrodylys my velykoyi hodyny"), "For Ukraine with the fire of ardor" ("Za Ukrayinu z vohnem zavziattia"), "Ukraine, beloved mother, we swear to you", ("O Ukrayino, liuba nen'ko, tobi ridnen'ka prysiahnem"). They also sang "Flag" ("Stiah"), by writer Borys Hrinchenko, as well as the march, "The ruin, covered with black clouds" ("Chornymy khmaramy vkryta ruyina"), written by Ivan Bahrianyi.

54  Liubov k otchyzni de heroyit'
Tam syla vrazha ne ustoyit',
Tam dukh mitsnishyi vid harmat.

In line with older kobzar tradition, these songs describe specific events and battles near Kyiv, in Irpin, Hostomel, and Bucha, as well as Okhtyrka in the Sumy region.

***

"We often say about our Ukrainian art that we need to finally 'stop crying' and create something optimistic. But in fact, tragedy is the highest form of art," said Taras, during his speech at the opening of the exhibition, "Invasion. Kyiv Shot," on 30 May 2022. "We remember Shakespeare's tragedies, but few remember his comedies. We have so many tragedies in our history that still have to be skillfully displayed in art."

After the exhibition, Taras and eight more people, mostly Kyiv artists, and the Deputy Mayor of Bucha Mykhailyna Skoryk-Shkarivska, went to the flat of Kyiv sculptor Bohdan Holoyad, which doubles as his workshop. The meeting quickly turned into yet another impromptu celebration of the recent victory in the Battle of Kyiv, featuring an informal concert by Taras.

Bohdan was a fan of the Renaissance and created his sculptures in a slightly more modern but still realistic, naturalistic, and emotionally expressive manner. A flat in the Kyiv city center hosts over 100 of his works, large and small, at various stages of completion. The largest sculpture, featuring three women representing the three virtues—faith, hope, and selfless love—was designed as part of the headstone for Holoyad's mother, Marta Hai, who served in the Ukrainian Insurgent Army during the Second World War.

"War is the continuation of politics, and politics is the continuation of culture," said Hryhoriy Lukyanenko, one of the artists present. He is a guitarist and composer for several Ukrainian folk-rock bands, including the band Ruthenia from the nineties, which was one of the first after the fall of the USSR to play Ukrainian military and other previously forbidden songs. "Even during times of war, it is critical to foster culture. Because we are primarily fighting for our culture," says Hryhoriy, recalling how several Ukrainian soldiers told him in 2014 and 2015, "If I hadn't listened to Ruthenia, I wouldn't have decided to fight." During the conversation,

Hryhoriy praises Taras for, "unlike many artists, finding strength early in the war to compose new songs," despite destruction and chaos.

\*\*\*

"The Russians came to destroy our very name, our culture — everything we have created — so that there is no emanation of the Ukrainian spirit. Thus, it really is genocide," Taras says, commenting on Russian atrocities and its deliberate policy to destroy Ukrainian books, eliminate the Ukrainian language and history at schools, and change public titling, signage and geographical names to Russian spelling in occupied areas.

He says Ukraine lost the 1917–1921 war because it was unprepared for the Bolsheviks' ruthlessness. However, in 2022, Ukraine was better prepared for the war while the truth about Russia's past atrocities turned against them.

"In 1917–1921, Ukrainian politicians and soldiers wanted to abide by the integrity of the Medieval Knights, by using fair and just means to display respect. And although they lost then — in the long run — the truth prevails."

# Acknowledgments

First and foremost, we thank Alya Shandra, enthusiastic founder and editor-in-chief of the independent English-language publication, Euromaidan Press, founded in 2014 in Kyiv, for her assistance in our work and the opportunity to record these stories. We extend our gratitude to all the members of the publication team who were willing to take on a significant part of the crucial tasks, enabling us to work on this book.

We are grateful to Sonia Maryn for committing an extensive amount of time to editing all the stories in this book, for her thoroughness, depth, keen interest, and feedback, which helped enhance the literary quality of these texts. Many thank you to Michael Garrood for proofreading and editing the stories in this book despite simultaneously having many other commitments, as well as for his valuable remarks and humor. We are grateful to Philip Melnychuk for proofreading and being the first reader of some of these stories, for his extraordinary attention to detail and support. We thank Andreas Umland, the editor of the Ukrainian Voices series, who immediately believed in the idea of this book as well as for many bright books he collected in the series. We appreciate the Ibidem Press team's efforts to bring the stories of this book to people worldwide. We also thank the cover designer of this book, Sofiia Afanasieva, who grasped our initial idea and transformed a crude version into a meaningful and beautiful cover.

We are immensely grateful to our family for their support and for spending time with our baby Severyn during some especially busy days of preparing this book. And to Severyn, for cheering us up every day.

It is a great honor for us that the preface to this book was written by a person who fought for Ukraine's independence and human dignity despite Soviet repressions and imprisonment in the Gulag, and who never gave up. For us, Myroslav Marynovych is a model of determination, sharpness of thought, humanity, and kindness.

This book would not have been possible without the heroes of these stories, who kindly agreed to share them in detail. We are grateful for their openness, trust, and time: many of these people dedicated an entire day to our conversations and visits to the sites of events, despite having many other important duties.

We greatly appreciate the interest in Ukraine from people all over the world, compassion for the challenges Ukraine faces, and support in its struggle for freedom. We are especially grateful to the patrons of Euromaidan Press, whose support means that we and our colleagues can continue telling the world about Ukraine.

These stories would never have been told or heard, and we would never have had the opportunity to write them, if not for the courage and efforts of Ukrainian soldiers who continue to hold the front line in the east at the cost of their health and lives, protecting the future of our country and its people.

# UKRAINIAN VOICES

Collected by Andreas Umland

11  *Oleksii Sinchenko, Dmytro Stus, Leonid Finberg (compilers)*
Ukrainian Dissidents
An Anthology of Texts
ISBN 978-3-8382-1551-8

12  *John-Paul Himka*
Ukrainian Nationalists and the Holocaust
OUN and UPA's Participation in the Destruction of Ukrainian Jewry, 1941–1944
ISBN 978-3-8382-1548-8

13  *Andrey Demartino*
False Mirrors
The Weaponization of Social Media in Russia's Operation to Annex Crimea
With a foreword by Oleksiy Danilov
ISBN 978-3-8382-1533-4

14  *Svitlana Biedarieva (ed.)*
Contemporary Ukrainian and Baltic Art
Political and Social Perspectives, 1991–2021
ISBN 978-3-8382-1526-6

15  *Olesya Khromeychuk*
A Loss
The Story of a Dead Soldier Told by His Sister
With a foreword by Andrey Kurkov
ISBN 978-3-8382-1570-9

16  *Marieluise Beck (Hg.)*
Ukraine verstehen
Auf den Spuren von Terror und Gewalt
Mit einem Vorwort von Dmytro Kuleba
ISBN 978-3-8382-1653-9

17  *Stanislav Aseyev*
Heller Weg
Geschichte eines Konzentrationslagers im Donbass 2017–2019
Aus dem Russischen übersetzt von Martina Steis und Charis Haska
ISBN 978-3-8382-1620-1

18  *Mykola Davydiuk*
Wie funktioniert Putins Propaganda?
Anmerkungen zum Informationskrieg des Kremls
Aus dem Ukrainischen übersetzt von Christian Weise
ISBN 978-3-8382-1628-7

19  *Olesya Yaremchuk*
Unsere Anderen
Geschichten ukrainischer Vielfalt
Aus dem Ukrainischen übersetzt von Christian Weise
ISBN 978-3-8382-1635-5

20  *Oleksandr Mykhed*
„Dein Blut wird die Kohle tränken"
Über die Ostukraine
Aus dem Ukrainischen übersetzt von Simon Muschick und Dario Planert
ISBN 978-3-8382-1648-5

21  *Vakhtang Kipiani (Hg.)*
Der Zweite Weltkrieg in der Ukraine
Geschichte und Lebensgeschichten
Aus dem Ukrainischen übersetzt von Margarita Grinko
ISBN 978-3-8382-1622-5

22  *Vakhtang Kipiani (ed.)*
World War II, Uncontrived and Unredacted
Testimonies from Ukraine
Translated from the Ukrainian by Zenia Tompkins and Daisy Gibbons
ISBN 978-3-8382-1621-8

# Book series "Ukrainian Voices"

Sergiy Korsunsky, Kobe Gakuin University, Japan

Nadiia Koval, Kyiv School of Economics, Ukraine

Volodymyr Kravchenko, University of Alberta, Edmonton

Oleksiy Kresin, NAS Koretskiy Institute of State and Law, Kyiv

Anatoliy Kruglashov, Fedkovych National University, Chernivtsi

Andrey Kurkov, PEN Ukraine, Kyiv

Ostap Kushnir, Lazarski University, Warsaw

Taras Kuzio, National University of Kyiv-Mohyla Academy

Serhii Kvit, National University of Kyiv-Mohyla Academy

Yuliya Ladygina, The Pennsylvania State University, USA

Yevhen Mahda, Institute of World Policy, Kyiv

Victoria Malko, California State University, Fresno, USA

Yulia Marushevska, Security and Defense Center (SAND), Kyiv

Myroslav Marynovych, Ukrainian Catholic University, Lviv

Oleksandra Matviichuk, Center for Civil Liberties, Kyiv

Mykhailo Minakov, Kennan Institute, Washington, USA

Anton Moiseienko, The Australian National University, Canberra

Alexander Motyl, Rutgers University-Newark, USA

Vlad Mykhnenko, University of Oxford, United Kingdom

Vitalii Ogiienko, Ukrainian Institute of National Remembrance, Kyiv

Olga Onuch, University of Manchester, United Kingdom

Olesya Ostrovska, Museum "Mystetskyi Arsenal," Kyiv

Anna Osypchuk, National University of Kyiv-Mohyla Academy

Oleksandr Pankieiev, University of Alberta, Edmonton

Oleksiy Panych, Publishing House "Dukh i Litera," Kyiv

Valerii Pekar, Kyiv-Mohyla Business School, Ukraine

Yohanan Petrovsky-Shtern, Northwestern University, Chicago

Serhii Plokhy, Harvard University, Cambridge, USA

Andrii Portnov, Viadrina University, Frankfurt-Oder, Germany

Maryna Rabinovych, Kyiv School of Economics, Ukraine

Valentyna Romanova, Institute of Developing Economies, Tokyo

Natalya Ryabinska, Collegium Civitas, Warsaw, Poland

Darya Tsymbalyk, University of Oxford, United Kingdom

Vsevolod Samokhvalov, University of Liege, Belgium

Orest Semotiuk, Franko National University, Lviv

Viktoriya Sereda, NAS Institute of Ethnology, Lviv

Anton Shekhovtsov, University of Vienna, Austria

Andriy Shevchenko, Media Center Ukraine, Kyiv

Oxana Shevel, Tufts University, Medford, USA

Pavlo Shopin, National Pedagogical Dragomanov University, Kyiv

Karina Shyrokykh, Stockholm University, Sweden

Nadja Simon, freelance interpreter, Cologne, Germany

Olena Snigova, NAS Institute for Economics and Forecasting, Kyiv

Ilona Solohub, Analytical Platform "VoxUkraine," Kyiv

Iryna Solonenko, LibMod - Center for Liberal Modernity, Berlin

Galyna Solovei, National University of Kyiv-Mohyla Academy

Sergiy Stelmakh, NAS Institute of World History, Kyiv

Olena Stiazhkina, NAS Institute of the History of Ukraine, Kyiv

Dmitri Stratievski, Osteuropa Zentrum (OEZB), Berlin

Dmytro Stus, National Taras Shevchenko Museum, Kyiv

Frank Sysyn, University of Toronto, Canada

Olha Tokariuk, Center for European Policy Analysis, Washington

Olena Tregub, Independent Anti-Corruption Commission, Kyiv

Hlib Vyshlinsky, Centre for Economic Strategy, Kyiv

Mychailo Wynnyckyj, National University of Kyiv-Mohyla Academy

Yelyzaveta Yasko, NGO "Yellow Blue Strategy," Kyiv

Serhy Yekelchyk, University of Victoria, Canada

Victor Yushchenko, President of Ukraine 2005-2010, Kyiv

Oleksandr Zaitsev, Ukrainian Catholic University, Lviv

Kateryna Zarembo, National University of Kyiv-Mohyla Academy

Yaroslav Zhalilo, National Institute for Strategic Studies, Kyiv

Sergei Zhuk, Ball State University at Muncie, USA

Alina Zubkovych, Nordic Ukraine Forum, Stockholm

Liudmyla Zubrytska, National University of Kyiv-Mohyla Academy

## Friends of the Series